MAGISTRATES' DECISION-MAKING IN CHILD PROTECTION CASES

In memory of my parents Mary and Michael Sheehan
Semper et ubique fidelis

Magistrates' Decision-Making in Child Protection Cases

ROSEMARY SHEEHAN
Department of Social Work, Monash University, Australia

Published with the assistance of the Monash University
Publications Grants Committee

LONDON AND NEW YORK

First published 2001 by Ashgate Publishing

Reissued 2018 by Routledge
2 Park Square, Milton Park, Abingdon, Oxon OX14 4RN
711 Third Avenue, New York, NY 10017, USA

Routledge is an imprint of the Taylor & Francis Group, an informa business

Copyright © Rosemary Sheehan 2001

All rights reserved. No part of this book may be reprinted or reproduced or utilised in any form or by any electronic, mechanical, or other means, now known or hereafter invented, including photocopying and recording, or in any information storage or retrieval system, without permission in writing from the publishers.

Notice:
Product or corporate names may be trademarks or registered trademarks, and are used only for identification and explanation without intent to infringe.

Publisher's Note
The publisher has gone to great lengths to ensure the quality of this reprint but points out that some imperfections in the original copies may be apparent.

Disclaimer
The publisher has made every effort to trace copyright holders and welcomes correspondence from those they have been unable to contact.

A Library of Congress record exists under LC control number: 2001086241

ISBN 13: 978-1-138-70673-6 (hbk)
ISBN 13: 978-1-138-70668-2 (pbk)
ISBN 13: 978-1-315-20166-5 (ebk)

Contents

List of Figure and Tables vi
Acknowledgments viii

Introduction 1

1 The Best Interests of the Child 10

2 Uncovering the Decision Process 29

3 Deciding Best Interests 77

4 Magistrate Decision-Making 144

5 Alternative Dispute Resolution 183

6 Future Directions 198

7 Conclusion 221

Bibliography 229

Appendices 249

Appendix 1 The Court Observation Sheet 251
Appendix 2 The Interview Schedule 253
Appendix 3 The Survey of Children's Court Records 256

List of Figure and Tables

Table 1.1	Total notifications received by DHS 1991–94	25
Table 1.2	Protection applications per year sought by DHS	25
Table 1.3	The grounds on which notifications were made to DHS in 1993/94	25
Table 1.4	Number of substantiated child protection notifications	25
Table 1.5	Grounds of protection application by age: 1993/94	26
Table 1.6	Grounds for protection and irreconcilable difference applications heard, Children's Court, 1997	26
Figure 3.1	Decision model proposed by Hogarth (1981:135)	43
Table 3.1	The grounds of the protection applications (CYPA 1989 s.63) in the study (n=89)	81
Table 3.2	Age of child compared with the grounds of the protection application	82
Table 3.3	Grounds for the protection matter before the court compared with the age of the child	83
Table 3.4	The child protection concerns based on the grounds of the protection application and the gender of the child	84
Table 3.5	Magistrate background	85
Table 3.6	Family factors in protection matters (no. families=84)	100
Table 3.7	Number of court appearances per protection application	122
Table 3.8	Parent income	138
Table 3.9	Parent relationship status compared with sex of child	141
Table 3.10	Child's place of residence at the time of the protection matter	141
Table 3.11	Child's siblings' place of residence	141
Table 3.12	The relationship of the perpetrator to the child	142
Table 3.13	Family history of welfare contact (no. of cases for which information was available, n=56)	142
Table 6.1	Types and outcomes of pre-hearing conferences held (n=228)	188
Table 6.2	The grounds of new child protection applications brought by the child protection service	188
Table 6.3	The ages of the children involved in the new child protection applications brought by the child protection service	188

Table 6.4 Decisions about new child protection applications (n=60); settlements achieved at pre-hearing conference   189

Acknowledgments

This book is based on a study of magistrates' decision-making in child protection cases brought before the Melbourne Children's Court, during 1993–94. The study could not have been undertaken without the support of the then Chief Magistrate of Victoria, Ms Sally Brown (now Hon. Justice Sally Brown of the Family Court of Australia), and the then Senior Magistrate of the Children's Court, Victoria, Mr Gregory Levine. The study was also made possible by the generous participation of Magistrates both currently and previously appointed to the Children's Court. I would also like to acknowledge the invaluable advice and assistance given to me by Mr Graham Freidman, a member of the Victorian Bar working at the Children's Court.

Professor Thea Brown encouraged me to submit a publisher's proposal for this book. I am also indebted to Dr Christopher Trotter from my own Department and Dr Roger Douglas, Senior Lecturer at Latrobe University and a member of the Victorian Bar. Dr Douglas provided me with considerable advice about the workings of the law. Acknowledgement is also paid to Professor Allan Borowski and Dr Martin Ryan for their advice at the commencement of the study, and to Dr Peter Hiller for his comments on the study.

I would like to thank Professor Christine Hallett, Vice-Principal (Research), University of Stirling, Scotland, who invited me to visit the Department of Social Science, March–May, 2000 and provided me with a congenial place to write this book.

I wish also to express my gratitude to my husband Gavan Martyn for his generous support and hours of babysitting. I would like to acknowledge the affection and tolerance of Melissa, Tim, Nicholas, and Maeve Martyn who withstood their mother's preoccupation with her desk and computer. I would like to thank my friends who have also tolerated this preoccupation and offered encouragement along the way.

Rosemary Sheehan
BSocStud (Syd), MSW (LaT), PhD(Mon)

Introduction

Children's Courts in Australia, as do the Family Proceedings Courts in England and the Children's Hearing System in Scotland, have a central role in the community's response to child abuse. Magistrates have considerable influence on the lives of children, and their families, who have been brought to court as a consequence of concern about child maltreatment. The decisions that they make about such children define the extent to which statutory welfare services intervene in the family's life and specify the changes parents must make in order to retain their children. Such decisions also impact on the wider community as it is the community that is asked to support policies which provide the resources for helping vulnerable children and families.

Children's Court work is psychological and social decision-making within a legal framework. Magistrates and judges must balance the often-competing interests of parents and the state, with the needs of children, to decide court outcomes. They must decide the balance of *parens patriae*, the legal principle which grants the state the right of intervention in family life to protect the interests of the child, against the legal and natural right of parents to raise their children in privacy without state interference (Carter 1983; Fogarty 1989; Kelly and Ramsey 1985; Parker, Sumner and Jarvis 1989; Wattam 1992).

Yet how these decisions are made is largely unknown. Little research attention has been given to the role of magistrates (or other judicial officers) in child protection cases despite the significance of their decisions and the view that, in these cases, 'social awareness is just as important as technical competence' (Richardson 1984:547). It is clear that legal and welfare professionals use different frames of reference to deal with child abuse cases (Parker, Sumner and Jarvis 1989; Brown 1991; Wattam 1992). This difference in outlook, and certain system difficulties, creates tension between welfare and legal professionals in child protection cases. Child protection workers, who are usually qualified social workers, often have difficulty understanding the decisions made about children brought before the Children's Court. Their professional training is different from that of magistrates, and this difference is apparent when issues of child maltreatment are debated in court.

I became aware of this, when I was working some years ago, in Victoria (Australia), as a Senior Social Worker for a non-government family welfare agency. Child protection matters were taken to the Children's Court by the local statutory welfare authority when they believed their investigations of allegations of child maltreatment or neglect warranted formal, statutory intervention. However, the court at times would take a different view of such intervention and decline to make the child protection orders that were sought. Child protection workers were often at a loss to understand why this had occurred. They interpreted this outcome as a lack of trust, by the court, in their assessments of child abuse cases, and their recommendations about the need for intervention.

I wondered whether the difficulty child protection workers had in understanding magistrates' decisions might arise from a lack of knowledge about the factors and processes magistrates use in judicial decision-making. It could therefore assist professionals, working with children in need of care and protection, if they had more knowledge about how magistrates respond to information that is presented to them in court. It could be useful also to have knowledge about the criteria that magistrates use, and the factors they look for, to decide what is an appropriate legal outcome for a child.

I therefore undertook a study, during 1993–94, in the Family Division of the Melbourne Children's Court, Victoria, the jurisdiction that hears child protection matters. The study involved interviews with magistrates, observation of cases in court and the analysis of court records, in order to explore the nature of magistrate work in child protection. My appointment as a Pre-Hearing Conference Convenor at the Children's Court (from 1995 and continuing) also provides information about how magistrates approach child protection decision-making.

Given the power magistrates have over the lives of individuals, it is important to know more about their legal decision-making. The community expects magistrates 'to dispose judicially and lawfully of all matters brought before them' (Carlen 1976:42). Douglas and Laster (1992) found that how magistrates viewed their judicial task, together with their individual attitudes and values, had a direct impact on their job performance and presumably on those who presented before them.

The legislative framework that directs the role of the magistrate, and the work of the child protection service, allows magistrates considerable discretion in the assessment of children's needs. What influences this discretion, what information is seen as relevant, what factors influence magistrates as they do their job, are of public interest; court orders both direct the future of the child and direct the work of the statutory services who are required to implement such orders (Asquith 1983; Brown 1991; Hogarth 1971; Parker, Sumner and Jarvis 1989).

Child abuse can be difficult to define; Boss (1995:133) describes it as both a temporal and culturally relative concept. It must accommodate what Harrison (1995:81) describes as 'the disparity of experiences of children' in a pluralist country like Australia. Whilst there is general agreement about broad definitions of what constitutes serious physical and sexual abuse to a child, it is difficult to achieve consensus on what constitutes physical abuse where a child is not seriously or gravely harmed and the child is not likely to suffer unnecessarily, or where cultural or other factors are put forward to explain the maltreatment. There is little community consensus about what is 'good enough' parenting (Stevenson 1996:15). Child rearing is still regarded as a private activity unless it is proven that there is child maltreatment (Garbarino 1995).

This lack of consensus is particularly evident in cases of emotional abuse and child neglect. Courts are reluctant to make a finding of child abuse in these cases because of the inexact measures that are used by child protection workers to define emotional abuse and neglect and because of the lack of legal criteria available to guide decision-making. This is despite what Garbarino (1995: 292) describes as the growing recognition that psychological maltreatment is 'the common thread that binds together all forms of maltreatment and accounts predominantly for developmental outcomes'. Child protection workers tend to focus on the context in which the child abuse occurs as much as on the abusive actions that are visited on children to explain and 'prove' child maltreatment (Adler 1979; Hallett and Stevenson 1989; Clark 1995:23). They refer to what normally happens in families to explain why a particular child's experiences are potentially or actually harmful. This presentation of social information as legal evidence in child abuse matters frustrates lawyers and creates misunderstandings between welfare and legal professionals. Child protection work requires professionals to work across inter-professional boundaries; yet this appears to be intrinsically difficult and is particularly evident in child protection matters (Hallett 1992).

Certainly, child abuse may not be as clear to the court as are other legal problems (Dingwall 1991). Moreover, decision-making in child protection is difficult because it often involves complex moral rather than technical judgements (Bullock, Little, Milham and Mount 1995:14; Clark 1995). It is difficult, also, because the values of protecting children at risk and respecting parental autonomy are in conflict. However, intervention on behalf of children who are abused and neglected is an important dimension of contemporary social policy (Boss 1995). There is now, less tolerance of family violence and an expectation that the problem of child abuse is alleviated, by the courts and government policy (Clark 1995:13). There is a strong community commitment to the belief in a child's right to safety, which is evidenced in current public health and education campaigns.

Children's Court Work

Child protection services are 'almost always services of last resort. Families who require these services are seriously troubled in one way or another' (Health and Community Services, Victoria, Annual Report 1993/94:103). The task of assessing whether a child is sufficiently at risk of child abuse in order to justify some degree of intervention is one of the hardest tasks undertaken in the welfare field (Community Services Victoria, Annual Report 1990–91:36). Moreover, the number of reports of child abuse have escalated over the last decade in Australia and the UK and this places considerable demands on the child protection services and the courts (Fogarty 1989). In the years 1993–94, in Australia, 74,436 cases of child abuse and neglect were reported to state and territory welfare departments. Of these, 28,711 cases were substantiated; however, few cases of substantiated child abuse reach court. In NSW in 1993–94, 5 per cent of all notifications ended up before the Children's Court (Angus and Woodward (1995:17). In 1997, in the Children's Court of Victoria, 3,115 child protection matters were finalised (Statistics of the Children's Court of Victoria 1997), which accounts for approximately 6.5 per cent of notifications about child abuse made to the state child protection service.

Conflicting philosophies and ideologies abound in child protection (Fogarty 1989). The issue of child abuse is powerful, both symbolically and politically, in arguments about the state and its right to be involved in family life, and in particular to intervene in the parenting of children (Parton 1985, 1991; Nelson 1986). There is a strongly held belief across society that the well-being of children, families and society cannot be separated (Community Services Victoria, Annual Report 1990–91:34). Yet, child abuse is now perceived as one of the major social problems of modern times and what behaviours constitute child abuse are more broadly defined (Parton 1985).

This increased awareness of child safety and child abuse has placed pressure on the legal process to pay more attention to the rights of children, and not to orient itself primarily to the rights of adult litigants. It is in the area of child sexual abuse that this awareness has been most concentrated.

Decisions about children in child protection cases must also take into account the increasingly limited alternative options for care of children as well as a strong societal preference for children to remain in the care of their family. These decisions therefore involve the court in the intimate world of adult/child relationships and, in so doing, make public what are essentially private matters (King and Trowell 1992). The courts and magistrates can therefore become easy targets for complaints most particularly when it is considered that the court has responded to a situation of child abuse in too limited a fashion. Yet there is a context of uncertainty and uniqueness in every child protection intervention and choices must be made, perhaps with little understanding of how best a child's interests can be met.

What behaviours are considered to constitute child abuse are drawn not just from what has actually happened to a child, for example a physical injury, but these actions are measured against what the community regards as normative standards of parenting behaviour. Clearly, such assessment is somewhat subjective and thus decision-making in child abuse cases combines the objective, or factual elements, in the case with a subjective interpretation of what behaviours place a child at risk of harm or neglect. Decision-makers are required to make what are essentially moral judgements about the culpability of parents where there are allegations of child abuse (Dingwall 1983). Moreover, these professional judgements and assessments must accord with what judicial and bureaucratic procedures have identified as evidence of child abuse (Howe 1994).

Magistrates depend on information provided to them by professionals 'to assist the court in reaching its judicial decisions' (Carlen 1976:42). This assistance is of particular importance in child welfare matters as magistrates are required to interpret social, as much as legal, evidence in order to decide what are the appropriate court outcomes for children (Clark 1995:17). Yet it can be difficult for magistrates to obtain this information in a manner which is legally appropriate. Moreover what is meant by the best interests of the child is ill-explained by legislation and is perceived as a 'vague and illusory concept which varies from case to case and depends on the context' (Kiel 1988:6). Nor, are there specific guidelines to decide what factors ought to preoccupy decision-makers: to what extent, and in what measure, should key childhood development factors such as emotional stability, social competence, physical well-being and intellectual development direct decision-making (Fernandez 1996:61).

Definitions of child abuse and neglect found in the literature do little to assist the explanation of best interests; they are often conflictual and vary in the emphasis they place on different aspects of child maltreatment (Batten 1988:247). Furthermore, although there is a considerable discourse on the incidence and prevalence of child abuse and neglect (Goddard and Carew

1993), the explanatory theories of child abuse that are expressed in relevant literature are often contradictory.

The Legislative Framework

Each State and Territory in Australia has enacted its own child welfare legislation that sets out the statutory requirements for child protection matters. In Victoria, it is the *Children and Young Persons Act 1989* that sets out the requirements for bringing a child protection application before the court; it also sets out the orders that can be made and the criteria which need to be met in order to establish whether or not there are grounds to justify statutory intervention in a family. The *Children and Young Persons Act* also sets out the factors magistrates must be mindful of when considering options for children. While child protection services are generally services of last resort and magistrates are dealing with families who have serious problems, the intent of the legislation is to preserve and maintain families and magistrates are directed to be mindful of this aim:

> The child's welfare and interest is to receive paramount consideration, without overlooking the rights of the parents and further potential harm of the child, by unnecessarily imposing forms of intervention (Blackmore and Horsburgh 1989:119).

The legislation requires court decisions to be legally justified and supported by evidence. Statutory welfare agencies must prove that abuse has occurred and that it is necessary for the state to intervene in the family for the child's protection (King and Trowell 1992:111). As a consequence the role of the legal profession is as central to the child protection process as is the role of the welfare practitioner (Thorpe 1994).

Statutory requirements increasingly define the day to day practice and context of child protection work. Thus, there is a greater need for child protection workers to understand the court decision process. Yet, welfare practitioners are frequently frustrated by magistrates' emphasis on the legal framework and apparent lack of use of the discretion available to them that could be used to achieve both justice, and welfare, aims for a child and their family. Parton (1991) and Breckenridge (1995) underlined the need for a more productive relationship between the judicial and the social representatives, aided perhaps by a better balance of power, discretion and understanding between the two groups of representatives.

Decision-making Studies

Little is known about how magistrates process information presented to them in court and even less is known about the ideas and predispositions which magistrates take with them into the courtroom (Brown 1991). Yet, as professional decision-makers magistrates would certainly develop strategies to process the information given to them, in hearings, into a decision about a case (Douglas and Laster 1992; Lawrence, 1981, 1987). Kapardis and Farrington (1981) and McKnight (1981) report that judicial decision-makers construct frames of reference, and decision rules and objectives, to assist their decision-making. Research attention to magistrate decision-making has largely focused on the adult and juvenile justice jurisdictions, on the descriptive aspects of such work, on sentencing patterns, and on the phenomenology of judicial decision-making.

Whilst ultimately it is case facts which direct court outcomes, it is acknowledged that magistrates do bring their individual approaches, experiences, and understanding of their role, to their work. Hogarth (1971) refers to sentencing as a human process and he, and other researchers, highlight the contribution that the individual values and views of decision-makers, combined with specific external factors such as the community context of the court, make to judicial makers' decision outcomes. Hogarth (1971) found that individual attitudes and beliefs did influence what information the decision-maker selected as relevant; Douglas and Laster (1992) found that magistrates and judges did refer to their own individual viewpoints when assessing information presented to them. Brown (1991), in England, found in her study of magistrates in the juvenile courts, that magistrates are very much influenced by their individual understanding of everyday life. Therefore, it must be expected that in child abuse cases, factors such as general social influences, organisational and institutional factors, beliefs about perpetrators, the purpose of the legislation, and the role of the court must all impact on court outcomes (Lawrence and Homel 1992).

The Structure of this Book

The next chapter discusses the thinking about children and their place in society that provides a statutory base for child protection. It refers to the child welfare legislative framework in place in Victoria, the *Children and Young Persons Act (1989),* which is representative of child welfare legislation throughout

Australia, and has some similarities with legislation in the UK. It also gives an overview of the work of the court and provides recent information about the child protection matters brought to the attention of the Melbourne Children's Court, Victoria, and information about those matters that came before the court during the study in 1993–94.

Chapter Two refers to studies of judicial decision-making, their findings about the culture of the magistracy and the tension that exists between legal requirements and the requirements of the 'welfare' jurisdictions. How the study of magistrates' decision-making was undertaken in the Melbourne Children's Court, during 1993–95, is explained. Details of what the study hoped to find, and why this mattered in understanding the difficulty magistrates have with child protection decision-making, are also provided.

Chapter Three presents the views of the magistrates about their work in the Children's Court and provides information about magistrate decision-making in child protection cases that is gained from courtroom observations, magistrates' comments about their work and court records.

Chapter Four discusses the implications of the study findings for child welfare decision-making and for the inter-professional cooperation that is essential for effective child protection. The chapter also includes examples of cases observed or comments made by magistrates and practitioners in order to provide a practical base for readers.

Chapter Five considers what other approaches might be used to decide child abuse cases and comments on the introduction of alternative dispute resolution methods, such as pre-hearing conferences and family group conferences, into the child welfare jurisdictions in Australia.

Chapter Six canvasses how other jurisdictions respond to child protection decision-making: specifically England, Scotland, Ireland; the inquisitorial approach of some European countries (Holland, Belgium, France) is compared with the adversarial approach of the Westminster system.

Chapter Seven concludes this book by noting that *Messages from Research*, the Department of Health (HMSO) study (of child protection practice) in England, Wales and Northern Ireland, came to conclusions not too distant from the Australian Law Reform report on children and the legal process. The aims of child welfare legislation fail to address the practical concerns of child protection. The study of the Children's Court, Victoria, and other related studies, reveal that effective child protection is a shared enterprise amongst the professions. The framing of child protection as a socio-legal enterprise limits this enterprise and distracts from a broader child welfare focus. The implications of this for child protection decision-making are suggested.

Study Considerations

When any research is undertaken in the area of child protection it is possible that numerous and potentially competing interests might emerge. Given that decisions made by magistrates have great impact on individuals, and their families, great care must be taken to view such decisions in context and to acknowledge that such decision-making is often not straightforward.

A study such as the one which forms the basis of this book has to be mindful of the sensitivity of the content of child abuse cases, and use case information gained ethically and appropriately. Child welfare decision-making is frequently commented on in the media, often along the lines of community views about the appropriateness of such decisions.

This book aims to make a theoretical contribution to knowledge of judicial decision-making in child welfare matters. In doing this it is hoped it will inform practice by professionals who work in this area and contribute relevant information to statutory child welfare policy and planning. It will also, it is hoped, contribute to debate about how our community protects children affected by abuse and neglect.

Chapter One

The Best Interests of the Child

> The fate of children is no longer exclusively in the hands of their parents, society feels responsible for children's welfare and is prepared to intervene in family affairs if that welfare appears to be threatened (Schaffer 1990:3).

The Place of Children

Contemporary child welfare policy debates the balance between parental and community responsibility for children. It also debates what are the exact rights of parents and children, the appropriate roles of the family, and what is the role of state intervention in family life. Parton (1983) emphasises that decisions about children's best interests remain a compromise between a family's right to parent their child and a child's need for protection. Contemporary child protection policy assumes that parents are the best carers of their children and emphasises that, where there are child protection concerns, it is better to support parents in their attempts to care for their children rather than removing them from their families and placing them in care.

Whilst attitudes to children have varied over time, according to their perceived utility to society, children have generally been viewed as of economic and social importance because they ensure the continuance of society. Children are therefore entitled to community support and the state imposes certain obligations on parents about the care of their children. Parents, however, still have the primary responsibility for the care of their children and are expected to behave in a way that protects, and promotes, their children's health and development:

> The duties of parents are to protect children's health and wellbeing; assist children to develop their physical, emotional and intellectual capacities; nourish their self-esteem and self-confidence; prepare them to take advantage of and responsibly exercise their rights and responsibilities as citizens; and provide them with conditions favourable to grasping the educational, occupational and other opportunities available to them in society (Family and Community Services, South Australia, 1990:4).

Structural changes in Western society, over recent decades, have had an impact on children and their families. Changes include an increase in family breakdown, and in subsequent poverty, in changing gender roles in families, and women's increased participation in the workforce. These factors, and others such as the impact of economic change on work opportunities, and the social mobility of families, have created narrower family structures; they have also led to debate about parental responsibilities and the extent to which the state is responsible for the care of children (Harrison 1988:23).

Research on the harmful effects of institutionalisation and the separation of children from their families has led to an emphasis on the provision of better support and assistance for families to care for their own children (ASLRC 1981: 207–8 in Carney 1984:284). Family oriented programs are therefore the major focus of child welfare legislation and child welfare services, and it is accepted that:

> the state should assist parents and guardians to care for their children so far as consistent with available resources and the child's welfare. It should do so in a way that does not stigmatise the parents and does not deprive them of parental rights. The model for support is the good neighbour, or the extended family (Institute Criminology Proceedings 49:39).

The Family Court of Australia asserts the need to give the widest possible protection and assistance to the family as the 'natural and fundamental group unit of society' (Family Court of Australia 1975:3).

The Ideology of State Intervention

The responsibility of the state to protect the welfare of children arises from the principle of *parens patriae*; the principle in English law which empowers the State to act as the parent of last resort when parents are unable to fulfil their parenting obligations (Carney 1983). Governments of the day have pursued this role, with varying degrees of vigour, depending on prevailing economic and social values of the times and the degree to which parents' rights or children's needs have been the focus of attention.

Social reformers of the nineteenth century, in Australia and in Great Britain, pressed for legislative provision for children who were ill-treated or deprived of the necessities of life as a result of industrialisation. They viewed children as the nation's salvation, with the need for a healthy, moral and secure home environment, adequate schooling and humane working conditions in order to ensure their survival (Tiffen 1983:7/8). In Australia, government interest in the quality of children's lives emerged some years after European settlement in 1788. The interest was driven by the need to deal with abandoned and wayward children as much as it was by paternalism and to improve the lot of children in society (Laster 1993). It was firmly believed however that children belonged with their families.

It was children who were isolated from, and out of the control of, their families, who were in need of state control (Laster 1993). Whilst in Victoria, from the nineteenth century, the rescue of neglected children was noted as 'a sacred and pressing duty (CSV Annual Report 1990/91:34); this interest appears to have been based more on a moral concern about parental behaviour than a sole concern for a child's needs and care.

The Victorian government introduced the Neglected and Criminal Children's Act in 1864 to deal with the large number of children who had been abandoned or neglected following the social instability of the gold rushes of the 1850s. The Act dealt also with young people considered to be at 'the first stages in the development of adolescent troublemakers' (CSV Annual Report 1990/91:6). In 1887, the Neglected Children's Department was founded to implement the Act and to care for children whose homes 'failed to fulfill their proper function' (Platt 1977:135). (In 1924 this became the Children's Welfare Department and in 1960 the Social Welfare Branch of the Chief Secretary's Department. In 1970 it was finally established as a separate department, known today as the Department of Human Services.)

The Children's Court of Victoria was introduced into the court system in 1906 as a direct response to the momentum of 'the child savers movement', the philanthropic groups which emerged in the USA in the late 19th century to urge the state to censure parents who had failed to protect their children (Carney 1984:284). They also urged that cases of child abuse and neglect should be dealt with separately from those of young offenders, who should also be dealt with in a separate jurisdiction from adults. The development of specialised jurisdictions for children in difficulty also took place in a number of European (France, Belgium, Germany, Poland, Portugal and Switzerland) and Scandinavian (Sweden, Norway), countries as well as Canada and Ireland at the end of the nineteenth and early twentieth centuries (Hallett and Hazel 1998:6).

In the 1950s English welfare reforms suggested a change in focus from a moral concern which emphasised the removal of children from unsuitable families or environments 'because of the wickedness or incompetence on the part of their parents' (Jamrozik, Drury and Sweeney 1989:4) and the placement of children in situations or institutions where they could be re-socialised, to concern about the social and psychological development of children. They suggested that problem families and young people ought to be viewed more as inadequate, rather than as immoral, and that skilled services could be provided to address this inadequacy and assist families. In the 1960s there was increasing concern about ill-treated children. Dr Henry Kempe, in the USA, published in 1962 in the *Journal of the American Medical Association*, a paper on what he entitled the Battered Child Syndrome – research findings about children whose parents had been referred for criminal prosecution for severely beating their children (ten Bessel 1985:1). This paper created widespread public and professional awareness of the problem of the physical abuse of children, and this concern later flowed onto other forms of child abuse such as neglect, emotional and sexual abuse (Hallett and Hazel 1998). A number of states in the USA subsequently passed laws obliging doctors and other health professionals to report children whom they believed were being abused or neglected. At the same time, in Victoria, the Doctors John Birrell and Dora Bialestock initiated public discussion about child maltreatment, although the focus of such discussion was mostly on young infants who had been physically harmed.

Responsibility for detection and intervention in matters of child abuse and neglect lay entirely with non-government bodies and the police, in Victoria, until 1985, when Community Services Victoria assumed this role (CSV 1989/90:42). At the same time a new framework for understanding child abuse and intervention emerged. It viewed actions that constituted child abuse not as solely caused by psychologically disturbed parents but more as a reflection of social problems that required a broader understanding (Giavonnoni and Beccera 1979). It was suggested that child maltreatment could be seen as either the result of social factors, such as poverty, or as the result of individual psychopathology, or a combination of both. Certainly there was a belief that the causes of child abuse were broader than previously presented and that there needed to be wider debate about the problem of child abuse (Boss 1981).

The new criterion for child protection became 'in need of care' rather than 'in need of control' (Smith 1982:43). There was greater community acknowledgment of the existence of child abuse and neglect and an acknowledgment of the economic and social costs of child neglect (Harrison 1988:232). Child protection is currently viewed, by welfare professionals, as best achieved when it is a partnership, or a shared responsibility, between the legal, health and welfare professionals, and between families and the community (Smith 1982:49). Contemporary social reform aimed to ensure that as much as possible a child should develop in their own family, albeit with the state providing the resources necessary to do so. If intervention in the family is necessary to protect the child then voluntary intervention is preferred; compulsory intervention is justified only when there are no other alternatives (Carney 1983:6).

Community attitudes about the importance of family preservation have led to the development of public policies that permit the state to intervene in family life only when it is detrimental for the child to remain in their family's care. Given the difficulties surrounding the distinctions between what is, and is not, child abuse and what is, and is not, an effective response to child abuse, there is considerable ambiguity about acceptable statutory responses. The state has been 'a reluctant partner in its relationship with the family' (Clark 1995:10). Intervention in families, whose care of children falls below minimum standards of care, is fraught with difficulty, and is:

> the battle ground for two powerful but contrary principles: on the one hand a belief in the privacy and autonomy of the family, and on the other the primacy of the rights of the child (Carney 1983:44).

The Development of the Child Protection System

The notion of children's rights is only a recent development in the legal system and parallels the concern for due process and children's and young people's rights to advocacy (Hallett and Hazel 1998). Previously, the traditional notion of parental 'ownership of children', and a parent's rights over a child, or, more particularly a father's rights, were almost always seen as superior to any children's rights (Carney 1983:110). Yet, contemporary legislation deems a child's welfare the paramount consideration of the state when deciding issues which affect children's welfare. The needs of the child must be the primary consideration when the interest of parents and children differ. This is most notable in claims surrounding the physical abuse of children, or child maltreatment and neglect (Family Court of Australia 1975:5; Family and Community Services 1990:12). Yet it is emphasised that a child must be seen as a member of a family group, and an integral part of a wider social network and culture (Schaffer 1990:235–6). Whilst the community acknowledges that children must be safe from detrimental conditions, beliefs about privacy and autonomy in family life and the importance of family, direct that intervention in family life must always be seen as a last resort.

Angus and Wilkinson (1993:8) report that in 1995–96, 91,000 cases of child abuse or neglect were reported to state and territory welfare departments in Australia; approximately one-third of these were substantiated, that is to say they were assessed as 'child at risk' (Australia has a population of around 18 million). This represented 4.9 in every 1,000 Australian children aged between birth and 16 years as at risk of child abuse and neglect. There were 22 reports per 1,000 children in Victoria (population almost five million and has mandatory reporting of suspected child abuse) who were believed to be exposed to child abuse or neglect (Australian Government Steering Committee 1997:535–6). Around 6.5 per cent of these notifications resulted in court proceedings.

It is generally accepted that child abuse and neglect occur across all socioeconomic and cultural groups and its causes are diverse. Finkelhor and Korbin (1983) report that different types of child abuse have different features. However, a lack of parenting skills, limited knowledge about children, relationship difficulties, overuse of physical punishment to deal with family problems, characterise child protection problems.

In the 1960s child abuse was seen as largely caused by psychologically disturbed parents (Boss 1987). Contemporary research offers differing perspectives on how child abuse should be understood (Goddard and Carew 1993). Batten (1988) and Garbarino (1977) suggest it is important to look for explanations in the environment as well as in the family. The inter-relationship between poverty on the one hand, and child abuse and neglect on the other, shows that an ecological perspective on child abuse is essential. Kadushin and Martin (1981) believe the social interactionist approach provides the best understanding of child abuse: it is the particular family dynamics and individual characteristics that explain the abusive behaviours.

Family system theorists support this view, maintaining it is family interactions, for example a high level of interpersonal conflict and domestic violence, and family socialisation and the modelling that parents provide children, that explain abusive behaviours by parents. Gabarino (1990) further suggests that some children are more physically and emotionally vulnerable than others to abusive and neglectful behaviour. Parton (1985) emphasises that socioeconomic factors such as unemployment, poverty, and poor housing etc., are also central to the cause of child abuse. Families living under the stress of poverty, in social isolation, with few personal resources, have a less materially favourable environment in which to parent and are more likely to come to the attention of welfare authorities. Otto and Melton (1997:61) comment however that family explanations, or family system explanations of child abuse, while providing important contextual information, fail to acknowledge the responsibility for causing harm to the child of the adults who have care for a child.

Child abuse is not a new social problem nor is it a haphazard or deviant activity. Unfortunately it has become an accepted part of our contemporary life. Wattam (1992:1–2) comments that 'the very terms 'child' and 'abuse' involve and invoke culturally understood and institutionalised categories and standards'. She further comments that although child abuse is almost universally acknowledged as a social problem, there is not complete agreement about what constitutes child abuse, although there is considerable research on the incidence and prevalence of abuse and neglect (Goddard and Carew 1993). This view, combined with the view that the family is traditionally regarded as a source of love and support has led to an element of denial at both the community level and at an individual level (James 1994:2b).

Furthermore, Wattam (1992) suggests that what is perceived as child abuse is culturally relative. There are different views on child upbringing that exist across the professions, and in the community, and different attitudes to children. Such differences in outlook and behaviour between individuals have important implications for those interpreting information about children in need of child protection (Dingwall, Eekelaar and Murray 1983). Fernandez (1996:8) cautions also that the notion of the 'state' as a unified entity is misleading, given that judgements about what is acceptable parenting and child behaviour are influenced by social, economic and ideological contexts. This is evident in child welfare policy in different countries (Hallett and Hazell 1998:15); some countries privilege the family and limit the authority of the state to intervene in families (e.g. Ireland), others expect the state to intervene authoritatively in child welfare matters (for example, Sweden and Denmark).

How individual professionals make such judgements about what constitutes child abuse is based on how they interpret facts about cases, the significance they attach to these and the explanations adults provide about the how the child abuse has occurred (Batten 1988; Clark 1995). Professionals 'draw on cultural knowledge about children, normal families, adults and particularly child abuse' to make these assessments (Wattam 1992:13). Making these judgements also involves making an assessment of the moral standing of the adults or parents who are involved in the care of the child (Fogarty 1989).

Assessments of child maltreatment are difficult, not only because they involve interpretation and speculation about outcomes, but also because they may come under the scrutiny of the legal system, which is now central to the operation of child protection (Parton 1994). The social evidence that is typically presented by child protection workers to support claims that a child is at risk very often fails to satisfy the needs of the legal process for concrete and factual evidence (Clark 1995). Smith suggests however such 'social' evidence is important to the understanding of child abuse and that the legal system will need to have some 'appreciation of the behavioural and social sciences to be able to adequately understand the implications of the evidence placed before them' (1982:70).

The politics of child welfare has had a major impact on community and professional perceptions of child abuse (Parton 1986; Frost 1991, in Carter, Jeffs and Smith 1992:3). In the United Kingdom, child abuse enquiries have, on the one hand called for more interventionist social work, and on the other hand, questioned the right of the state to intervene in family life (Frost 1990:17–18). The powerful ideology that all children prosper best in a family environment is the belief currently favoured by a number of governments, and the U.K and Australia are among these (King and Trowell 1992). Biological bonds are perceived as synonymous with psychological bonds (Fernanadez 1996:23). Whilst this is desirable for the majority of children it fails to consider the interests of the more vulnerable children and their parents. It is part of a larger debate about the changing role of the state in the family, and in parenting, and individual and family rights. Garbarino (1996:292) suggests it is centred in a debate about whether or not child rearing is a private activity until proven otherwise and indecision about the community's right of access into a family for the purpose of preventing child maltreatment. It is also part of a debate about the right of women to be seen as individuals separate from their male partners (Parton 1985, 1991; Dingwall 1989). Breckenridge (1995:38) argues, when writing about child sexual abuse, that issues of justice and equity are not properly addressed if a child's rights are still largely always identified with those of their family.

Child Welfare Legislation

> Children who are victims of avoidable, adult-inflicted harm and injury, now more than ever before, must make their case and have their case made for them by social workers, police officers, lawyers, judges and other legal practitioners who have the job of juxtaposing the competing needs and rights of children, with those of parents and those of the state (Wattam 1992:1).

The *Children and Young Persons Act* 1989 provides the legislative framework for child protection services in Victoria and similar legislation exists across the six states and two territories of Australia. Legislation allows for the removal of children, from their parents, if there is unacceptable risk of harm as a result of abuse or threat of harm to a child:

> if there is an unacceptable risk of harm to the child (CYPA s.87 (1)(j)) as a result of physical injury (CYPA s. 63 :(c)), sexual abuse (CYPA s.66 (d)), harm or threat of harm to a child's physical development or health (CYPA s.63 (f)), abandonment (CYPA s.63 (a)), or the child's parents are dead or incapacitated (CYPA s.63 (b)).

However the legislation also directs that the preservation of the family is fundamental to the court's decision-making, and that children's relationships with their family need to be strengthened and maintained. The court has the authority to intervene to protect children at risk, but intervention must not be beyond the requirements of the child's welfare. The court:

> must have regard to the need to give the widest possible protection and assistance to the family as the fundamental group unit of society (CYPA s.87 (1)(a));

> [and], have regard to the need to strengthen and preserve the relationship between the child and the child's family (CYPA s.87 (1)(b)).

Further, any order:

> must take into consideration the effect of the finding or order on the stability of family relationships (CYPA s.87 (1)(e)) and if a:

> child is removed from his or her family, to plan the re-unification of the child with his or her family, wherever practicable (CYPA s.87 (1)(f)).

The child protection service is expected to enhance the ability of parents to care for their children in a safe and proper way by implementing 'the services necessary to enable the child to remain in the custody of his or her parent' (CYPA s.86 (2) (b)) and that 'intervention into family life should be to the minimum extent that is necessary to secure the protection of the child' (CYPA s.87 (1) (g)).

When all steps reasonably possible have been taken by the welfare authorities (the Department of Human Services, Victoria), and, 'there is an unacceptable risk of harm to the child' (CYPA s.87 (1)(j)), and a child's best interests are served by the court making an order, then the court may make a protection order. The orders set out in Section 85 of the *Children and Young*

Persons Act 1989, are an Undertaking (l)(a) (iii), a Supervision Order (l) (a) (ii), a Custody to the Third Party Order (l(a)(iii)), a Supervised Custody Order (l)(a)(iv), a Custody to Secretary Order ((l)(a)(v)), a Guardianship to Secretary Order (l(a)(vi)), or an Interim Protection Order (l(b)).

The legislation includes provision for the court to make permanent care orders for children who have been away from their parents for two years and who cannot resume living with their parent either because it is not in their best interests or because their parent cannot resume the care of their child (CYPA s.112 (a)(b)).

The legislation uses the terms abuse and neglect to refer to cases of non-accidental physical injury to children, to refer to psychological and sexual abuse and, to parental failure to provide an adequate and acceptable standard of care for their children. Yet how child abuse is understood, and the criteria used to define it and measure it, are not spelt out in the legislation; rather, they are left to the discretion of the individual decision-maker. However, on balance, child abuse is generally understood to be:

> The physical or psychological damage caused to the child by the abusive behaviour of others or the failure of others to protect the child from such damage, (characterised by) the deliberate infliction of physical, emotional or sexual harm on the child. Child neglect is also included in this framework; it is conceptualised as a failure to provide conditions which are essential to the health, physical, and emotional development of the child. It is a failure to meet a child's basic needs for food, shelter/hygiene, health and the child fails to thrive as a consequence (James 1994a:2).

Physical abuse is typically understood as a physical injury that arises from deliberate harm to a child. Whilst the parent may not have intended to hurt the child the harm occurs and is an inappropriate response to dealing with a child. Emotional abuse is generally understood to be the consequences of parental behaviour that destroys a child's self-esteem and social competence. (New South Wales Child Protection Council 1993 in James 1994a:21). Sexual abuse is understood to occur when an older person uses their power over a child to involve the child in sexual activity to gratify the needs of the older person. This activity violates social taboos and/or family roles (NSW Child Protection Council 1993 in James 1994a:2).

Clark (1995:16) notes the cornerstone of these grounds is the need to prove the child 'has suffered or is likely to suffer significant harm' and 'the child's parents have not protected or are unlikely to protect, the child from harm of that type' (CYPA s.63 (1) (c) (d) (e)). How these terms are to be interpreted is not set out in legislation, rather it is left to the magistrate's interpretation and discretion.

The conduct of proceedings in the Family Division of the Children's Court, in Victoria, is undertaken in a more informal manner than in the adult jurisdiction (CYPA s.82 (l)(a)). This is to give magistrates greater scope to enquire into the evidence presented by the parties and to take a more interventionist role in the proceedings:

> to 'consider evidence on the balance of probabilities' (CYPA s.82 (l)(c)); and to 'inform itself on a matter in such a manner as it thinks fit, despite any rules of evidence to the contrary' (CYPA s.82 (1)(d)).

However, the complexity and vagueness about what constitutes child abuse and serious family and individual problems creates difficulty for a legal system that relies on precision in facts and evidence to decide cases (Adler 1979:48). The assessments that child protection workers provide for court are often perceived as being vague, woolly and difficult to pin down. These assessments are often more opinion than fact and the law finds this difficult to deal with (Adler 1979). This lack of factual information, combined with a lack of clear, and agreed, definitions of concepts such as significant harm, hampers legal decision-making. The limited availability of appropriate resources or facilities to address the variety of family problems which arise in child protection matters can make it difficult to decide on an order that is in the best interests of a child. It can be difficult also make orders that accommodate the autonomy of the family and the rights of parents (Frost in Carter, Jeffs and Smith 1989: Parton 1985).

The Children's Court

The Children's Court in Victoria, as it is in all Australian states, is a separate branch of the Magistrates Court, although the Victorian Government in 2000 aims to give the court individual status. The Children's Court has the same powers of the Magistrates Courts, although it has its own procedures as set out in the *Children and Young Persons Act 1989,* Section 18. The Children's Court is an open court unless the court orders otherwise. It comprises two divisions: the Criminal Division and the Family Division. It is the Family Division which has jurisdiction to hear child protection matters. Within the Family Division, a court is set aside as the Mention Court. It is in this court that the majority of child protection applications commence, where orders about cases are sought, warrants are sought, orders extended, pre-hearing conferences are ordered, and where the need for the hearing of a case is established. The majority of cases are dealt with in this court. The role of the Mention Court is to assess the immediate risk to a child and placement for a child pending investigation for hearing the child protection application. The *Children and Young Persons Act* 1989, established the Children's Court as a specialist jurisdiction. Indeed, Section 601t of the Family Law Act, Australia, gives precedence to proceedings being heard in the Children's Court.

The Children's Court is a high workload court: there has been a marked increase in the number of protection applications (H&CS Protective Services Statistical Report 1993,94:1), the cases have become more complex, and contested cases last longer (Fogarty 1993:140). This creates considerable pressure on magistrates assigned to the court:

> The work of the Children's Court is different. It deals with matters which are often more complex and the outcomes frequently more devastating in their consequences for young people and their families than the bread and butter cases of the adult summary jurisdiction (Laster 1993:41).

The *Children and Young Person's Act 1989* sets out directions for the appointment of magistrates to the court. Magistrates, in Victoria, are currently appointed from the ranks of practising legal practitioners. New magistrates are assigned to the court by the Chief Magistrate:

> In assigning a magistrate to be a magistrate, for the court, the Chief Magistrate must have regard to the experience of the magistrate in matters relating to child welfare (CYPA s11(2)).

Since 1984, a Children's Court Senior Magistrate (s.12) has been appointed to oversee the practice and procedure of the court. Magistrates assigned to the Children's Court generally work there for at least 12 months to gain familiarity with the jurisdiction. Magistrates hear cases in both the Family and Criminal Divisions of the court. Assignment to the Children's Court is not always voluntary. The Children's Court has low status in the judicial hierarchy, the work is complex, and the pressures on magistrates are greater than in the adult jurisdiction (Douglas and Laster 1992:23). Magistrates assigned to the court may have no prior knowledge or experience in the Family Division and may be unfamiliar with its specialist work (Fogarty 1977:135).

The Child Protection Process

Proceedings in the Family Division typically commence when the statutory welfare authority (the Department of Human Services, Victoria) lodges an application for a child protection order. The child protection service lodges a report setting out information relevant to a child's situation and the results of their preliminary investigations. In many cases, parents consent to the child protection service recommendations about their child. Where parents do not consent to these recommendations, the magistrate generally refers the case to a pre-hearing conference to see whether the parents and the child protection service can reach an agreement about child protection concerns. Pre-hearing conferences (CYPA s.82) are conducted by convenors and attended by the child's parents, their legal representatives, and by child protection workers. Child protection workers in Victoria are employed by the Department of Human Services, Victoria. They have social welfare qualifications and approximately half the practitioners have tertiary qualifications in social work.

Children have separate legal representation if they are aged seven years and over and can give instructions. Relatives of the child, or parents, representatives of the appropriate ethnic community, for example, may also attend the pre-hearing conference where necessary. If the case does not resolve at the conference then it proceeds to a contested hearing in front of a magistrate.

When a matter is listed for hearing, it is made out according to the grounds set out in the *Children and Young Persons Act 1989*, s. 63: a child is in need of protection as a consequence of physical or sexual abuse, emotional harm or threat of harm, lack of regard to a child's health, abandonment, or parental incapacity to care for the child.

In presenting the case to the court, the child protection service recommends a plan of intervention and recommends orders which are suitable, in accordance with the *Children and Young Persons Act 1989*, s. 85. Before an order is made, the court must find that the child is indeed in need of protection. New protection applications are made either by notification or by apprehension. By notification means that the child protection service advises parents that a protection application is to be sought. By apprehension means a child is removed from the family pending the hearing of the protection application. If a child is removed by apprehension, or the parents voluntarily place the child in foster care, then an interim accommodation order (IAO) is made. This order lasts for 21 days; it prescribes the placement of the child with a suitable person (who may be a parent) and sets out access matters. During this time reports are ordered and the investigation of child protection concerns is undertaken. When the IAO expires, the case returns to court and a decision is made. If the case is resolved, the order is struck out. If not, the interim accommodation order may be extended, to accommodate any problems with reports, with parent attendance at court etc., until a child protection order may be made.

Interim accommodation orders return to court every 21 days to be reviewed by a magistrate. Each case returns when a child protection order expires: be it an undertaking, a supervision order, a custody order. Cases return to court if there is a breach of an order, or where circumstances change and a different order is sought. Guardianship orders are reviewed by the court every 12 months (or two years in some cases).

The decision of the court to make a child protection order acknowledges that a child is at risk and that the child protection service has demonstrated this risk is real. It demonstrates that the parents have not been able to lessen this risk in the eyes of the court. A protection order allows a plan for a child to be set in place; the plan will aim to either maintain the child with the parents or to return the child home after a period of time. This allows parents to, for example, get into treatment programmes (parenting, anger management, substance abuse treatment etc.) and it allows the child protection service to set up support services for families.

Lawyers represent parties in contested matters or in complex cases. However, more straightforward matters are presented in court, on behalf of the child protection service, by court officers who are attached to the Legal and Court Advisory Unit (and employed by the Department of Human Services); court officers may be lawyers or social workers. Legal representation for children aged seven years and over, and for parents who qualify for legal aid, is provided by the Legal Aid Commission.

Cases Brought to Court

Section 63 of the *Children* and 28 Young *Persons Act 1989* sets out the grounds for a child protection application. Grounds involving emotional and psychological harm and jeopardy to the child's intellectual development were the basis of one-third of protection applications completed during 1993, followed by significant harm as a result of physical injury (27 per cent), and sexual abuse (11 per cent). The majority of these protection applications were proven (80 per cent) during 1993.

Custody and Guardianship to the Secretary Orders were 43 per cent of orders made by the court during the first half of 1994 (Protective Services, Statistical Report 1993/94:7–8).

The number of protection notifications for 1991/92, 1992/93 and 1993/94 are set out in Table 1.1 below. The increase in notifications in 1993/94 reflects the introduction of mandatory reporting of child abuse in Victoria. Notifications of physical abuse increased by 45 per cent and sexual abuse by 26 per cent in 1993–94.

Although not included in mandatory reporting, notification of emotional abuse increased by 58 per cent and neglect by 34 per cent in the same period (Protective Services Statistical Report 1993–94:1–2).

Forty per cent of cases investigated by the child protection service in 1993/94 were substantiated. That is to say that in 6,116 cases, it was confirmed that the child had suffered or was likely to suffer significant harm and the child's parents had failed to protect the child from harm (Protective Services Statistical Report, 1993/94:5). The outcomes of the child protection applications for 1992/93 and 1993/94 are set out below.

In 1993/94, 19,746 notifications were for children under 12 years of age and 6,311 for children aged 12 years and over. Children aged from birth to four years were more or less gender equal in terms of notifications; cases involving allegations of sexual abuse were the exception to the gender equality in notifications as 60 per cent of these notifications involved girls less than 12 years of age.

In 1997, 3,115 cases were completed in the Family Division of the Children's Court of Victoria (see Table 1.6). Nearly one-third (32.7 per cent) of the family cases involved children up to four years, less than one-quarter involved children aged five to nine years, more than one-quarter (27 per cent) involved children aged 10 to 14 years, and 15.9 per cent involved children aged 15 years or over. Slightly more male children (51.7 per cent) were represented in these figures. There was an increase in the number of family cases dealt with by the court: an increase of 4.6 per cent for male children and 9.6 per cent for female children.

The most common outcomes for child protection matters before the Children's Court in 1997, were Custody to the Secretary Orders (867), Guardianship to Secretary Orders (793) and Supervision Orders (792). These represented 27.8 per cent, 25.5 per cent and 25.4 per cent of all completed family cases.

Table 1.1 Total notifications received by DHS 1991–94

Period	Notification	% Change
1991/92	18,538	+3
1992/93	19,344	+4
1993/94	26,622	+38

Table 1.2 Protection applications per year sought by DHS

Period	Notifications	Protection applications	Protection applications as % of notifications
1992/93	19,344	1,191	6
1993/94	26,622	1,159	6

Table 1.3 The grounds on which notifications were made to DHS in 1993/94

	1993/94	
Abuse type	No.	% of total
Physical	6,657	25
Sexual	4,078	15
Emotional	5,888	22
Neglect	9,311	36
Other	645	2
Total	26,579	100

Table 1.4 Number of substantiated child protection notifications

Period	No cases investigated	No cases substantiated	Substantiation rate (%)
1992/93	10,027	4,198	42
1993/94	15,179	6,116	40

Table 1.5   Grounds of protection application by age: 1993/94

Age	Physical	Sexual	Emotional	Neglect
0–4	2,397	1,222	2,020	3,943
5–11	2,505	1,875	2,134	3,306
12 +	1,637	909	1,615	1,867
Unknown	118	72	119	195
Total	6,657	4,078	5,888	9,311

Table 1.6   Grounds for protection and irreconcilable difference applications heard, Children's Court, 1997

Grounds statutory reference	Males	Females	Total	% of total
Abandoned (89/56.63.a)	29	37	66	3.2
Parents dead or incapacitated (89/56.63.b)	84	65	149	7.1
Significant harm – physical injury (89/56.63.c)	482	412	894	42.8
Significant harm – sexual abuse (89/56.63.d)	60	92	152	7.3
Emotional, psychological harm (89/56.63.e)l	281	272	553	26.5
Physical development or health harmed (89/56.63.f)l	44	37	81	3.9
Combination of 63.e and 63.f (89/56.63.z)	93	100	193	9.2
Irreconcilable differences, person having custody (89/56.71.1)	1	0	1	0.0
Irreconcilable differences, child (89/56.71.2)	0	0	0	0.0
Total	1,074	1,015	2,089	100.0

Source: Statistics of the Children's Court of Victoria, 1997:18.

The steady increase in the number of child protection cases brought to the attention of the court confirms Fogarty's (1989) findings that it is a court with a high workload and an atmosphere of considerable pressure. The work is important and difficult, cases are increasingly complex and require specialised knowledge:

> it is a highly emotive jurisdiction and because many parents have limited social skills, this is an arduous and difficult task. Consequently the magistrates must have the qualities of independence and expertise and they need to be appropriately resourced and supported to carry out these duties (Fogarty 1989:140).

The Magistrate and the Children's Court

The Children's Court, Victoria, and the legislative framework which deals with child protection matters, has been the subject of a number of reports. Carney (1983) proposed changes to the Children's Court, Victoria, to better reflect the importance of children in our society. Most particularly he recommended that magistrates appointed to the jurisdiction have:

> an interest and enthusiasm for work in the children's court [and] aptitude for working with children and some training in behavioural sciences (Carney 1983:95).

He expressed concern about the inconsistencies in decisions made about children across different courts, in particular the difference between metropolitan and country Victorian Courts. He believed the status of the Children's Court ought to be enhanced to acknowledge the social import of the decisions made in this jurisdiction and the importance of the magistrates' work.

Justice Fogarty (1989, 1993) also expressed concern that the Children's Court 'is not at times accorded the status within legal circles, the department (DHS) and perhaps the community that its work justifies' (1993:147). Yet the work of the court is specialised and requires expertise in the evaluation of information about children. The need for this expertise has not been broadly recognised either within or outside the legal system.

The Victorian State Labour government, newly elected in 1999, undertook to address this concern. The Attorney-General will make the Children's Court a separate court and invest its chief magistrate with status equal to a County Court Judge (Mr Rob Hulls, Attorney-General, *The Age*, 14 April 2000).

However, the legislation enacted to protect children delivers potentially conflicting signals to decision-makers in children's matters (Fogarty 1993). Whilst the preservation of the family is generally the broad aim of such legislation, the court must also protect the child from harm. Yet, the legislation generally fails to give any clear indication of how the court decides the best interests of the child. In Victoria, the benchmark of significant harm is the criterion for establishing that child abuse has occurred. Definitions of what this means are not provided in the legislation and this may result in 'at times greater weight is attached to that word than was intended or is necessary so that an unduly heavy burden is required by the court before the ground is established' (Fogarty 1993:94).

This jurisdiction requires magistrates to put aside the approaches of the adult jurisdiction. The discretionary nature of the decision-making is more complex and requires experience and interest in children. Matters are:

> often more complex and the outcomes frequently more devastating in their consequences for young people and their families than the 'bread and butter' cases of the adult summary jurisdiction (Laster 1993:13).

How do magistrates go about judicial decision-making? Do magistrates and other professionals develop formulaic responses to the varying child welfare matters that arise in children's courts? Do they decide on combinations of factors and severity of circumstances which warrant the making of a child protection order? The next chapter looks at research into judicial decision-making and considers these issues in terms of this research.

Chapter Two

Uncovering the Decision Process

> a judicial sentence is an expression of power on behalf of society, made in its name (Fitzmaurice and Pease 1986:1).

The study of judicial decision-making has typically focused on specific aspects of judicial behaviour, most particularly in the area of sentencing disparity and sentencing behaviour. Much of the research is confined to the adult jurisdictions and to identifying factors that are significant in sentence prediction and outcomes (Konecni and Ebbeson 1982; Lovegrove 1988; Lawrence 1981 et al.; Kapardis 1981). The investigation of judicial decision-making has focused on three main areas. First, the frames of reference and information that magistrates and judges use to decide cases (Hood and Sparks 1970; Lawrence and Browne 1981; McKnight 1981). Second, the identification of the organisational and social-psychological variables that impact on judicial decision-making. Third, on developing decision-making models that could predict decision outcomes.

What was typically found was that the seriousness of the offence, and the existence of a previous record directly influenced judicial sentencing decisions. However, there was great variation in the weight that individual judges and magistrates attached to offender characteristics and to the offence. These variations were also influenced by magistrates' and judges' individual sentencing objectives, by how they used case information provided to the court, by their personal values and attitudes, and by the legal and external constraints that were placed on them.

This chapter looks then at what these studies say about the culture of the magistracy, the nature of discretion and what influences their legal decision-making. It also notes studies undertaken, predominantly in the juvenile justice area, that explore the tension that emerges when there are both legal and welfare matters to decide. The chapter also sets out how the study of magistrates' decision-making in the Melbourne Children's Court was undertaken and what it hoped to find.

Judicial Decision-making

> It appears from the analysis that we can explain more about sentencing by knowing a few things about the judge than by knowing a great deal about the facts of the case (Hogarth 1971:350).

The reasons for the disparity in sentencing decisions is generally explained by the variation of approach of individual sentencers, and by the case factors they look for when deciding case outcome (Hogarth 1971; Hood 1962; Tarling 1979; Ashworth 1984). Hogarth found, in his study of 78 Canadian magistrates, looking at the relationship between case facts, magistrate characteristics, and legal and other external variables to sentencing, that the individual penal philosophies and attitudes of magistrates might explain disparities in sentencing:

> once we knew the social purpose that a magistrate attempted to achieve through sentencing, the whole of the penal philosophy unfolded as a logical extension of it (1971:361).

Lawrence and Homel also found that magistrates' individual beliefs about the aims of sentencing influenced what case information they saw as relevant:

> a magistrate's or judge's views on the aims of sentencing and on the status of a particular offence as a crime may have direct effect on how he processes information about such matters (1987:157).

Bond and Lemon (1979, 1981) sought to explore the extent to which training might influence magistrate attitudes and, therefore, sentencing. In comparing two groups of magistrates, one which received training and the other which did not, they found magistrates with training had a more sympathetic view of defendants and this influenced their discretion in sentencing. Certainly, Lemon (1974) found in an earlier study comparing the sentencing decisions of recently appointed, and more experienced, magistrates, that experienced magistrates were more likely to have developed specific decision strategies. However, magistrates and judges, in the various studies undertaken, emphasised the notion of 'individualised justice' and that each case must be judged on its merits. This was found by Ashworth (1984), in a pilot study in the UK, who analysed 96 cases and, using sentencing vignettes, interviewed 25 judges about their sentencing practices. The judges emphasised the individuality of cases, and brought all issues about legal decision-making down to individual cases.

Hood (1962) and Tarling (1979) found that disparities in sentencing patterns could be explained not only by this individualised view but also by the characteristics of the local jurisdiction and its particular sentencing practices and approaches to dealing with offenders. Tarling (1974), in his statistical analysis of sentencing in 30 English courts, found that objective 'legal' factors could only partially account for disparities between the court's sentencing patterns.

Hood and Sparks (1972) found, when seeking to construct a theoretical model of judicial decision-making based on an archival study of case records, that it was impossible to make a connection between a judge's background and their case decisions because judicial attitudes varied according to the nature of the case. Combined factors such as legal environment, relevant statutes and conventions, the judge hearing the case, offence and offender variables, failed to uncover a decision-making model.

McKnight (1981) combined personal construct theory with multi-attribute theory to investigate whether various selected case and magistrate factors could predict sentences. Using a combination of quantitative method and conversational techniques, he asked nine magistrates from various UK courts to sentence cases from three case histories by rank-ordering a set of available sentences. He presented magistrates with simulated case histories that contained a brief description of the events leading to the charge, the plea, the finding of the court and the past record of the defendant.

He found that each magistrate had their own views about the relative importance of individual case factors, about rehabilitation, and about sentencing, and that these were weighted according to what each magistrate considered was important for the business of justice and the justice role. McKnight (1981) commented however that if magistrates were to occupy another role these same constructs might be weighted differently. McKnight suggested that his findings indicated the importance of personal construct theory to the understanding of magistrates' sentencing behaviour:

> choice results from a combination of beliefs and values [and] any differences between magistrates beliefs and values are likely to result in different choices. Inconsistency in sentencing is comprehensible and predictable because of the subjectivity in sentencing which the legal system allows (McKnight 1981:146).

Influences on Sentencing

A number of studies investigated whether particular factors, when combined, could predict sentencing outcomes. Hine, McWilliams and Pease (1978) and Hampson (1986) investigated the level of agreement between welfare recommendations to the court and magistrates decisions. Hine, McWilliams and Pease (1978) used a simulation exercise in which magistrates were presented with cases for assessment; some cases included a report with a recommendation, some a report without a recommendation, some without a report. They found that while pre-sentence welfare reports influenced dispositions, the magistrates commented that the simulation exercise did not accurately mirror court conditions. They could not be sure the simulated decisions accurately reflected real decisions.

Hampson analysed 982 children's court records at Wellington (NZ) Magistrates' Court to investigate whether social worker or probation officer recommendations to the court concurred with the magistrates' decisions. He found that the social work recommendations were indeed followed and wondered therefore if 'it is probable that the major determinant of any bias in sentencing comes from the social worker rather than the magistrate' (Hampson 1986:49).

He proposed a relationship between labelling theory and sentencing; particular theories about juvenile delinquency held by professionals shaped their view of the young offender and therefore influenced the court decision. He did not canvass whether social workers and magistrates operated according to similar formulae for determining outcomes; this is likely when professional groups work in the same domain.

Kapardis and Farrington (1981) used a simulated sentencing exercise to ask 23, then 168, magistrates in England to decide sentences for cases which had been before courts. By extracting the variables considered the most influential in sentencing, they aimed to develop a sentencing severity scale. Unlike Hine, McWilliams and Pease (1978), they found considerable similarity between real and simulated sentencing decisions. However, Kapardis and Farrington (1981) confirmed the difficulty in carrying out real-life sentencing experiments with magistrates and questioned the validity of findings from simulation cases.

The factor Kapardis and Farrington (1981) found most influential in sentencing was seriousness of the crime, particularly when offenders had a serious criminal record, were male and of a higher social status. The greater the harm caused by the offence, the more severe was the sentence. Factors such as age, race, breach of trust, prevalence of crime in the local area, were found not to be significant. The authors postulated that retribution, rather than deterrence, was, for these magistrates, the dominant aim of sentencing.

Kapardis (1985) later compared factors such as the magistrate's social background, age, gender, religion, politics and sentencing objectives in a review of 140 sentencing decisions. While he found older magistrates were more influenced by the offence than the offender, the relationship between other social background factors and the sentencing decision was inconclusive. Corbett's (1978) study of Magistrate Courts in England using case vignettes, to interview 23 magistrates and approximately 50 Clerks of Court, also showed little consensus across decision-making.

Carroll (1978) proposed that the way a legal decision-maker views the causes of crime influences their decisions. Whilst this finding emerged from a study of parole decisions, not judicial decisions, it mirrors the research noted earlier, that an individual decision-maker's beliefs on crime and sentencing influence their decisions. Carroll suggests the law looks for the objective causes of crimes; referred to by attribution theory as 'causality – forseeability – intentionality' (1978:253). Whether the legal decision-maker sees the cause of crime as internal to the individual, such as mental illness, or the cause as external, such as poor general economic conditions, will also influence the decision maker. So too does their view as to whether the crime is intended or unintentional.

However, when Carroll (1978) investigated the theories of crime held by law enforcement officials, in Pennsylvania, USA, and the effect on their parole decisions, he found that the most important consideration for parole officers was their view about the risk of the offender offending again. This exemplified his view that legal decision-makers develop decision frameworks that influence their response to the case. Thus, when decision-makers encounter certain case information or certain behaviours in a case, it triggers a cognitive schema, and this will include ideas about the responses to specific problems, predictions for the future, the origins of such criminal behaviour, and the like.

Fitzmaurice and Pease (1986) were also interested in the strategies of judgement, or heuristics, judges referred to when giving reasons for sentences. In their study of sentencing disparity amongst judges, they found that a judge's initial perceptions of a case and the issues important to it, determined what they perceived as relevant to the final decision. They found, as did Kahneman and Tversky (1982) and Ashworth et al. (1984), that judges were influenced by an individual's demeanour in the court, and by 'types' of defendants and these views influenced their decisions.

Fitzmaurice and Pease (1986) proposed that judicial decision-making is subject to the same kinds of errors which are commonly found in decision-making. They referred to the notion of illusory correlation, the idea that people assume facts are causally related to each other even when they are not. This is of particular relevance to judicial decision-making when judges believe particular relationships exist between variables which do not in fact exist. Since judges receive little feedback about their decisions, they rely on such perceptions which are difficult to challenge. These beliefs may also mean that reports to the court will have less effect than is desirable. Judicial decision-makers tend to overvalue the importance of individual case information and ignore the prior probabilities of outcomes and information in other similar cases (Fitzmaurice and Pease 1986:24).

Fitzmaurice and Pease (1986:19) also found that judges, as do many other people in the community, assume their views and values are shared more widely than they are and that their own judgments and choices are relatively common- what is referred to as the false consensus bias. This was reported also by Ashworth et al. (1984) who observed that judges, despite their social distance, believed they could identify what was informed public opinion.

Lovegrove (1989) sought to develop a conceptual framework of judicial decision-making which made explicit the rules of sentencing and explained the sentencing task as objective, quantitative and deliberative. He sought to address issues such as the appropriate goals for sentencing, the proper limits of judges' discretion, the weighting of information in cases, and what specific sentences ought to be given. The first issue for the judge to decide, however, was:

> whether the sentence should emphasise the seriousness of the offence or whether the rehabilitation prospects of the offender should be the salient determinant of sentence (Lovegrove 1989:9).

He found there was a direct relationship between the characteristics of a case and the sentence imposed on the offender and found seriousness of the offence indeed determined sentence. He achieved these findings using simulation cases, a method which gave him greater control over the presentation of case factors than statistical analysis of case records. Lovegrove found the study of judicial decision-making was particularly challenging:

> Winning the hearts and minds of the judiciary is part of the research challenge in the field of judicial sentencing and empirical psychology and it may sometimes

require both social as well as legal and political skills with no small measure of luck thrown in. One must be prepared to go forward slowly and graciously (Lovegrove 1989:68).

Judicial decision-making occurs in a framework of complex and authoritative rules. Richardson (1984:547) commented on the complexity of judicial decisions and that 'social inquiry does not sit well with the adversary system'. The primary function of courts is to determine disputes according to law. The law is unprepared when cases presented are welfare matters which may involve decisions about competing social values rather than specific disputes. In these cases there is little guidance on how to assess social data or how much material the court needs to decide a case.

Konecni and Ebbeson (1981, 1984 et al.) have undertaken a number of studies of the decision strategies of judicial and legal decision-making. They sought to discover what and how information about cases influenced sentencing, and what was the relative importance of these different factors, and whether there were causal relationships between factors 'to discover empirically the factors that sentencing judges consider in making their decisions and the relative weights that they assign to those factors ...' (Ebbeson and Konecni 1981:295).

Their 1984 San Diego study focused on the decision strategies of judges and which offenders attracted what sentences. They were interested also in how participants differed in the weight they attached to particular case information, and in their perceptions of the seriousness of offences, and what they perceived as mitigating circumstances. Ebbeson and Konecni used a multi-method approach of 'in-situ' research, archival analysis of case materials (hearing transcripts, court documents), interviews, questionnaire and observation of public hearings. They interviewed eight judges in chambers and sixteen judges completed questionnaires. Eight judges completed scales on which they rated the factors that influenced legal decision-making (for example, recommendations from parole officers or others, the existence of a prior record, the severity of outcome, etc.). Case simulations were also presented to three subject groups.

Ebbeson and Konecni (1984) found however, that the actual hearing of the case was in many ways simply a ritual as it was the recommendations by prosecutors and by probation officers that were influential. This was in direct contradiction to judges' strong beliefs about discretion and individualised justice. Ebbeson and Konecni (1984) found legal decision-making was more simple than the legal system suggested. These findings also reflected the researchers' conceptualisation of the court system as a network of decision points and that the judge is not the only decision maker in any case.

In Ebbeson and Konecni's (1975) studies of judicial decision-making in bail hearings (referred to by Konecni and Ebbeson 1984), they found the influence of the prosecutor's recommendations and the strength of the defendant's local ties were the significant influences. Eighteen judges were presented with simulated cases and the researchers aimed to predict bail decisions. Seriousness of the offence, and prosecution recommendations were found to be important to the judge; however there was no consistency between the simulation and the actual decisions. The researchers explained the reliance of judges on prosecutors' recommendations was the judges' way of dealing with conflicting inputs of information they received. It was also a mechanism for dealing with the cognitive and processing capacity limitations of individual decision-makers which makes it difficult to respond to more than one or two factors simultaneously.

Given the sources of information available to judges about a case e.g. type of offence, prior record, offender's social history, the various beliefs about offenders and offences, and the significance of judicial decision-making to the community, there would appear to be many interests to be balanced in judicial decision-making. Yet there were no guidelines as to how judges might weight the information relevant to a decision:

> what information about a case they must take into account, what relative importance they ought to attach to different types of information, what role, if any, social influence ought to play in a participant's decision (Ebbeson and Konecni 1984:8).

Ebbeson and Konecni (1984) suggested it was a combination of rules of law, discretion and the behaviour of the system participants, which produced judicial decisions. This was in contrast to the traditional view that it is the rule of law, due process, and administrative guidelines which determine decisions. Lovegrove (1989:67) believed however that this study failed to really understand the principles and conventions of the judiciary, and that its findings reflected the problems associated with the application of psychological research to sentencing.

Australian studies of the magistracy have also focused on magistrate sentencing decisions and their determinants (see Lawrence, various; Lawrence and Homel 1987, 1992; Lovegrove 1989; Homel 1983; Polk and Tait 1989; Douglas 1989). Douglas (1989) explored how magistrates made decisions in the magistrates' court by observing hearings and by gathering statistical data from court records. He chose this method both to witness the mechanics of the courtroom encounter, and because court records are often neither comprehensive nor accessible.

The study found that sentences were determined largely by the offence alleged, and by the offender's prior criminal record. He found that low socioeconomic status males were more likely to receive a sentence, and were also more likely to appear in court. Magistrates referred to defendant's records, to any mitigating factors raised by the defence, to reports, and to character evidence when delivering sentence. How guilt and liability were assessed appeared based on the magistrate's subjective criteria as well as on the objective criteria of offence and prior record. Magistrates were not obliged to give reasons for their sentences although the research found that many do. The data suggested differences between magistrates' sentencing outcomes but it was inconclusive. The most significant influences were those noted above:

> A defendant's fate will be rather more strongly influenced by what he is alleged to have done, and by his prior convictions and general character than it will by who happens to be sitting on the bench (Douglas 1989:97).

Douglas and Laster (1991) then sought to explore the more subtle aspects of the decision-making process. They used a qualitative approach to explore the magistrate's subjective reality in a way quantitative methods could not. In this study thirty magistrates (in Victoria, Australia), were asked about the individual qualities a magistrate needed in their work, about the influence of legal representation in a case, about legal concepts such as reasonable doubt and balance of probabilities, and about their relationship with other court participants. They were asked also if they had any particular sentencing frameworks, about the influence of appeals to a higher court about decisions, and what were the most difficult decisions and stressful aspects of the job.

They found magistrates saw themselves as part of a larger organisational culture. They were 'highly individualistic' (Douglas and Laster 1992:13), yet as a group held the law in high regard and saw their task as one of achieving a balance between legal considerations, societal expectations and the varying attitudes of people who appear before them. Magistrates had a diverse range of viewpoints, and range of backgrounds. There was little evidence that background, gender or age were connected to attitude. They saw themselves also as standing between the individual and the government to ensure offenders received 'fair' treatment. Douglas and Laster (1992) postulated that the strength of the magistrate culture meant the job of the magistrate was carried out in a legally uniform manner regardless of individual magistrate attributes.

Magistrates had little knowledge of how particular sentences were implemented or of the effect of these on the offenders or on society. They stated it is not part of their job to resolve the social problems of those who come before the courts. Court outcomes had to be legally justifiable and meet social expectations of deterrence, reduction and punishment of crime: 'There is among many magistrates recognition that many social problems can't be resolved or cured by the criminal system' (Douglas and Laster 1992:64).

Yet, magistrates are expected to make the 'right decision', and to seek out information that is useful for solving the particular problem before them (Kahneman, Slovic and Tversky 1982). Decision-making is therefore a complex process of gathering and interpreting information, perhaps under pressure, and at the same time recognising one's personal values and preferences yet keeping them separate from the decision situation (Hallett and Birchall 1992: 288). Decision theory examines the frameworks individuals use to solve problems and make decisions. It is interesting to explore this research in terms of the ideas that may inform magistrates' decisions in child protection matters.

Decision Theory

> [Decision-making is] a process by which a person, group, or organisation identifies a choice or judgement to be made, gathers and evaluates information about alternatives, and select from the alternatives (Carroll and Johnson 1990:19).

Decision-making is an interplay between information, interpretation and preference which the individual combines to produce judgements and choices. Carroll and Johnson (1990) found that individuals devise strategies, also referred to as heuristics, constructed from their personal characteristics, from their past experience and the current circumstances, in order to work through the alternatives pertinent to a problem and so make a decision. Individuals select the information they need about a situation based on their intuition and on sources they view as creditworthy. They developed a typology of decision-making which explained the decision process as a series of stages revolving around problem recognition and the generation of alternatives about problem outcome, the information which is sought, the judgement choice decided, and feedback about this outcome.

Certainty, uncertainty and risk play a role in decision-making as does the availability of information (Carroll and Johnson 1990). Decision-making in a context of uncertainty, which is typical of child protection matters creates particular tensions for decision-makers. They develop strategies to reduce this uncertainty when they may have little knowledge of possible alternative solutions or there is little information available to assist them, and where the decision maker has little control over the elements which are central to the problem's resolution. MacCrimmon and Taylor (1976) report that these strategies are influenced by the individuals' particular perceptions about the problem, their experience with this category of problem, and whether or not this has been successful.

Decisions were also influenced by the individual characteristics of the decision-maker, such as their risk-taking propensity. They found also that individuals might ignore, avoid, or absorb the uncertainty and delay the resolution. Jabes (1982) suggests that decision-making might be an unpleasant exercise when the decision alternatives are unattractive – which is characteristic of decision-making in child abuse matters. He describes child protection decisions as 'non-programmed' decisions, as distinct from 'programmed' decisions which are amenable to traditional problem-solving techniques (Jabes 1982:56).

MacCrimmon and Taylor (1976) found that how an individual dealt with information in contexts of uncertainty influenced their decision strategies. Individuals who take a concrete approach to problem resolution, and have less flexible belief systems, had difficulty with decisions. They managed the situation by seeking out information which was compatible with their particular decision approach. Hallett and Birchall (1992) and Lawrence and Browne (1981) noted that legal thinking and bureaucratic systems value the observance of rules to limit the varying organisational and political factors that may seek to influence decisions. Magistrates can be described as organisational decision-makers although the nature of their work is to decide individual cases.

Hogarth (1987) suggests that individual perceptions about problems and desirable outcomes are influenced by intuition and memory:

> When the degree of complexity of an issue exceeds the limits of cognitive abilities, there is a marked decrease in adequacy of information processing as a direct effect of information overload and ensuing fatigue (Lewin 1947 in Janis and Mann 1977:17).

Memory imposes limits on the amount of information an individual can manage. Hallett and Birchall (1992:288) referred to the study by Wells (1988) of American social workers' decision-making which showed only a limited number of factors about a situation could be processed by an individual. In such situations intuitive choices did influence decision-making particularly in unfamiliar circumstances. Carroll, Weiner, Coates, Gallagher and Alibrio (1982 cited by Carroll and Johnson 1990:31) found that decisions about a prisoner's appropriateness for parole were made by parole officers guided by 'intuition' and 'experience', and the view that 'every case is unique'.

Jabes (1982) suggested individuals in organisational contexts make decisions by 'satisficing', a concept devised by Simon (1960) to describe a process which enables an individual decision maker to deal with incomplete information about a situation by seeking out available choice alternatives which are 'good enough' and meet their individual minimum standard of satisfaction. Individuals simplify the world, and adjust it in accordance with their values and refer to available information or experiences, in order to make decisions (Jabes 1982:56; Taylor 1976).

This model is one of a number discussed by Taylor (1976:964) in his review of various approaches taken in strategic decision-making: decisions that provide direction for business organisations. Strategic decisions are important to an organisation's future yet they involve ill-structured and complex sets of problems; they have political implications, and are sensitive to the context around them. As such they provide a useful framework in which child protection decisions can be located.

The Process of Human Judgement

Hogarth (1981) investigated the strategies, or heuristics, individuals used to process information for decision-making. He found they processed information sequentially and that individuals select, even anticipate, information which is relevant to their needs and draw on their memory to reconstruct fragments of information. Memory is therefore important in predictive judgement as is the amount of information an individual can store and recall, and the meaning attached. Yet memory can be confused by the sequence of information and it can be biased by an individual's associations between items of information, and by the meanings attached to such information. Hogarth argued that

> to understand the basis of a person's predictive behaviour, it is necessary to understand the way that person conceptualises the world and the meaning s/he gives to information (1981:6).

Hogarth (1981) proposed also that choice is central to decision-making. Choice is affected both by personal and situational factors and by the meaning individuals ascribe to their experiences. If an individual is unaware of the environment in which the choices about behaviours are made then they cannot clearly understand the outcomes of the decisions. However, in judgement situations such as child protection decision-making, the individual may only be able to infer relationships between cues or factors which cannot be observed. Hogarth (1981:90) reported that people seek out information which confirms their views and remember positive feedback rather than negative feedback. However, individuals do not necessarily learn from experience.

Dhir and Markman (1986) also suggest that individuals look for similarities between past and present events to make decisions. While features of events may be similar however, the intent or context may differ. Saks and Kidd (1986) found that when particular events are connected by the decision maker a similar outcome is ascribed to the present event. People are inconsistent in their judgements often because they are not completely aware of the value of particular items of information selected as relevant to a decision.

Kahneman and Tversky (1986) suggested individuals select the outcome that is most representative of their past experiences, as well as considering what choices are available. This is one of the simplifying strategies individuals use to deal with judgements under uncertainty. Nisbett and Ross (1980) also found that these strategies or heuristics were used to reduce complex tasks into simple operations. Saks and Kidd suggested that when these heuristics were applied to legal decision-making, a task they described 'as an uncertain and probabilistic one' (1986:216), they can produce flawed judgements. This is because intuition and commonsense judgements differ from actual probabilities and the individual's simplifying strategies create errors. People are influenced by stereotypes to predict outcomes no matter how unreliable or scanty, or outdated, the descriptive material is (Saks and Kidd 1986:223). Hogarth (1981) noted that decisions are very often based on intuitive judgement and that intuition is in fact a powerful influence in stereotyping. Moreover, if an individual decision maker believes the information about a situation 'hangs together', then their trust in their stereotypical judgements is increased.

Saks and Kidd (1980) found that the ease with which an individual can recall an event has implications in decision-making. They suggested that in judicial decision-making the more salient an experience was to a judge the more readily it was recalled. Yet salience is not always a good measure as what is often most easily remembered is extreme or unusual or particularly vivid. A compelling personal experience readily remembered and recalled may have greater impact on a judge than an expert witness reporting scientific data. Anecdotal information also appeared to be more persuasive and readily processed than technical information. However, reliance on memory and salience of experience may lead decision-makers to make associations between events which may in fact not be linked. It is difficult to counter these associations in settings such as the magistrates' courts where magistrates receive little feedback about the outcomes of their decisions.

Furthermore, an individual's initial judgement is often resistant to further information because new information is not readily integrated. People find it difficult to discard information they already have. Nisbett and Ross found that when an individual committed themselves to a particular position, they had difficulty processing alternative information:

> It is not only people's eagerness to apply simple heuristics and immediately available knowledge structures that leads to grief, it is also the failure to make necessary adjustments of initial judgements. Once a simple heuristic or scheme has been used, subsequent considerations fail to exert as much impact as commonsense or normative considerations might dictate that is should (1980:41).

Saks and Hastie (1978) suggest that this should have particular implications for the courts. If individuals have difficulty integrating new information, most particularly when it is highly technical and quantitative information, then expert witnesses in court who present this information are not as persuasive as it is believed. Furthermore, people appear to prefer to rely on individual case information to make decisions rather than refer to more general information about other similar cases and outcomes. Kahneman and Tversky (1986) describe this as a 'perverse indifference to prior probabilities'. They report that judges decide a sentence on the basis of individual case information and their individual assessments of the defendant, a finding supported by Hogarth (1981). Therefore, why a person invokes a particular cognitive approach to deal with a given task and what influences are involved in their choice are essential to identify in order to understand the decision process.

The Use of Decision Frameworks

Mention is made earlier of strategic decision-making and that the courts might be viewed as strategic decision-making organisations. Mohr (1982) found it appropriate to apply an organisational framework to legal decision-making and presented a typology which reflected these organisational aspects. This approach accommodates the political or bureaucratic goals of the organisation and considers that the individual may need to discard outcomes which are undesirable to the organisation.

Hogarth (1981) suggested the consequences of alternative outcomes and the uncertainties in the environment around the decision were important influences on a decision maker. He presented the model outlined below which represents the decision outcome and includes the interrelationships between influences and how decision alternatives are evaluated.

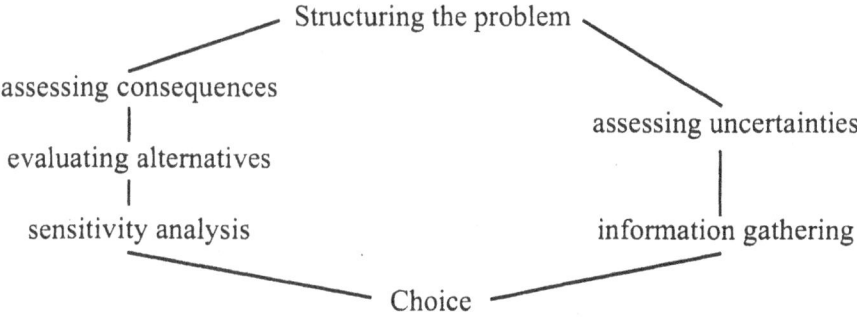

Figure 3.1 Decision model proposed by Hogarth (1981:135)

Sensitivity analysis refers to the need for individuals to select and balance different alternatives prior to making a choice and to ensure the alternative chosen is compatible with the preferred consequences of the decision. Hogarth (1981) notes that this is why conflict is inherent in decision situations. Janis and Mann (1977) had addressed this inherent conflict in decisions which require, for example, an individual to balance organisational or government policy with the welfare aims for a person or situation. They emphasise that this conflict arises also from an individual's need for satisfaction in decision-making. The decision framework they outlined concentrated on the gathering of sufficient information about the problem under consideration and outlined the process the individual decision maker uses to survey the alternatives, make a decision and adhere to it even in the face of negative feedback.

Carroll and Johnson (1990) suggested experienced decision-makers develop standard operating procedures to deal with problems and therefore reduce their difficulty. They outlined a process they described as the 'decision tree': a method which presents and compares the expected outcomes for each decision alternative. They quantitatively analysed the alternatives chosen within each of the four segments of the decision tree to discover how decision-makers assigned value to decision alternatives. The four segments of the tree were the decision problem formulation, the decision alternatives and the value of each alternative, the decision alternative with the highest expected value selected by calculating probabilities, and the analysis of conclusions.

Johnson (1988, cited by Carroll and Johnson 1990) found that expert decision-makers made quick, confident judgements under pressure. He undertook a study of expert judgement in practice by examining the choice of applicants for hospital medical officer positions by a committee of expert physicians. He also considered whether experts made decisions in a linear way as the decision tree model might suggest. Linear models in decision-making are straightforward and each dimension is weighed according to its relative importance. The decision response is the alternative chosen which has the greatest value. He found however that the committee of expert physicians did not operate in a linear way. Their exploration of alternatives and their selection of relevant knowledge was the key to their expertise, and mirrored the decision tree process. Lawrence suggested that the examination of decisions in linear and quantitative terms excluded the 'much richer matrix of relationships, causes and rationales for decision-making that is apparent ... in the criminal justice system' (Lawrence 1991 in Ballenden, Laster and Lawrence 1993:25).

Hogarth (1981) suggested linear models of decision-making assume all the dimensions of the decision process are independent of each other and inclusive of all relevant factors. The linear approach assumes that relevant information can be handled in a consistent manner. Tversky (1973) outlined a similar model known as the elimination-by-aspects model. This model outlined decision-making as a sequential order of alternatives in which each stage of the decision process is assessed according to its probable utility and fit with the decision outcome. The aspects which do not fit are discarded. Tversky (1973) found that the role of intuition in this process might lead a decision-maker to eliminate decision alternatives without a real examination of their merit.

These models present decision-making as goal-directed behaviour. When decision-makers are making decisions on behalf of society however, their own decision-making goals are governed by the larger influence of social policy (Fitzmaurice and Pease 1986). However, the frameworks individuals use as their guides to social reality are not always accurate. Individuals may have a common understanding of basic social concepts e.g. 'tree', 'chair', but do not necessarily share beliefs, values and theories about the world and the people in it.

The frameworks, or cognitive schemas, used are individual and powerful. They shape the explanations of causal relationships which individuals use to comprehend and predict behaviours and events. Lawrence (1981 et al.) has extensively researched the place of these individual frames of reference in judicial decision-making. Her studies, and those of Kahneman, Slovic, Tversky (1982), and Berger and Luckman (1967) suggest that judicial decision-makers depend on personal perspectives to make sense of information and arrive at solutions. Lawrence (1981 et al.) further suggests that the professional group culture is a significant influence on magistrate frames of reference.

Nisbett and Ross (1980:41) suggested individuals construct 'personae' within the cognitive schema they use in decision-making. These 'personae' or stereotypes comprise particular features and behaviours and are applied when a person is seen to resemble particular 'personae'; in judicial settings individuals construct stereotypes about people before the court who are, for example, worthy of trust, or of rehabilitation. The problem with cognitive schema is that they become fixed and individuals cease to make necessary adjustments to their initial judgements to accommodate new knowledge.

Kaplan and Schwartz referred to the zone of ambiguity which contributes to the complex nature of judgement tasks. This zone of ambiguity is the conceptual space between what can be observed about decision-making and what must be inferred because it cannot be observed (1977:3). Attempts to understand how individuals approach judgement decisions cannot be reliably replicated in experimental research because they do not allow for the ambiguity very often present in judgement tasks in the real world. The lack of feedback about the outcomes of judgement tasks adds to the complexity of decision-making.

How information is integrated to arrive at a decision outcome in court is a process which combines an individual judge's pre-existing biases, the values and weight they attribute to the testimony and observation of the defendant, with their belief about a person's ability to commit a crime. While cognitive schema are shaped by experience and exposure to new information, individuals resist new, or incongruent, information if it involves changing their existing perceptions.

Scott (1989:43) found however that professionals develop knowledge structures derived from their practice wisdom or tacit knowledge. Her study of hospital social work found workers looked for particular patterns of problems, or cues, based on previous similar cases, to assist their decision-making. However, the meaning individuals ascribe to situations is as much idiosyncratic as it is sociocultural and is influenced by the organisational context of the individual and their professional socialisation.

Professional Knowledge

Magistrates, as professional decision-makers, are expected to decipher what events mean to individuals who appear before them, as well as to others involved in the presentation of the case. Schon (1983:21) described legal decision-making as instrumental problem solving and suggested legal decision-making is guided by broadly determined principles that are based on prior court decisions. It is decision-making which follows rational procedures (Carroll and Johnson 1990). It is problem- solving which adopts a 'hierarchical' approach of first viewing problems in terms of general principles and then in more concrete terms (Schon 1983). This approach indicates a clear relationship between means and ends and any conflicts which emerge in decision-making are resolved by reference to empirical knowledge about the problem. The approach which relies on empirical observations to make decisions is also referred to as positivism; it is the philosophy which was influential in the foundation of legal knowledge (Douglas and Laster 1992).

In reality people simplify situations to reach decisions and what they describe as the facts of a situation are the meanings individuals create to explain the phenomena they observe. The problems an individual decision maker encounters in decisions, particularly when they are decisions about children, are often unique and uncertain and are not readily empirically categorised (Schon 1983:33). The technical rationality perspective matches decisions with an agreed, established end. However the uncertainty, the uniqueness and the conflicts inherent in child welfare practice, 'the confusing messes' (Schon 1983:42) are not readily dealt with by this prescriptive approach.

The tension between individual and institutional goals has particular implications for professional welfare practice in the courts. The technicalities of the law do not deal well with child welfare matters. Welfare views about families and child rearing differ markedly from the legal approach to such issues. The legal and welfare professional groups who work within the court have particular expertise and biases and they represent particular interests. However, they lack a common framework, with shared sets of assumptions, about children's needs and family functioning, which creates difficulties in decisions about children's welfare.

Decision-making about children is complex; while it is thoughtful and deliberate, it is not a rational process: 'Empirical knowledge about the nature of parenting plays little part in arriving at a decision, instead preconceptions are guidelines and override the requirements of particular cases' (Schaffer 1990:5). In children's matters there are powerful, possibly irrational beliefs and stereotypes, and ideologies, as well as administrative and financial pressures, which influence decisions. Moreover, child welfare matters are often ambiguous and the decision-makers must use considerable discretion.

Magistrates' Frames of Reference

Up to this point the study of judicial decision-making concentrates on explicating what factors predict sentencing decisions. Studies variously aimed either to construct models which would explain decision outcomes, or to predict associations between a combination of case factors, such as judicial attitude to sentencing, legal and social constraints, definitions of situations, and decision outcomes. There was an emphasis on the use of decision theory to do this.

Lawrence's Australian studies of judicial decision-making (1981, 1984, 1986, 1987) take this research in a new direction. Her various studies focused on magisterial decision-making as a problem-solving process:

> legal judging is a problem-solving domain where problems are always ill-structured, solutions are inconclusive and important features of the problem space only becomes apparent after initial processing (Laurence 1988: in Chi, Glaser, and Farr 1988).

Furthermore, magistrates are required to make significant decisions often in quite complex matters, quickly and clearly, with very little information (Douglas and Laster, 1992; Lawrence 1987, 1992), and to balance 'bureaucratic pressures in decisiveness and efficiency ... alongside community demands for impartiality and equality' (Lawrence 1988:2).

Lawrence (1987:19) aimed 'to identify the common, underlying patterns that specify how experts operate ... [so that] ... nuances of the institutionalised dispensation of justice is understood'. The notion of cognitive schema or working rules that magistrates develop to deal with cases, was central to Lawrence's research. These schema are the patterns or rules constructed by individuals from their knowledge, life experience, values and beliefs to solve problems. The study of these processes provides considerable knowledge of the operation of judicial decision-making.

In her various studies Lawrence uses a combination of methods, combining record analysis, interview, and observation, to capture the complexities of magisterial decision-making research (Lovegrove 1989:165). Archival analysis alone is more limited for the prediction of decision outcome than methods such as Lawrence's, which focus on understanding the decision process, and how this is influenced by the personalised styles of magistrates and their approaches to particular types of offenders and offences.

As a result of Lawrence's study (1981, with Browne, and 1984) Lawrence constructed a model of magistrates' thinking in court which she based on 'if – then' formal logic protocols (developed by Chi, Glaser and Rees and referred to in Lawrence 1988:4). This model combines the personal expectations, goals and perspective which form the frames of reference magistrates use to produce judgements. It combines also the external factors mentioned: statutory requirements, court system function, bureaucratic pressures and community expectations. These factors influence what magistrates see as relevant in a case and the inferences and decisions magistrates derive from that information (Lawrence and Browne 1981, McKnight, 1981, cited in Laurence 1988b:2)

Magistrates develop a particular mind set about crime and punishment, and the community, which is shaped by the knowledge they bring with them, and by their actual work and personal experiences (Lawrence and Browne 1981). This presumes that magistrates have certain prima facie strategies, or mental models, which they use to transform information into decisions. Lawrence's study with Homel (1987) combined this cognitive explanation with sociological and psychological explanations to explore magistrates' problem-solving strategies.

Lawrence and Homel (1987) found that experienced magistrates knew what to look for and were alert to unusual aspects of a case; they knew how to evaluate evidence. They had cognitive tricks for extracting information from cases. They approached each case individually however, and did not refer to them as typical cases. Magistrates did however look for what might be familiar about a case and then selected the significant facts and weighed up the value of these facts (Lawrence 1988b:4).

The contribution of cognitive psychology to understanding decision processes was taken up again by Lawrence (1987) in her study of magistrate' assessments in shoplifting cases. The seriousness the magistrate attached to the offence was a significant factor in explaining sentencing disparity. Lawrence (1987) and Lawrence and Homel (1987) used actual cases in these studies as several senior magistrates refused to work with simulation cases for it was their belief that 'construed cases had no reality to them and were not worth their considered attention' (Lawrence and Homel 1987:7).

Lawrence and Homel (1987:5) found judicial decision-making was highly personalised and magistrates gave different emphases to case details. One magistrate might focus on legal details in a case, another on the psychological background of the defendant. They found the decision-making was specific-case focused. Yet magistrate decision-making, and court functioning, is located in a broader context of social influences, institutional factors, beliefs about the purpose of legislation, and prevailing community norms. It may be viewed in Marxist terms which views the legal system as an oppressor of subordinate members of society. Or, it may be viewed as the mechanism which keeps people in their place in society. Lawrence and Homel (1987) confirmed that while any of these perspectives may impact on the court, court decisions are as much the product of the psychology of the presiding magistrate as of their sentencing aims and the facts in the case itself.

Lawrence's (1988b) study interviewed and observed magistrates at work. Her aim was to discover how magistrates balanced personal views, legal requirements and external constraints to arrive at a decision. She asked magistrates to make a decision, prior to hearing the case, based on the reports supplied and then observed the hearing and interviewed the magistrate afterwards to discover 'how cases are framed and set up in people's minds, and how their individual details are interpreted as the basis for decisions' (1988b:4).

Lawrence (1988b:7) found that the criterion of personal satisfaction for the magistrate was an important test of their decision-making. The lack of external criteria for a good decision and the lack of feedback meant magistrates relied on their own personal measure of a 'good' or 'satisfactory' decision. This does much to explain the disparity in sentencing decisions.

Lawrence developed another model of magistrate decision-making to show how cognitive processes are combined with personal and external factors to determine sentencing (Lawrence and Homel 1987). It illustrated that all the factors which influence decision-making are interactive: a magistrate's sentencing objective influences the information that s/he selects as relevant to their decision, and the information selection affects the inferences the magistrate makes about the defendant. It also illustrated that external or environmental factors both constrain and interact with magistrate decision-making.

Lawrence and Homel (1992) quantitatively analysed magistrates' penalties for drink-driving cases to discover how much magistrate determinations could be explained by offence and offender characteristics, such as gender and social class. It explored also the influence of legally defined factors, and magistrate sentencing orientations, on sentencing decisions. The study found disparities in the sentencing decisions that the researchers believed could only result from magistrate interpretation and discretionary powers. How conscious magistrates were that they selected out particular details for attention was unclear (e.g. young hooligan drivers attracted stiffer penalties). What was clear was that judicial discretion was highly individual and there was no 'regulation of that discretion' (Lawrence and Homel 1992:410).

What is also clear is that the studies of sentence disparity reveal a variety of theoretical approaches which reflect the problematic nature of legal research. Although the studies are numerous, they provide little agreement about the reasons for the disparity. A number of studies used an experimental approach to investigate the decision-making process by examining specific factors identified as influential in decision outcomes. These studies aimed to produce decision-making models which could predict decision outcomes (Hood and Sparks 1972; Tarling 1979; McKnight 1981; Kapardis and Farrington 1981; Lovegrove 1988; et al.). Studies such as McKnight (1981), Kapardis and Farrington (1981), and Lovegrove (1989), used experimental and quasi-experimental designs, such as multi-attribute utility analysis, which manipulated specific variables to find the factors which predict sentencing behaviour.

Hogarth (1971) suggested, however, assigning statistical weights to case factors does not reveal what weights the decision-makers themselves might attach to the same case factors. He therefore sought to predict sentencing decisions by constructing a phenomenologically derived model of sentencing outcome. He asked the decision-makers themselves to nominate the variables they believed were significant in sentencing, instead of the researcher analysing the variables and nominating those considered significant and the decision maker choosing from the researcher's list in order to decide sentence.

Simulation techniques have been a favoured approach to sentencing research as a method of identifying the decision strategies magistrates use (Hood 1962; Bond and Lemon 1981; Hine, McWilliams and Pease 1978). Lovegrove (1989) notes that the use of vignettes in simulation studies enables judges to look at cases at a distance and this assists them to identify the factors that are relevant to case disposition.

Approaches which focus on the individual decision-maker's cognitive frameworks are well-represented in sentencing research. These approaches variously include the use of case vignettes, and interview, to explore the decision-making process. Lawrence (1981 and various) focuses on the behaviour of the decision maker by trying to identify the decision strategies, or heuristics, magistrates use. She regularly employed in her research a 'conversational' or 'stream of consciousness' approach to assist the identification of these processes. Her research combined quantitative and qualitative approaches to capture the 'real-life' character of magistrate decision-making.

However, Konecni and Ebbeson (1984 and various) question the use of vignettes alone to predict sentencing behaviour. They suggest that as the simulation cases have no significant consequences, judges may give biased replies. Further, they suggest that although these cases might appear straightforward on paper, they might contain atypical characteristics, which could bias decisions. Legal decisions based on vignettes are made in the absence of court procedures, of testimony, of pressure to make a decision. They lack the impact of information overload that there is in complex cases, and the impact of legally immaterial factors which may be emotionally and personally compelling for the judge (for example, the presence of distressed relatives in court). They argue that 'individuals decision strategies are task and situation specific' (Konecni and Ebbeson 1984 cited in Lovegrove 1989: 190) and therefore the external validity of vignette research is very limited.

They argue that sentencing studies which combine archival data with interview and observation provide more complete data. Ebbeson and Konecni proposed that a multi-method approach better reflects what actually happens in the legal system. This approach also resolves problems with generalisability and external validity and makes study findings as accurate as possible (Ebbeson and Konecni 1984:33).

They suggest that research based on interviews alone can be biased by respondents. Interviews and questionnaires may not reflect what judges think or intend because their answers may be based on self-preservation, they may give certain answers for political reasons, or they may give politically acceptable answers (Ebbeson and Konecni 1984:34). Findings based on observations alone can also lead to wrong conclusions because relevant and influential information might be in the reports submitted to the court:

> In the area of legal decision-making as well as in many other types of decision-making the really important truths are to be found in the real world rather than in laboratory simulations ... we would prefer to base our conjectures about how people make various types of decisions in observations of actual people making actual decisions (Konecni and Ebbeson 1984:33).

The great variety of studies of sentencing all have as their common aim to understand the behaviour of participants in the criminal justice system. However what factors influence magistrate decision-making in jurisdictions other than the adult jurisdiction? The next section sets out the findings from studies undertaken in the juvenile justice jurisdiction.

Decision Studies in Juvenile Justice

Parker, Sumner and Jarvis (1989) investigated the sentencing of young offenders in England, specifically those young offenders at risk of custody. The study was undertaken in four courts from different parts of England. Each court was however of a similar size, in a metropolitan location and was the court which dealt with the majority of juvenile criminal matters. The research sought to explain disparities in sentencing across the different courts. It sought also to examine how magistrates dealt with decisions about custody for juvenile offenders and what were the influences on their decisions; it asked also how magistrates balanced the competing legal and welfare demands of their role. The magistrates were, as they are in England, lay magistrates appointed to the Bench because they have life experience and expertise, and a suitable position in the community. They do not usually have legal qualifications unlike magistrates in Victoria (Australia) who are appointed from the ranks of practising legal practitioners.

Parker, Sumner and Jarvis (1989) used a multi-method approach to gathering data. They interviewed magistrates, observed the work of the courts, surveyed social workers and probation officers, and analysed case files. They tracked 240 cases through the sentencing process and collected basic data about offence, defendant, age, sex, occupational status, and the seriousness of the offence. A seriousness score relating to offences was also constructed to assess the impact of different factors on the magistrates decision (Parker, Sumner, and Jarvis 1989:39). Reports associated with the cases, were also analysed. They were also interested in how magistrates evaluated information provided by other professionals such as social workers, probation officers, police and legal representatives. Magistrates were also asked about their perception of their role and the pressures and expectations on them.

The study found that magistrates' perceptions about the aims of sentencing and their interpretation of the relevant legislation were a significant influence on their decisions. These perceptions and interpretations were shaped as much by the social, as the legal, context in which the sentencing took place. Magistrates variously described the aim of penalties as deterrence, rehabilitation or retribution, depending on the situation. Magistrates reported also it was particularly important to consider factors such as seriousness of offence, the offender's previous record, and the public interest in deciding a penalty.

How magistrates defined their role, and their task, was also found to be important. They commonly defined it as maintaining a balance between the competing interests of the defendant and the general public within a legal framework. The study found however that what constitutes a fair balance was not defined the same way by the four courts in the study. Some courts noted it was their role to protect the interests of the person in the street. Magistrates saw themselves as having a responsibility to the community, unlike other court participants who represented the interests of the client. However, 'what passes under the guise of public opinion may well be the opinion of a particular social group' (Parker, Sumner and Jarvis 1989:79).

The authors referred to the finding of Ashworth et al. (1984) that the narrow social composition of the judiciary might distort what they understand as public opinion. This is the 'false consensus bias', referred to by Fitzmaurice and Pease (1986); the tendency for people to equate public opinion with their own, and to assume that their own views are generally held by the majority of the community. Yet, magistrates were rarely aware of sentencing patterns outside their own court. Each Bench had its own policies about sentencing options: what was to be the response to burglary, whether there was a clampdown on a particular offence. How these were decided depended on how local crime was perceived and on the social characteristics of the specific area (Parker, Sumner and Jarvis 1989:82). Magistrates described sentencing decisions as 'a very personal thing. It has to be directed to the individual' (Magistrate X cited in Parker, Sumner and Jarvis 1989:83)

The magistrate's judgement of a defendant's behaviour in the court was a significant influence in two-thirds (68 per cent) of the cases in the study sample. Magistrates reported that their knowledge of local problems, for example whether there might be industrial problems in the community and instability of employment, was important to their perspective in a case. The seriousness of the offence and the offender's likelihood of committing another offence were also important factors. Welfare reports prepared for the court were very influential in two-thirds of cases, though magistrates were sometimes critical of them. School reports were usually found to be helpful.

Magistrates were critical however of the unrealistic recommendations which they identified as made more often by social workers than probation officers. Some recommendations were seen as biased and an intrusion into the magistrate's domain. If the author of the report was trusted by the Bench then greater value was attached to the report.

Magistrates viewed their position as unique; they alone had all the facts of a case before them, and could decide the competing interests. Parker, Sumner and Jarvis (1989) expressed concerns about this perception as it allows no opportunity for criticism of a decision. Furthermore, deciding each case on its merits means 'it is difficult to ensure any level of consistency in the way cases are dealt with' (Parker, Sumner and Jarvis 1989:106). Most particularly when 'magistrates have a sublime disregard for treating like cases alike. Most do not refer back to previous decisions' (Parker, Sumner and Jarvis 1989:117).

Magistrate trust in their own assessment of a defendant's demeanour was a particular influence on sentencing. Their assessment included a moral categorisation about family background, and what makes a good family, as well as an assessment of welfare-oriented factors relevant to the defendant's behaviour. It included beliefs held by magistrates about how specific problems e.g. drug problems, were best processed by the court:

> Who the defendant is thought to be, as well as what he or she has done, is a central factor in the sentencing decision. It is no wonder that sentencing patterns are so difficult to explain when at the heart of the process is the belief that sentencers, and they alone, are uniquely placed to understand the uniqueness of the events which constitute the offence but also the true character of the individual who has committed it (Parker, Sumner and Jarvis 1989:116).

While they found offence seriousness was a specific influence on magistrates, they found the 'mind-set' of the particular local Bench and its magistrates was of great importance. Of central importance however, was how magistrates perceived and interpreted information about cases and the interaction of this with their personal assessments of offenders.

Brown (1991) further explored magistrates' perceptions of a defendant's background and how the role of social information influenced magistrate decision-making. Her study took place in six juvenile courts in England between 1985 and 1988. She interviewed ninety magistrates, observed the work of the six courts, and analysed 122 social inquiry reports. Magistrates reported that their task was to decide culpability and to decide which of the range of penalties available was appropriate. It was not for them to take a welfare orientation, although the social data relevant to the case was measured against the nature of the offence (Brown 1991:27). Magistrates looked for information from social reports about the family lives of defendants both as an explanatory and mediating factor. Magistrates expected information to be presented in an acceptable way and were often frustrated by social workers lack of familiarity with courts and by the jargon they used in reports.

The magistrate's view about what they hoped their penalty could achieve for the juvenile offender was important to their decision. Generally magistrates aimed to deter and rehabilitate young offenders although no clear link was found between sentencing objectives and general ideas about punishment.

What was significant however, was the nature of the local community and the magistrates involvement in it. However, Brown (1991) challenges the idea that magistrates represent the community:

> the magistrate is not grounded in the community; their legitimacy as a representative is as mythical as the 'normal family'. The community which it represents is a notion (1991:112).

The Ideology of the Magistrate and Child Protection

The legal focus on children who are abused or neglected is a relatively recent phenomenon (Edwards 1992:14). Mandatory reporting of child abuse is very recent in Victoria; 1994 saw police, doctors, nurses and teachers for the first time legally required to report suspected cases of child abuse or neglect. Increasingly the Children's Court is asked to review the care of children and resolve problems of family dysfunction (Edwards 1992:1; Swain 1989:229). Yet what constitutes the best interests of children is unclear, and best interests is 'a vague and illusory concept which varies in meaning from case to case, depending on the context in which it is applies' (Butz 1982 in Kiel 1988:8).

However, the role and task of the children's court presents magistrates with considerable difficulty. The Children's Court is perceived more as a social than legal court and so does not enjoy a high status in the legal hierarchy (Swain 1989). An assignment to the Children's Court separates magistrates from the mainstream magistracy and from the broader legal community.

Legal practitioners, and magistrates in Victoria, are qualified lawyers, who observe the principle that it is the role of the court to find the truth in a dispute and to decide on any redress (Swain 1989:230). An individual's day in court is seen as an important right in a democracy (King and Trowell 1992). The rights of parties are protected in court, most typically through legal representation, and each case is regarded as unique and is judged on its merits (Carson 1990; Parker, Sumner and Jarvis 1989). The court emphasises due process and proper procedures; legal sanctions such as punishment, and intervention in people's lives, are undertaken only when guilt is clearly proven.

However, the principles of the least intervention and individual rights which are pre-eminent in the adversarial setting are not compatible with the interventionist and needs based approach of child welfare matters (King and Trowell 1992:3). The legal principle of parens patriae directs the court to make children's rights its primary concern (Smith 1982:39). This principle allows the state to intervene in families when parents neglect their duty to their children (Tiffin 1982:143). This principle also allows for flexibility in judicial principles about evidence, as child abuse cases demand a degree of subjective evaluation in order to make a finding. However:

> the releasing of formal procedures, the growing importance of social workers, the dispositions of an indeterminate nature (which were designed to meet the needs of individual children) made for a very different approach and a very different language of justice from the adult court (Pratt 1992:42).

Blackmore (1989) emphasises that the child welfare court is still a court of law with a judicial function to weigh the evidence of submissions and arrive at legally correct decisions. It must ensure natural justice principles are upheld and families have a chance to be heard. Any such intervention must be legally justified and a last resort in order to protect the child's welfare:

> in child abuse and neglect cases, it is up to State agencies who wish to intervene in family life to prove in law that abuse has occurred and that action by the State is justified and necessary for the children's protection (King and Trowell 1992:111).

Furthermore, the resolution of a child's problems must focus on the preservation of the family whenever possible whilst ensuring the protection of the child. However the dependent status and different developmental needs of children give the children's court a different purpose from that of the adult court: 'The juvenile courts are society's means of holding itself accountable on behalf of its children and families' (Edwards 1992:23).

However the ambiguity and uncertainty in child welfare matters makes the magistrate's task difficult. The legislative framework does not provide definitions of child abuse, or guidelines to say how a child's emotional, intellectual or physical development, or parental responsibility is assessed (Ronnau and Poertner 1989). It does not assist lawyers with the gathering of evidence from children, especially when the child is very young. Moreover, definitions of child abuse are often not shared by the professional groups interested in child protection. Also, in children's matters there are very often a great number of individuals and child protection professionals who come to court to present their views about what is in a child's best interests.

The rules of evidence allow 'hearsay' evidence to be presented, as long as it is relevant, so that the court can hear about a child's developmental needs, and what assistance is critical for them to receive (Carson 1990). Magistrates rely on this information to make decisions about children. However, Ballenden, Laster and Lawrence suggest significant decisions about welfare matters may be substantially made prior to court: 'in so many instances the real gatekeeper is the step prior to the law maker or law keeper' (1992:3). This clearly has implications for the availability and quality of information supplied to the court, as it is this information, combined with the magistrate's discretion and other relevant personal or external factors that influence the magistrate's decision-making process.

Few magistrates have a particular background in child welfare law and so it takes considerable time to develop the necessary knowledge of human development, family dynamics and available community resources to be skilled in Children's Court work (Edwards 1992:36). The magistrate's legal training in child welfare may not be of great assistance in deciding child protection cases. They must rely on knowledge and skills, other than their legal training, to assess child protection matters: 'It is essential that lawyers have an appreciation of the behavioural and social services to be able to adequately understand the implications of the evidence placed before them' (Smith 1982:70).

Foucault (1980) referred to the 'modern episteme': the new modes of discipline in society which are no longer dependent on the traditional methods of law. These mechanisms do not focus on rights, as does the law, but more on personal regulation. Social work is part of this modern episteme. Certainly, there is an increased presence of social workers in children's courts who see the welfare of a child as the sole consideration for the court. Yet, the law prefers to remain separate from the welfare professions, which now have a role in family law, and rely on the certainty of legal principle, and evidence, to decide child welfare matters. This is preferable to accepting the welfare assessment without question, particularly when magistrates perceive the welfare bureaucracy as having too much discretionary power that may undermine the power and the authority of the judiciary; a bureaucracy 'which sees itself as autonomous and which may have quite different aims from those of the courts' (Blackmore 1989:136).

Yet it is difficult to obtain clear answers in child abuse cases (King 1991). The complexities of these cases make it difficult to narrow, to a small range of issues, the broad range of factors which affect a child's welfare:

> to transform the complex, messy situations involving intricate human relationships and a multiplicity of possible causes and effects into a simple story which makes sense and holds a moral for everyone (King and Trowell 1992:1).

The imprecision of existing knowledge about children and predictions for their future, and the difficulty welfare practitioners often have explaining case issues, create considerable frustration for magistrates trying to establish facts and find the right outcome for a child (King 1991:312).

Child Abuse Decision-making

How best interests is defined varies considerably across professionals. Ronnau and Poertner (1989) investigated the degree of consensus among social workers, lawyers and judges about intervention in cases of child emotional abuse. Public policy and state laws about abuse provided little assistance with decisions about intervention and so decision-makers in this area developed guidelines they believed were appropriate. The study found the professional groups differed significantly in the concerns they raised about child abuse cases. The lawyers and judges were concerned with legally admissible evidence, with statutory definitions and legal standards, and finding cause-effect relationships. Social workers were concerned with describing the behaviour of the child and parents, their individual and environmental influences, their needs, and the help they required (Swain 1989:231). The study remarked that each profession does have different roles to play, however the lack of consensus on what constitutes child emotional abuse and good child rearing complicates decisions about intervention.

Seeking to establish definitive criteria about child abuse however may overlook the differences in family functioning. Child rearing is a variable process and defining, for example, 'emotional maltreatment' is a mix of factors based on culture and science, values and expertise. However, when the complex issues of child abuse enter the legal arena:

> [they] are so easily transformed into simple questions of whether the abuse did or did not take place and the outcome for the child depends much more on the answers to that question than in a careful analysis of the child's needs (King and Trowell 1992:6).

The need for child welfare concerns 'to be constructed according to the demands of the legal discourse' (King 1992:312) narrows what should be a broad examination of the problems affecting the welfare of a child, to only those problems which can be proven. Decisions in child welfare are often moral decisions about child rearing and child-parent relationships. The view that children prosper best in a family environment is a powerful ideology.

Equally powerful is the belief that contemporary welfare authorities have the potential to 'impose patterns of family behaviour on the community and displace parental judgement about how their children should be socialised' (Donzelot 1980 in Eekelaar 1984:2).

The view that a child's rights be viewed solely within the context of the family is not necessarily shared by legal and welfare professionals. 'The current practice of supporting families first and removing children as a last resort' (King and Trowell 1992:53) means there is less acknowledgment of the more vulnerable children whose best interests may lie outside their families. This response may also place parents in an impossible situation. The pressure for parents to be seen as capable of meeting their child's needs leads parents to deny, in court, the problems they may have and they may not, therefore, receive the supports they need.

How best interests is decided by welfare and justice professionals is central to studies by Craft et al. (1980, 1991). In 1980, Craft, Epley and Clarkson investigated factors that influenced the disposition recommendation in child abuse cases. They asked 38 child protection workers to weight the relative importance of four factors in recommending court action: previous injury, severity of injury, consistency of explanation, parental reaction. They found there was substantial disagreement among child protection workers about what constituted a risk to the child and therefore justified court action (1980:43). They found also that recommendations for court action were influenced by the parent reaction to the child protection worker; a negative reaction meant there was more certainty of court action. The individual biases of the worker, about a case, were more important to decisions than were the characteristics of the case. Di Leonardi (1980) had also found that a parent's receptiveness to help was significant in whether or not they received support services.

Craft and Betten (1991:108) investigated the particular factors selected, and their significance, in deciding cases of physical abuse to a child. They asked 41 graduate (USA) social work students to examine four case vignettes and decide which cases ought to be investigated and what disposition they would recommend. The case vignettes contained basic information about the child and their injury and study participants could request more information about these. The severity of injury and risk to the child was the major factor chosen as significant to the decision to investigate. Cases that were assessed as high-risk and low-risk were considered more straightforward. Decisions about medium-risk cases were inconsistent, reflecting the lack of consensus among professionals about what is a significant injury and the variability in the subjective assessments used to decide about intervention.

Drew and Dalgleish (1986) examined Children's Court decisions (in Queensland) about separating children from their families, when children were assessed to be at risk. The study found that it was the severity of abuse and the family's lack of cooperation were considered the strongest indicators of risk to the child and the need to the remove the child from their family. It was these factors, rather than the type of abuse or the age of the child that were considered the important predictors of risk and subsequent separation of the child from parents.

The importance of the court system in child protection is acknowledged by Kelly and Ramsey (1985) in their study of cases where a child was removed from their home, or where child-family reunion was a focus of the court's attention. They found that cases in which the court ordered extensive services, or which were energetically legally represented, moved more quickly to child-family reunion. Assessments by the court about which families received services were based on what the court decided was the family's problem. Families in which there was violence, substance abuse, poverty and abandonment were more likely to have their children placed in care and the child's return to their family was slower. They were cases that were difficult for the court: 'the central values of protecting children at risk and respecting parental autonomy are in conflict and that any attempt to satisfy one, necessarily undermines the other' (Kelly and Ramsey 1985:27).

Wattam (1992:5) investigated what factors child protection workers, in the UK, used to decide to bring a child protection application before the court. She found that cases which 'made sense' or, had 'real issues', and in which evidence could prove harm received attention. Dingwall, Eekelaar and Murray (1983) found that 'cultural relativism' explained why incidents that cause harm to a child may not be defined as child abuse. They found that particular ideas about families and children, for example that there is 'natural love' between mothers and children, influenced professional judgements; beliefs about 'parental love will excuse a wide spectrum of behaviour which, would otherwise adversely affect the child' (Eekelaar 1984:656).

Dingwall, Eekelaar and Murray (1983:79) also found that child protection workers used the rule of optimism in their assessments: they tried to think the best of parents in their treatment of their children. This meant that, in some cases, the possibility of child abuse was minimised. This was as much because child protection workers found it difficult to transform their judgements about social problems, or 'social evidence' into legal evidence of child abuse as it was because of system preferences to think the best of parents.

Clark (1989) investigated child protection workers' decision-making to explain how and why they chose a particular course of action. Her study asked workers to assess 'real-life' referrals to the child protection service for investigation. Konecni and Ebbeson (1982:53) had earlier referred to the 'subjective uncertainty' in decision-making that postpones decisions until the professional's uncertainty falls to an acceptable level. With this in mind, Clark (1988:84) asked workers to decide whether they would substantiate a notification of child abuse, based on the information in the study cases. They were also asked to decide the level of risk to the child, and decide an appropriate plan for the child that might include court action.

Clark (1995:18) found that child protection workers searched for 'confirming information', or the negative aspects of a situation, to support the need for court action. They felt pressured to put aside the uncertainty and ambiguity that is endemic in child protection decision-making, as:

> abuse and neglect are the products of complex processes of identification, conformation and disposal, rather than inherent in a child's 'presenting' condition, and, are at best in some sense, self-evident (Dingwall, Eekelaar and Murray 1983:31).

The need to be certain about a case reflects the current emphasis of child maltreatment which is to be sparing about blame on parents for maltreating their children and to ensure that the child protection service can justify its actions (Clark 1995:23).

Clark (1995:13) proposed that families who come to the attention of protective services are those whose 'social credit' has run out. She found that approximately three-quarters of the children who are the subject of child protection applications in Victoria each year came from families in poverty. The dimensions of child abuse would appear therefore to be as much structural as they are personal. Solutions to child abuse are therefore not simply a matter of 'finding better checklists or new models of psychology or technical forces' suggest Dingwall, Eeekelaar, Murray (1983).

However, the legal system plays a central role in the response to child abuse. Weil (1982) confirmed what has been noted above: that child protection workers find it difficult to translate concerns for a child's welfare into a basis for legal action. The legal process preference for the least stigmatising interpretation of evidence and the least coercive disposition created difficulties for social workers. Their explanations of injuries to a child had to be supported by legally admissible evidence rule while at the same time shedding the best light possible on the competence and character of the parents. Social workers believed this process did not always achieve a proper balance of children's rights and adults' liberties.

Palmer examined the diversion of less serious cases of child abuse away from the adversarial system and the use of mediation to resolve them. This was to avoid the combative nature of the legal system and the 'win or lose' approach to cases which often involves seeing welfare as an enemy to be beaten. The differences between welfare and justice approaches to decision-making about created an approach that was based more on confrontation than on cooperation. Social workers in her study believed that the '[i]ncreasing emphasis on client's legal rights may be undermining social workers' roles in protecting children' (1989:25).

Morris and Giller (1987:26) suggest that professionals decide 'what type of case is this' based on choices, discretion and value judgements. Professionals develop practice frameworks to interpret people, behaviour and events and these are influenced by the 'moral character and practical contingencies affecting what can be done about the case' (1987:74). Scott (1989) had also found, in her study of hospital social workers, that individuals ascribe meaning to particular actions or events based as much on their personal views as on the values and norms of their broader culture. This is as significant as the influence of professional knowledge on the recognition and response to child abuse.

The individualised nature of child protection decision-making hampers a common understanding of what constitutes child abuse. Parker, Sumner and Jarvis (1989), Blackmore (1989), Brown (1991), all suggest that the discretionary powers, the lack of definite objective criteria, and the different professional ideologies of law and welfare are important determinants in child abuse decision-making. Justice and welfare approaches do share a common aim in the area of child abuse: the resolution of complaints of child abuse (Swain 1989). Yet the roles of law and social work in child protection differ considerably. Both may appear to differ in terms of deciding who is the client in the matter, and whose interests are to be protected: the child's, the family's, or the community's? (Swain 1989:231). Laster (1990) suggests the adversarial nature of court hearings fails to accommodate the complexity of child abuse decisions, and the range of decisions which may differ at various times in the life of a case. Yet, the legal and social welfare systems are interdependent in child protection and need to collaborate if cases are to be managed effectively. The different professional cultures and approaches to such cases is discussed next.

Justice and Welfare Approaches to Child Abuse Cases

In the adversarial system, the law resolves conflict in cases by seeking out the facts: 'the belief that an examination of the external facts can lead to solutions in situations of conflict' (Smith, Lane and Walsh 1988:14). Parties come to court and their legal representatives represent their interests '... to utilise the available law to achieve for one's client the most favourable legal outcome possible in the circumstances' (Zifcak 1995:278).

The court 'privileges legal knowledge above other knowledge' (Beckenridge 1995:34) in making its decision. The primacy given to the law and the consequent limits this places on social work autonomy are sources of frustration for social workers (Smith, Lane and Walsh 1988; Braye and Preston-Shoot 1990). They believe also that the legalistic model does not take into account that child abuse cases often are irrational and unreasonable (Braye and Preston-Shoot 1993). Moreover, the legal involvement with a case is limited to the achievement of a legal solution. Social work purposes are however more complex and necessitate longer-term relationships with families than a single court appearance (Zifcak 1995:278).

Welfare practitioners have difficulty with this conflict model, preferring mediation and agreement between parties, as much as possible. They also have difficulty with the court confining their role to that of the legal appearance. Social workers who have child protection responsibilities at court very often also have a dual responsibility to protect the child and assist parents to achieve the return of their child. They find the law's need for facts and firm judgement incongruent with the complex and multidimensional problems of child maltreatment. They also have difficulties with the need to bring all the information about a family into the open in court as evidence, particularly when they will have to continue to work with the family after court (Smith, Lane and Walsh 1988). Trying to make children's disclosures about abuse legally viable is particularly problematic as children, especially sexual abuse cases, often disclose information in indirect ways.

Magistrates place great emphasis on child protection workers having a clear understanding of legal procedures and the relevant skills to work appropriately in the legal system (Braye and Preston-Shoot 1990). Magistrates are often uneasy about how evidence in child abuse cases is gathered and about its reliability. Hearsay evidence, that is 'information reported by someone other than its author and offered to demonstrate a point' (Braye and Preston-Shoot 1993:145) sits uncomfortably with magistrates, even though child welfare courts allow for this. Magistrates express concern about whether the rights of defendants are properly accommodated when such evidence is admitted. The judicial approach is to focus on dealing with the offence whilst the welfare approach is to examine what the child maltreatment signals in terms of help for a child and their family (Hardiker and Storz 1979:29).

The Provision of Information for the Court

The provision of social information about children and families is of immense significance to judicial decision-makers in child maltreatment cases. The lack of clear agreement about what constitutes child maltreatment makes it important that as much information as possible is provided to assist magistrates making these decisions (Schroeder 1982:97). Judges and magistrates depend on welfare assessments to provide not only the pertinent facts about a child but also to contribute the knowledge of child development and family functioning which is not part of their legal training (Spakes 1987:35). Magistrates however still turn to their own training and experience when selecting an appropriate decision option (Albert 1986; Brown 1991:109).

Magistrates have difficulty with welfare reports which are incomplete, lack fact and relevant explanation, and do not provide a comprehensive picture of a child's situation (Smith, Lane and Walsh 1988:18). Yet child protection workers often have difficulty getting access to all relevant family members and sources of information which are necessary for a complete investigation. The ambiguities in child abuse cases can make it difficult to find the right answers for court social work reports (Braye and Preston-Shoot 1990:5).

Child protection workers comment that they have found magistrates reluctant to accept research about child maltreatment and about what is significant harm; information which is unfamiliar to magistrates. Whilst indicators about family breakdown and about threats to child development have been developed (Bentovim et al. 1987), it is often difficult to communicate these to the court in legally acceptable terms. What also creates difficulty for child protection workers and magistrates is the lack of general agreement in the community about what is 'good enough care' for a child (Braye and Preston-Shoot 1990:39). There are many subjective, or moral, evaluations made in child abuse cases and: 'what matters is that we should not disguise this and pretend it is all a matter of finding better check lists or new models of psychopathology' (Dingwall, Eekelaar and Murray 1983:244).

The Ideology of the Family

The legal system supports the autonomy of the family and their right to privacy. Children's rights are believed to be best met when they live with their family (Breckenridge 1995:38). Children's Court decisions can sanction intervention in family life. Legal practitioners are uncomfortable about such intrusion in family life and have a general concern about the trend to greater statutory intervention in other areas of family life, such as in health and education (Smith Lane and Walsh 1988:9). Such a position may fail to give:

> proper attention to the complex relationship between the family and the state, the dependent and vulnerable status of children, and the balance between individual freedom and the necessary regulation of social behaviour (Smith, Lane and Walsh 1988:9).

Beliefs about the primacy of the family in their children's lives is strongly held within the legal system, and within the community and those who challenge this are viewed with suspicion. The view that children's interests can be considered separately from the family is not readily acceptable to magistrates. Welfare practitioners believe the view of the primacy of the family is somewhat idealised and is held by magistrates 'because the magistracy is not grounded in the community: its legitimacy as a representative (of the community) is as mythical as the "normal family"' (Brown 1991:112).

The belief of primacy of importance of the family may promote an unrealistic optimism about the care available to a child within their family. This optimism may reduce an individual's belief in the reality of child abuse and can create difficulties for the court and for lawyers when they are required to make decisions in child abuse cases (FACS, South Australia 1990:21). Moreover, the legal system's concern about 'foster care drift' (Harris and Webb 1987:85) supports the belief that families must be preserved at all cost. Social workers however believe the legal system has failed to take into account the great social changes which affect families' abilities to care for children. Changes to the permanency of the family unit and the subsequent impact on the continuity of care of children appear little acknowledged by the legal system (Carter 1983:1).

The Role of the Social Worker and the Court

The court looks to child protection workers to provide solutions in child abuse cases. Certainly there is a perception that if social workers managed cases better, and observed legally derived guidelines and procedures, then cases might be more clearly presented in court and appropriate decisions easier to achieve. Zifcak summarised magistrates' views about child protection workers:

> their lack of clarity and rigour, their lack of adherence to procedural and evidentiary rule, their ill-founded certainty, their trust and credulity, led them into error. It was implicit that such error would not occur if the strictures of the law were properly observed (1995:275).

There appears to be a lack of sympathy in the legal system for the reality of the practice of child protection workers. There appears to be a dichotomy between what the child protection worker has experienced in a case and what the law establishes as the truth about a case (Smart 1992). Child protection workers believe their task is poorly understood by the courts and the community. The lack of agreement about what is risk to a child and the lack of agreement about the amount of investigation and bureaucratic intervention the community really wants creates major difficulties (Braye and Preston-Shoot 1990:342). The belief that social workers do not give expert testimony and cannot often provide the clear evidence about families that magistrates need further undermines the child protection worker's task. Yet there may be a number of different views about a family's problems and competence which cannot be reduced to an either/or account.

The law operates under a system of opposites, the presentation of opposite accounts in a case is how the truth is established. This approach does not accommodate the different nature of child abuse cases in which the evidence is often a range of opinions rather than fixed accounts. The legal view of the adjudication process as a fair and neutral process is generally not shared by social workers who work in child protection. The lack of trust child protection workers have in the adversarial system in child protection matters is a source of concern for magistrates. It is not always possible to be neutral towards parents whose behaviour puts their children at risk and the decisions which must be made about this may not always be fair. Social workers are seen as too ready to be agents of social control and to rescue children from unfortunate homes. There is a belief amongst members of the legal system that social workers 'are permanently and selectively attuned to discovery of breaches of statute' (Dingwall, Eekelaar and Murray 1983 cited in Freeman 1990:109). Yet, for social workers recourse to the law is only one mechanism for dealing with social troubles (Dingwall, Eekelaar and Murray 1983). Social workers are concerned that the shift to a legalistic model as the primary way to interpret child abuse cases reduces the range of responses they may make in cases of child abuse and reduces the contribution of their professional judgement (Freeman 1990).

Magistrates express concern about the power of the welfare bureaucracy, and therefore the power of social workers who are its representatives. Magistrates emphasise that it is the court's role to control this power and make welfare practitioners accountable for their actions (Harris 1983; Freeman 1990). Concerns about the power of the welfare bureaucracy arise also from the encroachment of welfare principles into the domain of family law. Magistrates have no wish to be seen as an extension of the welfare system (Smart 1992:4). Yet, this distance between the law and welfare is unhelpful for the court. Social workers do have training in areas which can provide direct assistance to the court. A lack of acknowledgement of this leads King and Trowell to ask:

> why the system employs highly qualified people to evaluate parenting ability and assess where the best interests of the children lie if their advice is then rejected by a bench of magistrates with limited training in these matters (1992:4).

How magistrates decide cases which come before them and the factors which influence these decisions is described next.

The Study of Magistrate Decision-making

Decisions about the care and protection of children impact not just on the children themselves but also on their families and on the wider community. Studies of child abuse decision-making (Craft et al. 1980, 1985, 1991; Bentovim 1987) have generally focused on developing scales of indicators of child abuse to improve the recognition of abuse and to arrive at appropriate court dispositions for such children. However, what is also needed is to discover the criteria magistrates use to make child protection decisions, and to discover the factors which influence them in this decision-making.

The study undertaken in the Melbourne Children's Court set out to investigate what factors influence magistrates in their decisions in child protection matters and the decision-making process they use to do this. The study comprised observation of the work of the magistrates at the Melbourne Children's Court, interviews with magistrates assigned to the Children's Court and analysis of court records of cases observed.

Quantitative and qualitative approaches have both been used in legal decision-making research; the studies all attempt to clarify the decision process and the significant factors judicial officers use to make decisions. Studies using a quantitative approach have used case record analysis, scales, or simulation exercises to study the decision process. Studies using case vignettes, or simulations, presented respondents with a range of factors in a variety of combinations for them to select what factors they believed were relevant to the case decision.

However, variables other than specific case factors have considerable influence on judicial decision-making (Ebbeson and Konecni 1982; Lawrence 1981, 1984; Lawrence and Homel 1992). Decision-making in the judicial context is in reality based on a combination of case factors, of organisational factors and specific individual decision-maker variables. Studies of judicial decision-making that used experimental designs to study sentencing decisions found it difficult to establish consistent cause-effect relationships between variables. The facts of cases were not always true and the same for all judges and magistrates, all the time. The quantitative approach did not accommodate the individualised nature of judicial decision-making and it was difficult to control variables to the extent required by an experimental design in order to reliably identify causal relationships.

Qualitative studies of legal decision-making sought to identify this range of variables using participant observation and interview methods and 'unobtrusive research' in the field (Kellehear 1993; Brannen 1992). It is an approach that is useful in an unfamiliar research context, and, where the researcher has little control over the research situation (Epstein 1985:273). Denzin (1994) suggests that a combination of methodologies offers a better approach to the study of judicial decision-making. This study takes a multi-method approach and combines observation, interview and archival survey to identify the characteristics of judicial decision-making. It is an approach that accommodates the social reality of the court and the most appropriate aspects of qualitative and quantitative research 'to treat classrooms or courtrooms as natural and experiments as artificial is to forget that social research is itself part of the social world' (Hammersley 1992:44).

Clearly, there are ethical issues involved in the study of magisterial decision-making in child protection and these influence the choice of research methods. The need for precise data about Children's Court decision-making and child abuse must also be balanced against the needs of magistrates and how they, and others at the Children's Court, might be affected by the research process. Methods chosen had to preserve the confidentiality and anonymity of participants; they had to respect the decisions of magistrates, not interfere with them or compromise them, nor intrude too much on their time. The cooperation of study participants and others in the research setting was essential; the study could not proceed without it. It was important therefore to be clear about the purpose of the study: that it aimed to advance knowledge about child protection issues, not to judge or expose individual decisions or decision-makers. 'The researcher's goal is to describe the symbols and values of such a culture without passing judgement based on his personal cultural context' (Marshall and Rossman 1989:72).

Feasibility

Before the proposed study could commence it had to be established that it was possible for it to be undertaken. There is considerable interest in magistrates' decisions in the Children's Court both from the community, concerned about child abuse, and from child protection practitioners and other professionals. How far this interest could be translated into 'doable' research had to be explored.

Consultation with legal and welfare professionals found support for the study. Approval was gained from the relevant official agencies. Meetings were held with magistrates at the Children's Court to explain the study intent and procedures, to reassure them that the study would not be disruptive to people's work, would respect the magistrate position, preserve their anonymity and respect the sensitive nature, and confidentiality of their work. Magistrates were initially ambivalent about the study and their participation in it. One magistrate noted that if the researcher was familiar with the legislation then that was how decisions were made. Interviews would not reveal anything different. However it was suggested that the researcher could observe hearings in the court and a few magistrates said they were prepared to look at an interview schedule prepared and provided by the researcher to see whether they might be prepared to answer the questions.

The Chief Magistrate of Victoria, wrote to the Senior Magistrate at the Children's Court in support of the study and nominated six magistrates who had been at the court since the implementation of the *Children and Young*

Persons' Act 1989. These magistrates then nominated others who had worked at the Court and who might be prepared to be interviewed. The significance of formal support of the Chief Magistrate of Victoria cannot be underestimated. Such formal support gave the study legitimacy. It would have been extremely difficult to proceed with this study without it.

The Study Setting and Participants

The study took place at the Melbourne Children's Court. The Children's Court is one of the three fora for decision-making in child protection matters. The Children's Court is however the 'public welfare' court, the jurisdiction that considers all applications for child protection. However the Family Court of Australia also considers children's matters, but only in relation to how children's welfare and interests relate to adults (that is their parents). The Family Court is a court of 'private law' and children come to its attention as a consequence of their parents' matrimonial dispute. Most typically child protection matters are raised as issues in access and custody decisions. Where there are child protection concerns, these are referred to the state child protection service for investigation. Where action is warranted, they are brought before the Children's Court of Victoria. Whilst the paramount welfare of the child is foremost in the Family Court disposition, parents' interests must also be considered.

The Civil and Administrative Appeals Tribunal hears cases where parents are in dispute with the statutory welfare authority about, for example, case planning decisions. However the Children's Court is the primary forum for the resolution of child protection matters.

The Melbourne Children's Court, at the time of the study, comprised four main courtrooms and one supplementary courtroom. Two courtrooms were usually allocated to juvenile justice matters (Criminal Division), and two allocated to the Family Division. One court in the Family Division is set aside as the Mention Court in which the majority of cases commence, where orders are sought or reviewed, cases are directed to pre-hearing conference, or to contest. The other court in the Family Division is set aside to hear contested matters. The supplementary court is set aside for part-heard matters, including directions hearings.

The Court is administered by the Registrar. Offices are allocated at court for the clerks of the court, the Legal and Advisory Court Unit (administered by the Department of Human Services and employing welfare practitioners and lawyers who represent the Department of Human Services), and for legal representatives. The Legal Aid Commission also has an office. So too, does the Salvation Army which provides voluntary support for families attending court and who assist any individuals in custody.

The Children's Court is a busy court. People wait, often for long periods of time, for their case to be heard. There are sparse facilities for families and few distractions for children. The numbers of people in this area, the often obvious distress of parties, the busy noise level creates a tense atmosphere. Within the courtroom the magistrate sits behind a bench, with the clerk of court's desk and the witness stand at the side. In front of the bench is a table for legal representatives to sit facing the magistrate. Behind the legal representatives are rows of chairs for the parties to proceedings and for court visitors.

All individuals who attend the court proceed first to the registry window to seek information about cases, relevant documents, to book times for hearings. The queue of legal personnel, parents, police and child protection workers in front of this window, making their enquiries, became a familiar sight during the fifteen months the researcher attended the court.

The Study Participants

Fifteen magistrates participated in this study. Five of the magistrates were at the Children's Court at the time of the study. The other 10 magistrates had worked at the Children's Court for specific periods of time between the years 1987 to 1993. The study included almost the entire number of legally qualified magistrates who spent at least 12 months at the Children's Court, Victoria in the years 1987 to 1993. The participants were suggested to the researcher initially by the Chief Magistrate, and then by the individual magistrates so that all possible participants for the study were included. As a group they are representative of magistrates in Australia, appointed to similar children's court jurisdictions.

The Commencement of the Study

The study commenced with a three-month observation period (September–December 1993) and the researcher attended the court approximately three days a week during this time. During this three-month period the researcher observed 92 cases. Seventy-three cases were observed in the Mention Court and the hearing of these matters could last anywhere between five minutes and a few hours. Nineteen contested cases were observed. The majority of contested matters were cases in which sexual or physical abuse was alleged.

Hearings were often held over four to five days: a number of cases lasted for 10 or more days and one case lasted in excess of three weeks. However, the majority of child protection cases proceed through the Mention Court, often in quick succession, when the child protection service recommendation is accepted by parents and the court.

Cases observed were those before the Mention Court on the days the researcher attended court, what would be described as an availability sample. There was more throughput of cases in the Mentions Court and so a greater number of cases were observed in this court. The researcher did follow the hearing of a number of contested cases. It was not possible to select a random sample of cases heard because cases are not given fixed appearance times, because of the unpredictability of the child protection cases before the court, and because of the time taken to hear each matter.

During the observation period the researcher sat at the back of the court and observed court activity. The researcher had minimal interaction with other participants in the court process: most usually it was to explain her presence to legal or welfare representatives. At times magistrates noted her presence or commented to her when the court was clear. The value of observation was the opportunity to experience the nature of the court, to observe the setting in which magistrates work, the activities which take place, who participates in court activity, and obtain individual perspectives on what is happening that are offered by those in and around the court. 'The first hand experience ... allows ... the observer to make inferences without relying on prior conceptualisations' (Patton 1984:204).

It was not always possible or appropriate to take notes in the courtroom. Where there was considerable tension in the court, or the case was of great sensitivity, or large numbers of people were present, note taking was not appropriate. However notes were made as soon as possible after a hearing or during temporary adjournments.

No matter how objective the researcher is however, it has to be acknowledged that there is the unintentional bias in how s/he constructs the meaning of behaviours. The opportunity to check out these observations with other participants in the court, and with study participants (the magistrates), assisted the validity and reliability of these perceptions. It was important to find out about the myriad of things that happen inside and outside the court. The researcher spoke to legal practitioners, to child protection workers, to get explanations of terms, processes, and the meanings of orders made.

The researcher made a point of not specifically asking about cases unless information was offered. Such information was always about orders sought or departmental concerns: no confidential personal information was offered or sought. The researcher had basic information about what cases were being heard in what courtroom from the court's daily running sheet.

An observation sheet was constructed to record the court activity (see Appendix One). The observation sheet recorded the participants in each case, case characteristics (order sought, grounds and reasons for application, basic child and family details, court history of the case) and the court decision order and conditions. Noteworthy interactions between participants were also recorded. The time taken in a case and the frequency with which some cases appear before the court was also noted. So too were the sources of information for the court and legal representation. The idiosyncratic nature of cases presented made it impossible to predict categories for such information. Simple note taking was more useful.

Observation sheets were often incomplete. Cases which were returns for orders, or roll over orders (that is continuations of interim accommodation orders), typically had little information presented. The observer was entirely reliant on information provided to the court and any serendipitous comments made which were relevant. The researcher had no access to reports which could have provided case details. Thus the researcher could only record what was spoken about in court. The researcher limited the observation record to the categories chosen in order to systematically describe the participants and their behaviour for the study, and also to be realistic about what was available to be recorded. As well as obtaining information for the observation sheet the researcher noted other data relevant to the research issues, issues relevant for the magistrate interviews and, what beginning propositions could be developed about magisterial decision-making in this jurisdiction.

The observation data was qualitatively analysed, using content analysis to look for patterns in the data: recurring themes in cases, in allegations, in orders sought, in family characteristics, legal and welfare representation, and issues which appear to be related; the 'who/what/where/when/how/why questions' (Burns 1994:285).

Magistrate Interviews

Interviews with magistrates based at the Children's Court took place in their chambers at the court. Interviews with the other magistrates took place in various suburban Melbourne courthouses.

A structured interview schedule was developed for interviews (see Appendix Two). It contained 21 questions based on key issues identified in the literature and by the observation stage of the study. The schedule questions were designed to clearly address the research aims and were directly related to the work of the study participants. Sensitive items were kept to a minimum, acknowledging the highly personal nature of the magistrates work. Open-ended questions were chosen to gain as much information as possible in an area where little is known about what alternative choices would be. Open-ended questions or free-answer questions created a more natural situation for respondents (Minichello et al. 1993:90). The order in which the questions are presented in the schedule was carefully developed to maximise study participants' cooperation and interest.

Questions were grouped along particular themes of the study so that each area was covered on one segment and the magistrates did not have to switch from one topic to another from question to question. The questions which clearly related to the research problem were asked of the magistrates first. Questions that are potentially more personal or sensitive were asked halfway through the interview. Individual demographic information was sought at the end of the interview schedule as is suggested by Gochros (1985).

The interview schedule was pre-tested by one magistrate who was not one of the study participants, to ensure it would be understood by participants and would be interpreted similarly by participants (Dillman 1978). Questions were positive in their framing. It was important also to be sure questions were seen to be free from perceived interviewer bias (Mindel 1985). This was pertinent given the social work qualifications of the researcher. Such interviews involve considerable personal interaction and so cooperation with the respondents was essential, most especially when there was no compulsion for them to participate nor were there immediate payoffs for them (Marshall and Rossman 1989).

The face to face interview allowed the researcher the opportunity to clarify questions for the respondents; it also meant interviewees might be more willing to answer sensitive questions, a number of which were included in the study's interview schedule. Clearly, there is a potential for bias in face to face interviewing; there is no anonymity for respondents and they may answer to please the interviewer, or give answers which are generally felt but which may withhold particular personal ideas or views or beliefs (Gochros 1985).

The interview questions commenced with four questions about the frames of reference magistrates use in child protection cases: the weight they attach to specific criteria, how case characteristics affect factors selected, how magistrates operationalise the notions of 'significant harm' and 'best interests'. The next three questions (5, 6 and 7) asked magistrates about influences other than case factors which impact on their work, and gave them the opportunity to comment on other professionals in the child protection field. The next three questions (8, 9 and 10) asked about the magistrate's work in the Family Division of the Children's Court. The next questions (11, 12 and 13) asked magistrates about the particular beliefs they have about the role of the court in child protection and personal views they rely on to assess cases before them.

Questions 14, 15 and 16 asked about inter-professional collaboration, in particular their views about the information welfare practitioners provide. Questions 17 and 18 asked about feedback magistrates receive and information about child abuse they are given, to canvass how magistrates acquire knowledge about child welfare matters. Questions 20 and 21 sought some demographic information.

Before any interviews took place the researcher gained written consent from each magistrate. Interviews were recorded on a small cassette recorder and later transcribed and word processed. This allowed a complete and accurate record of magistrate responses and allowed the researcher to concentrate solely on the interview process. Interviews were at times interrupted by court officer enquiries or a magistrate's need to briefly return to court. Taping interviews dealt more easily with these interruptions.

The data analysis of interview transcripts initially looked for preliminary themes and points of interest that emerged in the responses to each question. From this question-by-question analysis, specific concepts were constructed from the data (e.g. 'job context', 'professional ideology', 'views about child abuse') according to their salience to the study interest (Patton 1984). The data was then examined for linkages or associations between issues that appeared significant to magistrate decision-making. This analytic deduction method allows the researcher to accumulate information from respondents about whom little is known and to progress from outlining general themes to more specific propositions about how magistrates make decisions in child protection matters.

Excerpts from the interview transcripts are provided in the next chapter to convey how magistrates described the factors that influenced their decision-making. The examination of these excerpts also allows one to discover what similarities and differences there are in interview responses and what patterns and associations emerge to explain decision-making.

Court Record Analysis

The court records analysed in the third stage of the study were the records of the 92 cases observed by the researcher at the commencement of the study. However, only 89 case records could be analysed as no information was found in three of the cases: they had been either withdrawn or struck out. The case record data collection took place over a three month period (June to September 1994), in the Registry of the Children's Court.

Data recorded on the survey sheet included information about case features: the grounds for the child protection application, family details, prior history, other agency involvement (see Appendix Three). It also recorded the family problems noted by the child protection worker and their recommendations to the court about a case. The number of appearances of a case and decisions in the court life of a case were also noted. The data was quantitatively processed using SPSS.

The court record for each case generally comprises the magistrate's decision sheet and the court report prepared by the child protection worker. The magistrate decision sheet typically contains very little information except to record the court decision and any conditions on an order, and a return hearing date. The quality and content of child protection reports varied according to their author, the haste with which the report was prepared, and the information which was available to report about the child and family, and whether the author had access to family members. The lack of computerised or centralised information about cases meant court records were at times incomplete. Files could also be absent, being used by magistrates or court staff. As mentioned earlier, the child protection reports were variable and at times it was not clear what were the significant issues or problems in a case. This meant court records could be very limited and while the aim was to collect as much information as possible about study variables, the survey questionnaires were often incomplete. However, it provided a data source that could support other findings and possibly provide data about other relevant variables.

The next chapter describes how magistrates' perform their work in the Children's Court and combines the author's observations with magistrate comments about their work. It provides information about how magistrates approach cases and decision-making. It also reveals their views about the professionals who attend court and the families who appear before them. This chapter integrates data obtained from court records to compare with the magistrates' views about child protection cases.

Chapter Three

Deciding Best Interests

Decisions about children are always difficult because you can do something that alters a child's life (M 13).

In this chapter magistrates describe the nature of their work in the Children's Court. Their views about the families who appear before them, their views about the professionals who attend the court and, my observations about how magistrates go about their work in the Court, are included. Magistrates' comments are identified in the text thus: (M 01), or other number according to which of the 15 magistrates has made the comment.

Inside the Children's Court

The Children's Court in Melbourne is a purpose-built court near the centre of the city that hears juvenile justice and child welfare matters in metropolitan Melbourne. Outside Melbourne, regional courts have designated Children's Court sitting days to hear child protection and juvenile justice matters. Child protection matters are dealt with in the Family Division of the Children's Court; juvenile justice matters (for young people up to the age of seventeen years), are dealt with in the Criminal Division of the Children's Court but are also heard in other Melbourne suburban courts to ease the burden on the Melbourne Children's Court. All child protection matters that arise in metropolitan Melbourne, a city of some three and a half million people, are heard solely in the Family Division of the Melbourne Children's Court.

The Children's Court sits between 10 a.m. and 4 p.m., Monday to Friday. About 9.30 a.m. each morning, families and professionals involved in Children's Court matters start to gather at the court. Legal practitioners, child protection workers, family members, and other interested parties queue before the enquiries window seeking information from Court officers about hearings, court times, documents etc. Child protection workers meet families and legal representatives to discuss cases, to negotiate their recommendations to the Court and to ensure reports and necessary witnesses are available. The Legal and Court Advisory Unit (run by the Department of Human Services, Victoria), deals with child protection workers' and legal practitioners' enquiries about cases, responds to telephone enquiries from regional Human Services Victoria offices and organises representation for child protection workers in court.

The waiting area at the Court is busy with individuals waiting for their case to be called and trying to locate who they need for their case. There are rooms available for families and professionals to consult; however, they might wait hours for their case to be called. Everyone is thrown together in this atmosphere; there is little protection for distressed, or fearful, family members as they, and other witnesses, may need to wait in close proximity to each other.

Cases commence in the Mention Court when the child protection service sets out their concerns about a child, and the grounds of the application according to the *Children and Young Persons Act (Victoria) 1989,* so that the magistrate can assess the immediate risk to a child and decide on the need for interim orders. The Mention Court hears short matters, reviews cases and gives directions as to how the Court will manage a case. Cases are dealt with swiftly if parents agree to the child protection service recommendations. The majority of cases, anecdotally reported (in 1994) as 80 per cent by the senior magistrate, are in fact decided by agreement. If parents do not agree with the basis of the child protection case, the magistrate directs the family and the child protection workers to attend a pre-hearing conference, run by a court-appointed Convenor. If parents and children and the child protection service do not reach an agreement at the pre-hearing conference the Court sets a date for a contested hearing. Child protection disputes occur most often after initial orders are made, although interim orders are also contested, usually when there is disagreement about a child remaining out of the parents' care until the case returns to court. Child protection applications on the grounds of child sexual abuse are usually contested because of the likelihood of criminal charges against the perpetrator if the case is found proven. The four contested cases of sexual abuse that I observed lasted between six and 15 days. Each case was not necessarily heard on consecutive days; they often lasted longer than expected, and remained part-heard for a longer period of time than other cases. One magistrate described sexual abuse cases as like runaway trains: cases that gather up great amounts of information, time, and energy, yet often with little resolution for the family, apart from an increase in family tensions.

There was great variability in how matters proceeded at court and so there was considerable uncertainty about what process a case might follow. Court hearings might be delayed by a number of factors other than a parent's wish to dispute the child protection concerns. There might be problems with the availability of legal representation for clients, the availability of relevant parties to attend court, or necessary court reports might not be ready. Cases are adjourned while these matters are attended to and cases might be adjourned a couple of times before these matters are resolved and the case can be heard. These delays and the need for numerous adjournments made court hearings appear very fragmented. The busy turnover of cases in the Mention Court, the adjournment of cases and the procession of professionals in and out of the court is bewildering for families, who were unfamiliar with court processes, with the language of the court, who did not know how to behave in court, or when to ask questions. The cross-examination of witnesses in contested hearings is followed often with great difficulty by families, if followed at all. In contested cases I observed, parents often appeared disengaged by the judicial process, alienated by legal argument that was conducted in language which was often difficult to understand. No matter how concerned a magistrate might be about this, it appeared there was little that could be done to redress it. The Children's Court is a magistrates' court and legal requirements had to be satisfied.

This disengagement and alienation was exemplified during the lengthy hearing of a sexual abuse case. The alleged perpetrator was the children's father. He spent a considerable amount of time outside the court, often caring for the two younger children (his three daughters were the subject of the court hearing). He appeared distanced from the court process not just by the difficulty of the case but also by the protracted and acrimonious cross-examination of child protection workers and his stepdaughter, about whom similar concerns had been brought to court 12 months previously.

Cases varied in terms of the amount of court time they occupied and in the number of participants involved. Cases might return to court on a number of occasions to vary access arrangements between children and parents, or to change where a child was to reside, or to review if parents had made the specific changes recommended by the child protection service, if they had accepted family support services or undertaken treatment programmes, for example in anger management, parenting skills, substance abuse etc.

Court appearances in child abuse cases create considerable tension for families; hearing their private life made public is difficult enough but it is made more difficult by an unfamiliar environment and dealing with the professional and other witnesses who might be unsympathetic towards them. It was clear the court, in reality, could do little to ensure the personal safety of court participants or deal with disruptive behaviour, or to deal with threats made against witnesses, family members, or child protection workers by angry parents. Likewise, waiting outside the courtroom could be difficult, and feel unsafe, when one party in a case is confronted by the opponents in their case. In one case observed, where sexual abuse was alleged between a father and his daughter, and her mother had a criminal conviction for physical injury to the child, the mother attended court with numerous supporters who made hostile gestures and comments to the father, who had no support, both inside and outside the court during the case hearing. The magistrate spoke sternly to the parties involved but the hostility made it difficult for the court to debate the case issues and negotiate about conditions for a court order.

Child Protection Applications

The child protection applications taken out in the Children's Court, during the time of the study (1993–94), were predominantly for children aged between birth and five years and were more or less evenly divided between male and female children (56 male and 63 female children). The applications generally involved one child of the family (in 64 applications) although the cases also involved 23 sibling groups, on average three children per sibling group. The young ages of children subject to child protection applications was also found to be the case in the study by Sheehan (1998): children aged between birth and eight years of age comprised 65 per cent of the group of children for whom the child protection service took out a new protection application in the Children's Court during the first six months of 1997.

Problems with family violence, with physical and emotional abuse of children, were most commonly the basis of a protection application across all age groups, most particularly for children aged one year to 10 years. Table 3.1 shows that the child protection cases included in this Children's Court study were predominantly taken out on the grounds of both the likelihood of physical and emotional harm, or actual physical and emotional harm; emotional abuse as the primary ground for child protection mostly appeared in cases involving children in the five to 10 year age group. The grounds of child protection applications did vary and very often two, perhaps three grounds, were included in the one application which reflects the multifactorial nature of child abuse.

In terms of ages of the children involved in protection matters, Table 3.2 shows that risk of, or actual harm to, a child's physical health and development was the major reason for a protection application for a child under 12 months old. Sexual abuse of a child, coupled most often with emotional abuse, was

Table 3.1 The grounds of the protection applications (CYPA 1989 s.63) in the study (n=89)

Reason PA sought	No. sought
Parent absent (s.63a)	0
Parent incapacitated (s.63b)	0
Physical abuse (s.63c)	5
Sexual abuse (s.63d)	3
Emotional abuse (s.63e)	12
Threat to child development (s.63f)	2
Section b & e (incapacitated and emotional)	3
Section b & f (incapacitated and developmental harm)	2
Section c & e (physical and emotional)	20
Section c & f (physical and developmental harm)	2
Section d & e (sexual and emotional)	7
Section d & f (sexual and developmental harm)	1
Section e & f (emotional and developmental harm)	3
Section b, c, e (incapacitated, physical and emotional harm)	1
Section b, c, f (incapacitated, physical and developmental harm)	2
Section c, d, e (physical, sexual and emotional)	1
Section c, e, f (physical, emotional and developmental harm)	3
Guardianship	6
Breach of Order	2

the second most reported ground of a child protection application for a child aged between five and 16 years. Twelve protection applications were made solely on the grounds of emotional abuse, recognising that emotional harm is perceived to be as injurious to a child as is physical maltreatment

Table 3.3 sets out the child protection concerns that formed the basis of the child protection matters included in the study. Parental substance abuse and psychiatric problems were both frequent grounds for seeking a protection application. Such problems were often interrelated when the parent's transient lifestyle contributed to child neglect and to emotional harm. Children abandoned by parents, or were neglected, or who failed to thrive, formed another significant group in the study. In children less than one year of age, these grounds were particularly pronounced. Some grounds appeared more age-specific; 'incapacitated parent' (s.63f) is most numerous for very young infants. 'Runaway child' is specific to children aged between 11 to 16 years – they are old enough physically to remove themselves from their family. Two children in this group were intentionally homeless – and at immediate risk to themselves.

Table 3.2 Age of child compared with the grounds of the protection application

	Age groups								Total	
	Less than 1 year		1–4 years		5–10 years		11–16 years			
	N	%	N	%	N	%	N	%	N	%
Reason seeking PA										
section 63b	4	33	2	11	1	5	1	4	8	10
section 63c	4	33	8	44	10	45	9	33	31	39
section 63d			3	17	3	14	5	19	11	14
section 63e	8	67	13	72	18	82	18	67	57	72
section 63f	8	67	5	28	2	9	4	15	19	24
s107	1	8	1	6	3	14	2	7	7	9
Breach			1	6	1	5	1	4	3	4
Other	1	8					2	7	3	4
No. of children per age group	12		18		22		27		79	

Note: given that often two grounds are included in the one application, on occasion more than two, the percentages in the table do not total 100%; rather, they indicate the number of times the ground appears in an application.

Table 3.4 compares the grounds of the protection application with the gender of the child. This table cross-references the previous table and enables comparison of the reason for the protection application with gender.

Family violence, physical abuse, injuries to a child, feature as reasons for protection applications in more than half the cases included in the study. In about half of the child protection applications (n=47 cases, 52.8 per cent) the application was as a result of the apprehension of a child (removal from parental care) rather than by notification of the parents that an application would be sought because of risk to a child or inadequate care of a child (n=24; 27.0 per cent). Child protection work was perceived very much as crisis intervention, with children removed from parents because of immediate risk and/or harm.

Who is a Magistrate?

Magistrates in Victoria are required to have a law degree. Indeed all the magistrates who participated in the study had the University qualification, the Bachelor of Laws (LLB). Three of the 15 magistrates also held a

Table 3.3 Grounds for the protection matter before the court compared with the age of the child

	Less than 1 year		1–4 years		5–10 years		11–16 years			
	N	%	N	%	N	%	N	%	N	%
Grounds for PA										
Family violence	3	21	4	22	2	9	7	25	16	19
Phys abuse of child	1	7	8	44	11	48	8	29	28	34
Emot abuse of child	2	14	7	39	12	52	10	36	31	37
Sex abuse of child			3	17	4	17	5	18	12	14
Parents relationship	2	14	1	6			1	4	4	5
Parent-child problems					2	9	5	18	7	8
Irreconcilable differences							3	11	3	4
Incapacitated parent	10	71	4	22	9	39	6	21	29	35
Abandoned	1	7	1	6	2	9	4	14	8	10
Neglect	1	7	5	28	3	13	3	11	12	14
Failure to thrive	5	36	2	11	1	4			8	10
Developmental delay	1	7	3	17	1	4			5	6
Illness in child	2	14			2	9	2	7	6	7
Illness in mother	3	21	1	6	1	4			5	6
Intellect disability – parent	3	21	2	11					5	6
Transient lifestyle – parent	2	14	3	17	5	22	3	11	13	16
Excessive discipline					3	13	4	14	7	8
Runaway child							4	14	5	6
Child exposed to unsuitable people			2	11					2	2
Child associated with unsuitable people					1	4	4	14	5	6
Inadequate food			1	6	2	9			3	4
Leave child in locked car			1	6					1	1
Injuries to child	1	7	5	28	3	13			9	11
Other					6	26	6	21	12	14
Psychiatric problems – parents	5	36	3	17	6	26	3	11	17	20
Breach			1	6	1	4	1	4	3	4
Substance abuse	5	36	4	22	7	30	5	18	21	25
Total no. children per category	14		18		23		28		83	100

Note: the total number of court records for which this information was available is 84.

Table 3.4 The child protection concerns based on the grounds of the protection application and the gender of the child

| | Sex of child | | | | Total | |
| | Male | | Female | | | |
	N	%	N	%	N	%
Grounds for PA						
Family violence	10	27	6	13	16	19
Physical abuse of child	16	43	12	26	28	33
Emotional abuse of child	15	41	16	34	31	37
Sexual abuse of child	5	14	7	15	12	14
Parents relationship	4	11			4	5
Parent-child problems	3	8	4	9	7	8
Irreconcilable differences	1	3	2	4	3	4
Incapacitated parent	11	30	18	38	29	35
Abandoned	3	8	5	11	8	10
Neglect	6	16	6	13	12	14
Failure to thrive	5	14	3	6	8	10
Developmental delay	4	11	1	2	5	6
Illness in child	2	5	4	9	6	7
Illness in mother	2	5	3	6	5	6
Intellectual disability – parent	3	8	2	4	5	6
Transient lifestyle – parent	6	16	7	15	13	15
Excessive discipline	1	3	6	13	7	8
Runaway child	2	5	3	6	5	6
Child exposed to unsuitable people	1	3	1	2	2	2
Child associated with unsuitable people	2	5	3	6	5	6
Inadequate food	1	3	2	4	3	4
Leave child in locked car			1	2	1	1
Injuries to child	8	22	1	2	9	11
Other	5	14	7	15	12	14
Psychiatric problems – parents	8	22	9	19	17	20
Breach	3	8			3	4
Substance abuse	7	19	14	30	21	25
Total no. cases	37	100	47	100	84	100

postgraduate diploma in an area related to the law, most notably in criminology. One woman magistrate had trained as a teacher prior to undertaking her legal training. Table 3.5 provides some personal and professional information about the five female and 10 male magistrates who participated in the study.

Table 3.5 Magistrate background

Magistrate	Gender	Magis. Prior	Time at Children's Court	Bar/solicitor	
01	m	2.8yrs	12mths	solicitor	52
02	m		6yrs	solicitor	49
03	m	12mths	2yrs	bar/dpp/solicitor	42
04	m	3yrs	18mths	solicitor	
05	m	2yrs	2yrs	fam.crt./bar/prior	48
06	f	yes	3yrs	tribunal member	47
07	f	2yrs	18mths	bar	52
08	m	5yrs	12mths	solicitor	46
09	m	2yrs	18mths	bar, then solicitor	
10	m	12mths	10mths	bar	54
11	m	no	2yrs	bar	47
12	m	3yrs	2.9yrs	solicitor	
13	f	3yrs	4mths	bar	56
14	f	6mths	15mths	bar	41
15	f	no	18mths	solicitor	43

Nine of the magistrates had practised as solicitors, six of the magistrates as barristers at law, prior to their appointment to the Magistracy. Three of the six women magistrates were appointed directly to the Children's Court as their first appointment. This, they suggested, was done by the Chief Magistrate in order to provide a better gender and life experience mix amongst the magistrates already working at the Children's Court.

Magistrates tended to have relatively short appointments: the mean time spent at the Children's Court by the male magistrates was 25 months, for the female magistrates it was 20 months. However, one of the male magistrates had spent six years at the court; if his period at the court is excluded from the mean time, then the average appointment time for a male magistrate was 18 months. This meant that by the time magistrates had developed expertise in children's matters they moved to the adult jurisdiction.

All the magistrates, when interviewed, referred to the work of the Family Division of the Children's Court, as quite unlike that in any other jurisdiction. Whilst three of the magistrates had worked in community or Government legal agencies prior to their appointment: organisations such as Aboriginal Legal Aid, the Office of the Director of Public Prosecutions, the Crimes Compensation Tribunal and, one magistrate was a Registrar of the Family Court prior to the magistracy, eight magistrates had no experience of family law matters and so the work of the Children's Court was quite unfamiliar.

Seven magistrates had worked in areas with some exposure to family law and 12 magistrates had worked in the adult jurisdiction prior to their appointment to the Children's Court. Yet, magistrates felt their prior experience did little to prepare them for the work of the Children's Court.

The Nature of the Children's Jurisdiction

The Children's Court is a specialist jurisdiction, very different from the adult courts. The work is emotionally difficult, magistrates receive no specific training for the jurisdiction, the procedures and dispositions are different, the Act provides for the more informal conduct of hearings, lawyers are often unfamiliar with the jurisdiction and magistrates who are assigned to the Court say they feel isolated from mainstream magistrate work.

> The whole Family Division is different from anything else you do in the Magistrate's Court ... procedurally the Family Division has rules of evidence which mean you don't have to apply the strict rules of evidence ... you conduct the hearings informally (M 09).

> It's like trying to describe the difference between chalk and cheese. It couldn't be any more different. They are utterly different functions. There is no other line of work that corresponds in even the least way in the Family Division (M 12).

> The atmosphere of the court in that it is more informal ... we sit close together – in some ways it makes it more difficult because of the intimacy, it's more difficult for me to distance myself from the parties (M 01).

> I think most courts are fairly detached but you are sort of sitting – the legal expression – at arms length from the parties, you sit back and listen and you make a decision. Here it is a much more sort of closeness, it does not always appear in other courts (M 02).

> ... if you are doing a civil matter it doesn't matter about the personality, about anybody in the courtroom, but in these cases you are watching everybody (M 06).

The decisions magistrates make in the Family Division have a major impact on children's lives. Magistrates said the decisions are not so much legally difficult as psychologically and cognitively difficult. They are decisions that involve balancing the competing interests of parents, the child protection service and other parties, dealing with the distress that inevitably surrounds child protection cases and ensuring parents understand decisions and are treated appropriately; they are also cases that often lack clear and available evidence:

> In terms of the day to day decisions and the enormity of decisions you have to make, it is extremely difficult. It's not because there is a lot of law in it, it's social-based decision-making which over time I found more and more awkward to do (M 07).

> Children's Court – not complex legally but difficult work because of the kind of work it is. In the adult court a case is presented and decided on the balance of probabilities. There are evidence rules. And even if you get it wrong as a magistrate it doesn't really matter – it's not life and death but it does matter if you get it wrong in the Children's Court. You are making difficult decisions in the best interests of the child and family (M 05).

> There is a clear difference in the process necessary between the Children's Court and the adult courts. If you don't have any, as I had not, exposure to the Children's Court, then you just walk in there and you don't really know what you are walking into (M 03).

> The thing I found so hard in Children's Court was on top of trying to make the right decision and keep everyone calm, I was always conscious of trying to salvage a bit of psyche in the whole thing. I think one of the greatest skills in that court is to take someone's child from them nicely or put them under supervision in the most caring way. If you are trying to help a young mother who has no skills to parent her children better it's not a great help to have her sitting in court for three days listening to how dreadful she is (M 14).

What made work in the Children's Court so challenging was that it calls on expertise other than legal training:

> It's difficult in a different way. It's difficult, it's very emotional, it's not really law. You are not using legal training other than training for magistrates to make decisions. There is not much case law to know about so it's not testing you as a lawyer which the criminal jurisdiction does – its using your experience of life, trying to be objective as you can. It uses different skills altogether (M 11).

The impact of this work weighed heavily on magistrates:

> I felt terribly ill-equipped ... I'm sure I have sublimated the whole experience because it was so painful (M 15).

> Knowing the decisions you are making are going to affect the child's life and the life of the family for maybe the whole term of the child's life, you are really making very major decisions. Whereas in the other courts generally the decisions you are making don't have that sort of dramatic impact (M 02).

> It's the emotional strain that's implicit in working in the Family Division. It's much more difficult to make a child a ward than send someone to prison so I think it's a much more difficult area and of course it's much more specialised ... and that involves a lot of extra work and everything (M 15).

The majority of the magistrates (13 of the 15 magistrates) said their work in the Children's Court had a significant personal impact on them: a pressure to make the correct decision, not only because of the consequences of such decisions but also because of community reaction to such decisions:

> You are worried about making a decision which could go wrong if a child was returned to a family and you woke up the next day, saw the headlines 'Mother/ father kills child' (M 09).

> ... I found the Family Division very demanding, I didn't like decision-making in the Family Division, I found it very difficult (M 15).

The youth and vulnerability of children before the court impressed on one magistrate the need to 'get it right':

> You are dealing with people [who are] so young and have such little opportunity or experience in life (M 13).

> The people who you deal with really need protection – it's an entirely different situation to dealing with independent adults (M 15).

Work in the adult jurisdiction is more routine and predictable, and straightforward: magistrates can rely on case law, on laws of evidence and case facts, and on their legal training to assist decision-making:

> In the adult court the magistrates there have got enormously wide work requirements ... but in effect most of the work they do is reasonably predictable and it tends to be fairly routine particularly in the Magistrates Court ... there is not the sort of pressure, the importance ... it doesn't have the consequences of what we do here ... the impact on the parties is nowhere near as great as when you have to decide whether or not to put children back into families where they may be at risk or whether to take children away from families because of abuse,

making those decisions which may well have long term impact (M 02).

... in the adult court you just sentence (M 07).

In the Children's Court, however, decisions are about the best interests of the child and magistrates had to consider family and parent wishes as well as the recommendations of the child protection service when deciding best interests. Families and professionals looked to the court outcome to address child protection problems. Yet magistrates said they were powerless to address such complex problems. What they could do was make orders requiring parents to attend treatment or counselling programmes. Whilst they had the legal power to change a child's circumstances this change was often short-term and, magistrates said, probably made little overall difference to a child's life:

Often what you do or don't it doesn't make much difference (M 05).

... [It was a] frustratingly futile sort of exercise because I'm not able to right the wrongs of society and that's what brings the business to that court ... I couldn't fix it up for these children, I never felt I could achieve anything there (M 14).

One magistrate, however, found work in the jurisdiction less routine and therefore more intellectually interesting than adult court work:

There was a possibility of being more creative here because of the greater options of orders trying to find out what's going on in a person ... it's more intellectually interesting in the Children's Court (M 06).

Children's Court cases seemed, to magistrates, to take longer to resolve than those in the adult courts. Difficulties with the nature of the cases, with obtaining reports, getting witnesses to court, with changes in cases: parents separating, new child protection notifications, for example, delayed hearings. One magistrate said the Court seemed to operate on a time scale that was different from the adult courts:

The Children's Court runs on a totally different time frame, pressure. People don't seem to be in a hurry to get to court in the first place, they are not in a hurry to get their matters on. Everyone is hampered by the fact that there is insufficient legal aid. There is a system where the social workers who deal with the legal work hand over contests. They for a long time haven't been handing them over until too late so the whole thing runs in a very disjointed and irregular way ... (M 07).

Evidence

Magistrates spoke about the different procedures in the Family Division of the Children's Court; one significant difference was the admission of hearsay evidence and, deciding cases on the balance of probabilities, rather than the adult court's measure of beyond reasonable doubt. Magistrates also felt the availability and quality of accurate evidence for child protection matters often fell short of what was necessary:

> There are problems with evidence in this process ... although normal evidence rules don't apply ... there is still the need for relevance ... they really are problems for social workers to do with evidence; they have no legal training and in my view they present as fearful, arrogant, give often one-sided reports and that can be very difficult when you are trying to assess evidence. Social workers don't understand the concept of 'hearsay'. In the Children's Court while there are not rules of evidence yet social workers don't understand they have to report what they observe (M 05).

> Evidence which is inadmissible is admitted. One then has to assess the weight of that evidence and in turn what the probabilities are ... You would look at the papers in the file, look at the alleged facts and say, I need more information here. Go and investigate. Then I would hear and test the evidence – that's the approach that appeals to me. I was powerless in obtaining material and information I really wanted (M 01).

> The need to explore issues and satisfy oneself that a claim is properly brought is frustrated by the difficulty of fact-finding where there are competing versions of a situation, where evidence is problematic, it is underlined by the court's reliance on hearsay evidence particularly when it is the hearsay evidence of very young children (M 12).

The admission of hearsay evidence allowed child protection workers to present their accounts and reports about children as evidence of child protection concerns. Magistrates were uneasy about this and believed that child protection workers did not give proper attention to legal requirements about evidence. One magistrate commented that child protection matters attract people who 'have axes to grind in this jurisdiction' (M 12). This, combined with magistrates' unfamiliarity with welfare terminology, the professional practice of protective workers and the conditions under which they worked, meant magistrates felt they could not always rely on the evidence of child protection workers.

What was plain was that it is often difficult to articulate welfare issues and child protection concerns into legal facts. What was also difficult for child protection workers was not only the nature and amount of evidence required in child protection matters but also the public exposure, for the purposes of legal debate, of confidential personal information about clients in order to substantiate child protection concerns.

Concerns about evidence and differences between legal and welfare approaches was particularly apparent in cases of sexual abuse and physical injury. Magistrates made it clear that evidence presented had to be legally relevant and reliable because of possible criminal action. Concern was also expressed about false allegations and about how much the court ought to rely on children's disclosures. While the court takes very seriously what children say in such cases:

> It's difficult in sexual abuse cases to know what really did happen – those are very difficult – sometimes they are quite easy – but often difficult to decide depending on the evidence about the family (M 06).

> I don't think many contested sexual abuse cases were found proved in this court last year (M 10).

Training for Magistrates

> ... you are making decisions which are going to affect their lives forever and I sometimes wonder whether we shouldn't have more training in what we are doing. Specialist training in order to be able to appreciate the effects that our decisions have (M 07).

Work in adult courts does not prepare magistrates for work in the Children's Court and the majority of magistrates said they had little, or no, exposure to the Court prior to their appointment:

> You can't do a crash course in social work and child psychiatry – it's not feasible and especially because it now appears to be the policy; the people don't stay at the children's court now for more than a year. Just when you are getting good they are leaving. By the same token you can't take more than two and a half years of it, I was going crazy by the end and the cases were getting longer when I left (M 12).

One magistrate noted that the Act requires magistrates who work in the Children's Court to show a particular qualification for the appointment although it was not happening with the current magistrate appointments:

> I don't bring any training. I've got no psychology nor child welfare training, I don't bring any qualifications to making those decisions ... I know the Act says people who work in a Children's Court ought to be people who have shown a particular qualification ... I don't really believe that's how it happens with magistrates going to the Children's Court (M 03).

Three magistrates said their lack of psychological knowledge or familiarity with child welfare, combined with frequently not having all the information about a case that a magistrate believed was necessary in order to understand child protection concerns, was a source of frustration:

> You've got someone like me, young, untrained and trying to make the right decision, trying to feel that I've listened to both sides, now what am I going to make about it? (M 03).

A number of magistrates noted how different were their life experiences from those of the families who appeared before them. Whilst magistrates relied on their legal background, their own reading and their experiences with families, they relied on their discretion to decide whether or not what was alleged constituted child abuse. At times, two magistrates said, it was difficult to decide about a family given the different values, the lack of opportunity, and different ethnic backgrounds of the range of families who appeared in Children's Court cases. However, a number of magistrates emphasised the importance of trying not to have preconceptions or fixed positions about particular types of cases and the importance of having flexible views about families:

> None of us [magistrates at the Children's Court] is committed to any particular line of treatment or theory of psychological development or theory of families which I think is good – it's very much just looking at the story as it comes out (M 06).

> You go to a third world country and see what constitutes a family and then you go to Glen Waverley [a comfortable middle-class suburb] and you see what constitutes a family. You have to be aware that the social textbook family isn't the only family. You have to be aware of the incredible diversity and possibility of care. The basic tenet is that love and support and stimulation – that's critical (M 05).

Yet seven magistrates believed there was a pattern to child abuse cases seen by the court:

> The mother would often herself have been abused as a child, abused by her father, uncles, brothers, etc., and then would have a child or children and then attract men to her life who would be sexually abusing of the children and then the mother would deny the man would behave in such a way (M 01).

One magistrate said it was important however to be on the lookout for particular ideological positions on child abuse held by some professionals appearing in the Children's Court who would attempt to persuade the court:

> to fall into an ideological position and to make quite outrageous generalisations like this woman cannot protect a child because she was abused as a child and she is attracted to violent men (M 11).

And, professionals who might be selective about the information they sought, to confirm a particular view about a case:

> But then how do you know that this case fits in the pattern ... in these [difficult] cases it's a common trap to fall into to make a decision in a difficult case and then seek to substantiate it (M 05).

> Why should the court be hobbled by hearing just what either interest group wants to tell you – maybe its the one area where the court should be able to say 'could you please interview this person and check that out' (M 14).

Magistrates said they received very little feedback about cases they decided so it was difficult to develop frameworks for Children's Court practice. Appeals in cases are heard in the County Court although that court is not specialised in dealing with family problems. However, a number of magistrates did want to know more about what happened to children after court:

> It would be very nice to know sometimes whether the decision you made in terms of placements worked (M 05).

> to appreciate the effects our decisions have ... if there were feedback and training to understand where our decisions lead and the results of them (M 07).

Most of the magistrates commented that the work of the Children's Court is not highly regarded in legal circles. This lack of status in the legal system meant there was insufficient recognition given to the Court's important purpose:

> If we don't get the recognition or the attention we deserve, I think that's very unfortunate. If we don't have that recognition it affects our capacity to be able to sometimes make the best decision (M 02).

It also meant legal and other professionals who appeared in court might have insufficient understanding of child welfare legislation and, perhaps, little interest in the nature of the work:

> there are people who come here who don't appear to have any real understanding of what the real issues are (M 05).

The Ease or Difficulty of Decision-making

> ... it is a jurisdiction in which you are playing God more than any other, I find it much easier to send people to prison than it is to take people's children off them ... [because] there is enough independent objective material there to show that's [prison] what must happen ... taking someone's child off them is very much harder because it's a value judgement (M 14).

The Children's Court tries, as much as possible, to achieve agreement between parents and the child protection service, without recourse to the adversarial process. Yet, despite magistrates' efforts, child abuse cases can very quickly become polarised when parents and the child protection service are unwilling to compromise. Some cases were more amenable to settlement than others. Cases where there was clear evidence of child abuse, or were based on one significant incident of child abuse for which the parent was now contrite, or cases in which the parents' problems are serious, and obvious, were easier to decide:

> The most straightforward ones are the clear cut ones. The parents are absolutely hopeless and there is nothing going for them (M 05).

> Those sort of ones where the action is momentary or the mother has left the child because she is working ... they're not matters that are serious enough to warrant the child going into care ... where the mother has had a lack of judgement (M 07).

> The obvious one is physical abuse. They were obvious. A child at risk to its life and limb where the mother wasn't simply protecting and is careless of her responsibilities, that wasn't difficult, particularly if they were warned and given opportunities (M 11).

Or, cases in which parents were agreeing to the conditions the child protection service was asking the court to impose:

> Those that were easy to decide were where the mother was cooperating with the carers (M 01).

Cases that were difficult to decide were those in which the child protection concerns were not obvious to the magistrate and there was limited evidence to support protective concerns. Magistrates said this happened in cases when child protection concerns were based on the emotional abuse of a child:

> The more difficult ones were psychological abuse where there is nothing obvious like bruises. I was always troubled that sexual abuse always got the headlines and possibly the greater funding compared with psychological abuse (M 11).

> The ones I found difficult were the ones where it was very difficult to know who had caused the harm (M 15).

Cases involving adolescents could also be difficult, especially when they were estranged from their parents or were homeless and they did not accept that they needed care and protection. Making orders in such cases, said one magistrate, compared with Tolstoy's *War and Peace*. The different needs of adolescents, from those of younger children, are not catered for by the legislation and magistrates felt there were fewer resources available to the court to assist these cases.

Cases that featured a high level of family violence were also difficult for magistrates. A number of cases observed were based on excessive discipline of a child. Magistrates said they had few options in these cases; they could insist parents change their parenting practices or remove the child from their care. However, it was difficult to challenge parent beliefs, that the physical discipline of their child was unacceptable and parents had to change. In one case I observed, a young girl of five years with unexplained burns was returned to her mother and stepfather with a condition on the court order that they not hit her. The mother of the child asked in court: 'How do we discipline her?' The magistrate asked her: 'Is that the way you were brought up?', and to her answer of: 'Yes', responded that 'We don't hit kids'. The magistrate did not feel removing the child was the step to be taken in this case.

Magistrates referred to inconsistency with cases brought to court: some child abuse situations were more readily identified than others and could more readily be articulated into the specific legislative grounds for a child protection application. Yet magistrates were aware that there were cases in which children were enduring painful and harmful situations but the lack of certainty and clarity about what constitutes child abuse, the narrow legislative categories and the lack of guidelines for the assessment of significant harm or unacceptable risk to a child made it difficult to act in these cases. Magistrates commented on the fact that cases involving the physical and sexual abuse of children often received a greater degree of attention from investigating authorities, given the criminal implications in these cases. This concerned three magistrates who felt all allegations of child abuse should receive equal status in terms of community concern and investigation.

The Case Hearing

Magistrates commented that initial decisions are significant as they can set the direction of a case and the course of action for the child:

> You need to be much more careful with the initial consideration of taking the child away ... my concern is that either way a child can be left in a unsatisfactory situation for a very long time, be it with the family or foster care ... The first decision you make is so important it creates a huge strain (M 05).

Magistrates said initial decisions about a case are challenging because there might be little available information about the family, and, if the child is apprehended and the application is urgent, little information about the what the family will want to do:

> Interim accommodation orders is a holding operation. I find them difficult simply because its all so immediate and quick and people haven't had the chance to rally themselves. It sets in place a change in the structure which can become the status quo ... this can affect the whole character of a situation (M 08).

However, initial decisions did provide magistrates with the opportunity to investigate a family's circumstances and willingness or ability to deal with the child protection concerns:

> With the first time you can experiment more, you can see how things might work. Once you've got the end result you can't. Sometimes it's marginally easier at the end of the road in that a lot of things have been tried and you've got a lot more information about what worked and what didn't work (M 05).

Two-thirds of the magistrates (n=10), said that cases concerning physical abuse were often more straightforward, especially when there was clear evidence and witnesses.

> (In) physical abuse cases you are often shown photographs, so you are more likely to have some actual evidence ... (M 13).

> Physical and sexual abuse are easily measured and you can see with physical harm with photos, for example ... (M 09).

Magistrates were more hopeful about the possibility of change in such situations and believed they were cases that were likely to be remedied by welfare intervention so the child could remain living with their family:

> People are more optimistic about the problems that have led to the physical abuse, may be fixed up by counselling, by anger management courses, and all those sorts of things. People at least feel as though these things may work, whereas with sexual abuse cases you feel as though once an abuser always an abuser ... (M 02).

However, magistrates found cases involving emotional abuse were troubling. They did not have the same stigma, or possible criminal consequences, as cases involving sexual abuse, yet were difficult to decide:

> A lot of people feel that somehow emotional abuse wasn't as bad as physical abuse because you couldn't see it (M 15).

> ... if it were emotional abuse it's not the same stigma. I find less of a problem branding someone an emotional abuser than a sexual abuser (M 12).

There were no clear definitions about what constitutes emotional abuse, for magistrates to refer to; this made it difficult for magistrates to judge the impact of emotional abuse on a child and therefore find it proven:

> ... with suggestions of psychological harm ... you are more inclined to want fairly clear proof of those sets of issues ... be satisfied fairly clearly in your

own mind that there really was significant risk of harm. It's an easy allegation to make that the child is suffering in some way from emotional harm – but you really would have to be clearly specific about it and also prove it as well (M 09).

The emotional abuse is much harder because there is so many value loaded judgements on the part of social workers and on my part, too ... they are very different fact finding exercises ... the emotional abuse cases are by far the hardest from a judicial point of view because you are being asked to make Godlike judgements, I think (M 14).

Given the uncertainty about what actions or circumstances constitute emotional abuse magistrates said it was particularly important in such cases to look for all available information about a child rather than rely solely on the facts presented in court reports. Three magistrates said one factor they looked for when assessing the merit of allegations of emotional harm was whether or not the child was appropriately nurtured:

... you can have situations where children are never hit – there is no question of sexual activity but that child may be being treated, intimidated, rejected without the parent realizing it ... but in fact they are behaving in a way that's incredibly damaging or rejecting. The sort of evidence will simply be different and with sexual abuse cases and physical abuse cases obviously most of the evidence tends to be on trying to prove that the events occurred ... (M 06).

Cases of sexual abuse of children were both personally and professionally challenging, six magistrates commented, because they were cases that challenged their personal values, beliefs about families and views about child abuse. They also challenge justice principles:

What I find in these cases is the vehemence with which people want to adopt causes and never worry about the foundations (M 08).

A number of magistrates said sexual abuse cases exemplify the complexity of child protection cases and the difficulties they have with finding proof, especially when allegations of sexual abuse rely on a child's disclosures or a professional's interpretation of a child's actions and, they are cases that are almost always contested:

... in sexual abuse, very rarely is there any actual evidence other than what you are being told. Physical abuse cases you are often shown photographs so you are more likely to have some actual evidence (M 09).

> ... sexual abuse cases, there is often no actual evidence ... so when you have this situation you are really relying on making a decision about the reality of the allegations and its very difficult, but again you have to weigh up on the balance of probabilities in this court ... (M 13).

> I don't have special frameworks. Sexual abuse is alleged so often with no proof, no evidence, and it is very difficult when there is no physical evidence that they have been interfered with. Just because someone has interpreted something the child has said and I often read the so-called 'disclosures' and I don't feel that they are (M 07).

Four magistrates said that cases involving the sexual abuse of children bring to the court

> ... families who otherwise may not have contact with the system (M 02).

These magistrates believed that there had been an increase in the number of sexual abuse cases appearing before the court, possibly because of greater community acknowledgment of child sexual abuse:

> I suspect very much the number of cases involving sexual abuse has increased ... the publicity of sexual abuse and people's preparedness to come out in the open more now (M 02).

Three magistrates also said they found sexual abuse cases difficult because of the often different consequences for families and alleged perpetrators if the allegations are found proven:

> ... the problem with sexual cases is whilst you are doing that [your job] and while you are trying to divorce that from your thought process you realise once you find those things proved it really is a slur, a very bad slur on the alleged perpetrator (M 12).

Magistrates were less optimistic about maintaining a child with, or returning a child to, their family because necessary changes in the family functioning or successful treatment for the perpetrator was often difficult to achieve:

> ... in sexual abuse cases there are certain characteristics of some of the perpetrators that make rehabilitation very difficult, where it is unlikely that the child would be protected from harm if returned to that particular abuse whereas there's more likelihood of it being in circumstances of physical abuse (M 02).

Yet the child's interests are paramount and four magistrates said they had to put aside concerns about repercussions for the perpetrator.

> ... you must not be weighted down with the repercussions of finding the facts because the child's interests are paramount ... but it is much easier said than done. I'm sure it has and had a lot more effect than any magistrate would admit too. I took no different steps in sifting through it but obviously there was that undercurrent all the time (M 12).

Problems with poverty, unemployment, illness, intellectual disability and substance abuse featured strongly in families involved in child protection cases, as set out in Table 3.6.

Table 3.6 Family factors in protection matters (no. families=84)

	Factors common to families	
	N	%
Child sex abuse	12	13.5
Child physical abuse	33	37.1
Child emotional abuse	33	37.1
Psychiatric disorder	14	15.7
Failure to thrive	8	9.0
Developmental delay	3	3.4
Family violence	14	15.7
Drug abuse	16	18.0
Intellectual disability	7	7.9
Child neglect	25	28.1
Homelessness	5	5.6
Runaway child	1	1.1
Parent non-cooperation with DHS	19	21.3
Threats of violence to DHS	8	9.0

Parents with an intellectual disability presented magistrates with specific difficulties. They were a group of parents who came to the attention of the Court not because of a lack of love for their children but rather because of their limited parenting skills and difficulties learning adequate skills. They were parents who also had more difficulty obtaining supports or resources that could help them with their problems:

> Those cases are terribly sad because you've often got a person who has lots of strong love feelings ... but they are incapable of meeting that child's needs and

that is different from somebody who perhaps is quite a wonderful parent except when they go on a binge (M 06).

Magistrates had a similar view about parents with psychiatric problems who might have:

> ... nothing intrinsically wrong with them as parents, other than their own difficulties (M11).

but whose parenting was impaired by their condition. Even so:

> ... even if the mother was imperfect as a parent it's all a matter of degree ... I take all those things into consideration ... particularly in psychiatric illness, as long as the mother, parent, recognises that she needs treatment, that can usually be contained or managed through proper medication and therapy ... (M 01).

Parents with considerable psychiatric problems could not always engage in rational discussion about court orders and the conditions which accompanied them. They often had difficulties accepting the limitations these conditions placed on their own behaviour. Further, their own problems very often made it difficult for them to understand how their behaviour negatively affected their children. Magistrates were rarely provided with information about the impact of psychiatric problems of parents on their children which meant they had to make decisions without the benefit of such assistance. This lack of information about the nature of psychiatric disorder was evident in the case of a ten year old child, settled with extended family. The child wanted to see her mother but not for overnight access for fear of a return to a physically and emotionally abusing situation. The mother's volatility in and outside court and unwillingness to negotiate with child protection about times for access suggested the child's concerns were well founded. The mother's legal representative asserted the mother's right to overnight access and argued it could occur at the child's grandmother's home. Neither the child nor the grandmother were consulted about this; they were both fearful of the mother's aggressive outbursts. Yet the court acceded to the mother's wishes

Ten magistrates commented on the difficulties parents with substance abuse problems present to the court:

> Substance abuse rules their life. They aren't able to control their parenting... People who were abusing heroin and other drugs were not very good parents (M 09).

Yet 11 magistrates noted that:

> People can abuse substances and still be capable. I'm sure many people abuse alcohol and still function as parents. I don't see that it itself is a reason for protection. But when the children are starting to be affected and the whole fabric of the family starts to fall apart, then something has got to be done (M 07).

The Difficulty of the Work

The specialist nature of Children's Court work presents magistrates with particular difficulties, a number of which have already been noted: lack of training for the area, different procedures, isolation from mainstream magistrate work, the emotional difficulty of the work. Magistrates also referred to the difficulty of child abuse cases, the lack of agreement about what behaviours and situations constitute child abuse, difficulties with obtaining enough information about cases and in obtaining the resources a case might need. Broader issues such as sensitivity to the sociocultural differences of families, to community attitudes to child abuse, to the availability of the welfare system to respond to children and, the often unsatisfactory options for children, also impacted on the work of the Court.

Magistrates saw themselves as having dual responsibilities both as a community representative and a judicial officer and believed the community expected magistrates' decisions to reflect community attitudes to child abuse:

> We are constrained ... by the way in which the community views child abuse ... when we have to make decisions about whether we return a child who may have been physically harmed by parents, obviously you've got in the back of your mind 'what would the community think about this?' (M 02).

> The Act [CYPA] in itself is far more rehabilitation based ... so you're faced with the dilemma of thinking of things not only from the way the community would look at them but also in the way the community is best served ... It presents a lot of difficulties which you don't have in the adult court because you just sentence (M 01).

Yet magistrates said whilst they have power in the legalistic or curial sense, the orders and conditions they can impose on parents and children are constrained by the resources that are available:

> At the back of my mind was this concern about how well the orders can be implemented. It is difficult for DHS with huge caseloads ... families are going to suffer and the objective of the Act will not be obtained (M 09).

> [There are] times when you like to make certain orders which we can't make because there are not the facilities (M 02).

However, five magistrates said it was their job to make the orders and it was up to the Department of Human Services to make the resources available:

> ... but that was their problem, they had to do that, that was the only way you could operate ... this is what's best for the child now you've got to do it (M 11).

Child Abuse Explained

> It's absolutely critical we know about research but we have to follow up ourselves ... It's important we know about the research to enhance the professionalism of this court. There needs to be increasing expertise among magistrates in this area (M 13).

Two magistrates emphasised it was important they knew more about child protection issues in order to increase their expertise in the jurisdiction. There was some material available to them at the Court, and eight magistrates commented that they had sought out material to prepare and inform themselves prior to coming to the jurisdiction:

> When you work in the area you tend to look for things to read to inform yourself and when you are doing cases, you get a lot of material to read in the course of the running of the case (M 09).

However the utility of such information was always qualified by how much it could assist a magistrate with a particular case:

> Sometimes it's useful to have research quoted, but if it's a professional who is not impressing me generally then I am probably not going to be that impressed by the research (M 14).

Children and the Court Process

The focus of the Children's Court is on the best interests of children and ensuring these interests are met by parents, other interested parties, and the statutory welfare authority. The Act urges the participation of children in decisions made about them particularly when these decisions might involve changes in their lives. Magistrates prefer that children, as much as possible, attend court so they can contribute to these decisions. Yet, such participation by children, especially in contested matters, though desirable, may require lengthy attendances at court that disrupt daily routines, such as school, and can heighten their vulnerability. There appeared to be little thought given to ensuring that children understood what was happening while they were in court. Children aged seven years and over have separate legal representation (CYPA s.20). When children are younger or are unrepresented it is expected that Department of Human Services' representatives look out for their interests. Legal Aid represents eligible parents and children in child protection matters and DHS retains legal counsel to represent its interests in court.

Five magistrates commented on what they observed as a greater involvement of legal practitioners in the Children's Court and a subsequent increase in the number of contested cases, creating a more adversarial approach to child abuse hearings. Parents were now more likely to dispute welfare concerns and recommendations and less likely to simply accept intervention in their family:

> Now there is much more involvement with lawyers who have given them [parents] stronger advice to fight about their rights and their likelihood to disprove allegations and matters of that type (M 02).

Legal representation therefore was a significant influence on court outcome. Strong legal representation appeared often to persuade the court that DHS recommendations should be put aside. Legal representatives measured their expertise in terms of how well they negotiated the adversarial process in order to resolve the case in hand. There appeared to be particular influences on the vigour of legal representation: cases in which it was believed that DHS was unsympathetic to particular parent problems, that might be alleviated if enough support or treatment services were provided. This was particularly noticeable in cases where parents had an intellectual disability. Representation in these cases argued that parenting courses and parenting assessment, and 'short term' orders should be the court outcome. They would argue that family preservation should always be attempted even when DHS argued that current circumstances and previous history clearly indicated the need for more long-term alternative care arrangements for such children.

Cases involving the children of very young parents were also vigorously defended. DHS sought an interim protection order for a four month old baby whose mother was transient and whose infant had experienced 10 or 11 placements in his four months of life. His teenage mother, herself on a guardianship order, had been living on the streets, and had come to court with her mother to retain the custody of her infant. She had already unsuccessfully attempted living with her mother, and attempted a residential parenting program for teenage mothers. She appeared to have considerable mental health problems and little understanding of the needs of her very young child. The important issues in this case were the young woman's incapacity to parent and obvious mental health problems, not DHS being judgemental about the mother's lifestyle choice, as was asserted by her legal representative. Yet the magistrate was persuaded that the infant should be returned to his mother's care.

Legal representatives appeared very often to focus primarily on the wishes of parents, especially when they were particularly demanding parents, over and above the interests of children. A 13-year old girl had an extremely vexatious stepfather who declined to allow her to have treatment for her physical health problem. This girl appeared not to have a voice in the court, which appeared powerless to deal with a stepfather whose legal manoeuvres and appeals prevented the court implementing any orders. The child remained without medical treatment while the stepfather exhausted all appeal processes available in the court system.

There was considerable variability in terms of the legal representation cases attracted. Cases involving allegations of child sexual abuse were strongly represented, and contested, because of possible criminal action against the perpetrator. They were cases that involved not only male adult-female child sexual abuse but also male sibling-female child, father male-child sexual abuse and female parent-male child sexual abuse. They were cases that attracted considerable professional attention and tended to be heavily attended by families and their supporters. Magistrates' varied in their attempts to maintain calm in the courtroom, given the often tense atmosphere, often between counsel and child protection workers. Parents with substance abuse problems and parents with an intellectual disability were often vigorously defended, even when their problems were long-standing, the child protection concerns seemed clear and parents appeared to accept the need for intervention.

The parents of a three-month old child, failing to thrive, parents with long-standing addiction problems and an older child placed out of the mother's care were vigorously defended. Legal representation successfully emphasised the legislative aim of family preservation and resisted DHS attempts to investigate the parents' capacity to care for the infant. This appeared to persuade the magistrate to maintain the child with the parents. Equally, the vigorous legal defence of the mother of a three month old infant who herself had significant brain damage and drug abuse problems, and was not long out of prison, ensured the child returned to her care. The magistrate was persuaded that a parenting course and new accommodation for the mother could resolve the child's problems.

Magistrates' concerns about family preservation and the right of the state to intervene in family life was evident in a case that involved two children of seven and five years, out of their mother's care for two years, now wanting to be permanently placed in their grandmother's care. The mother's legal representative vigorously sought to prevent this case plan. Whilst the mother was currently imprisoned, her representative stated it was the mother's intention to contest any application for guardianship for the girls as she wished to have them in her care when she was released. The persuasive legal representation combined with the magistrate's belief in the mother's right to continue to parent her children ensured the mother's wishes were upheld by the court. The children and their grandmother were unrepresented. Legal representation is such an influence on the court that the absence of it in this case greatly disadvantaged the children.

Yet, there were cases that received little legal representation although the issues for the children involved were of considerable importance. Often there appeared to be little legal interest in extension of guardianship applications. Although these extensions were most often sought for children who had been in care for a considerable amount of time, and parents were usually consenting to the order, the issue of children remaining in care for long periods of time is significant yet was an issue that failed to attract the same level of attention from legal representatives as was given to other cases outlined above.

Legal practitioners were not always familiar with the Children's Court jurisdiction. Those who were used to the adult courts were less at ease with the more informal atmosphere of the court and were more likely to be legalistic in the conduct of cases and in their demeanour in court. Legal practitioners, who were unfamiliar with child development theory and knowledge of child abuse, appeared to more readily argue case issues in terms of parents' rights rather than the issue of risk to a child and, to place the locus of responsibility for abusing behaviours outside the parent. Legal debate was more likely to focus on exactly what behaviours or circumstances could be considered to constitute child abuse or normal parenting behaviour. Protective workers' work practices were often challenged most particularly on the criteria they used to substantiate child protection concerns. Legal representatives appeared to pay little attention to the likely need for the family to work with the child protection service post-court, nor did they appear to take responsibility for the fact that their behaviour in court had a direct influence on the attitude of parents to accepting services, and to working with the child protection service, after the court hearing.

In a case of physical abuse to three children the legal representatives for the parents asserted that the physical injuries sustained by the children indicated simply that they were very active children. The concept of developmental delay which the child protection service introduced in court to support their concerns was trivialised by legal representatives as too rigid and unscientific a measure to apply to all children. Delays in speech, in toilet training, in motor coordination, in weight gain were, they suggested, were variations in childhood development. The child protection concerns were challenged as overprotective or zealous. The legal argument ensured that the larger picture of long-standing physical abuse of these children was put aside and not considered.

Legal representatives who regularly appeared at the court developed considerable expertise in child welfare matters. The barrister retained by the child protection service (DHS) during the researcher's time at the court, who appeared in a wide range of consent and contested matters, had considerable expertise. He also used mediation skills to resolve cases which might otherwise have been contested – at great emotional and financial cost to the parties. It was not infrequent that child protection workers' concerns for children could not be translated into a successful application because of a lack of evidence, available witnesses, or because legislative criteria could not be met. His capacity to explain these legal implications to protective workers was greatly valued by the court.

How children's interests are presented and their instructions sought appeared problematic. Legal representatives who were familiar with the jurisdiction modified their practice to sensitively take instruction and present them in a sensitive manner in court. The cases in which this did not happen were all the more obvious because of their contrast to those cases where children's interests were sensitively handled.

However legal practitioners who were inexperienced in Children's Court work approached taking instructions from children as they would in the adult courts. This led to children being asked questions in court by their representative in full view of their parents with the questions very often heard by other family members and by observers. How children can really be separately represented when they are seated with their parents, hear difficult evidence about themselves, and continue to live at home is questionable. The concept of taking instruction is an adult one; it assumes the children understand what is meant, feel free to make choices, trust the adult concerned, and believe they can be protected. In a case concerning three children of 10, five and four years, counsel sought the children's instructions in full view of their parents. This was a case which had considerable forensic evidence of physical abuse of the children by their parents and the children not only heard the forensic evidence but saw photos of their injuries. Their mother had made several angry outbursts during the hearing. The children had not seen their parents for some time and desperately wanted their approval. They were in no position to give instructions in this atmosphere and little was done to alleviate the children's discomfort.

The process which seeks to establish a child's best interests at times operated in ways which intensified the distress and disadvantage experienced by children in need of care and protection. The capacity of children to evaluate evidence they hear in court and give considered instructions in court in full view and, most often in full hearing, of their parents, must be doubted. One must question whether children are really being represented if legal representation is conducted in this manner. A lengthy and strongly contested case of sexual abuse was attended daily by the children and their parents. The children were constantly addressed by their representative, who at times, chided them for their inattention. Her questions to the children could clearly be heard in court and she expected the children to confirm or deny child protection workers' testimony as it was presented. The representative expected the children to understand the language being used in court and expected also that the children could speak openly in court in front of their parents and others.

Magistrates, who are qualified lawyers, look to the legal framework to assist their decision-making. Legal representatives, who share the same training, and are familiar with legal procedure, clearly influenced court outcomes. Therefore, magistrates were less than positive about the use of specifically appointed court-based social workers to represent the DHS in consent matters, rather than legal counsel who are briefed, by DHS, to appear in contested cases. It was their view that these court officers, and legal representatives who were unfamiliar with the Children's Court, or with child representation, might hamper the court process because of their lack of familiarity with the legislation and the jurisdiction. It is a situation that does not exist in the adult jurisdiction and was therefore a source of frustration for magistrates.

Magistrates at Work

> We've got a responsibility to defuse the anger and frustration and make an order which we hope in a sense will please everybody so that's basically our responsibility (M 02).

Magistrates said they looked first to legal factors to make decisions. However, it was apparent that there were other influences: magistrates' individual beliefs about families, about judicial objectivity, magistrates' personal views on child abuse, views about individual rights and state intervention in family life, attitudes to protective workers and their work practices.

The role of the magistrate in the Family Division has different dimensions from that in the adult arena. Children's Court magistrates are expected, in uncontested matters, to be more participatory, to provide direction in hearings, and to speak to parties:

> [there] is a lot more pressure on the magistrate here to be able to deal with this work and that's why most magistrates don't want to come near the place ... [In adult courts] you tend to be more distant ... just sitting there as an arbitrator you listen to what's going on and make a fair decision. Here there is much more complexity to what you have to do, the issues we have to go through, the things we have to do (M 02).

As well as the expected functions of hearing the evidence and ensuring parties interests are represented, magistrates in the Children's Court must look out for the child's interests:

> Everyone is there to represent someone else and the person who is left there for the child is the magistrate (M 10).

Magistrates need to attend to welfare concerns when making decisions and, to consider a child's future options and the impact of adult parents or custodians on the lives of the children in their care. This requirement to be 'welfare-minded' is uncomfortable for many magistrates. It is quite unlike anything they experience in the adult jurisdiction. Two-thirds of the magistrates (n=10) stated they balanced these competing demands in child protection matters by focusing on the evidence in the case before them. They refrained from looking at the larger picture for the child. The very different approaches of the Children's Court is referred to by a third of the magistrates:

> We train to be objective and not be influenced ... social workers and lawyers have different models. I think this is a matter of personal opinion. Some magistrates say that they don't want to know what happened afterwards because we just have to make our decision on the evidence before us and then forget about it. But I think in the Children's Court it's different. We are talking about the whole system, the adversarial versus the inquisitorial system ... we are talking about a completely different system where you make decisions and follow them up and you get reports to say what's been happening (M 01).

Magistrates on occasion were observed to assume an advocacy role on behalf of children to ensure their interests were properly addressed. In one case before the court, the parents of children aged five, four, and three years, had placed them in care. Protective services sought to establish and regularise access between the parents and the children, to encourage the parents to reconnect with the children. The parents, now separated, preferred that the children remain in care. An incredulous magistrate asked the children's parents:

> Is that what you want to happen? (M 07).

In another matter the parents of a young infant who had medical problems, the parents themselves having a significant drug abuse problem, were loudly protesting the short-term foster care and assessment plan for their child. They saw no need for the child's health and physical care needs to be assessed. The magistrate stated to the parents:

> The welfare of the child is the first priority, the child must have proper care ... H&CS [DHS] is not out to break up the family (M 09).

Counsel for parents of a badly injured ten week old infant, argued that the child's 'bonding' would be disrupted if the child were not returned to the parents. The magistrate firmly reminded counsel, and the parents, that the injuries were extremely serious for a young and fragile child and that this concern was the priority of the court.

> In hearings for guardianship extensions at which parents quite often were not present, magistrates would ask the protective worker, or the child: 'do the children know what they are agreeing to?' (M 04).

Magistrate concern that children's wishes were properly established was evident in the case of two girls of 12 and eight years. Their parents had been absent for much of their lives, and the father now sought that they live with him in another country. The magistrate firmly asked their legal counsel:

> What were the children's instructions? (M 08)

and asked protective workers:

> What can be achieved for these children? (M 08)

The magistrate was clearly concerned that any plans for the children must be in the children's, not the father's, interests.

A number of magistrates advocated for children in cases where there were court orders that required a particular family member to live out of the family home. This order was made most often in cases of sexual and physical abuse. Very often, some or all of the family members might be ambivalent about such orders. When this occurred, the magistrate's emphasis on the seriousness of the allegations, and the child's right to be free from harm, was an important voice for the child. This advocacy role was of particular importance in contested hearings when legal debate focused mostly on the adult interests in a case. When a magistrate reminded parties that deciding the best interests of children was the purpose of the court it had considerable impact on the running of a case. This response however was irregular and occurred when the welfare concerns appeared to be of particular significance to the particular magistrate. Cases of sexual abuse, cases of significant harm would evoke this response.

This response also occurred when a particularly valued belief of a magistrate was challenged by the child protection service's intervention, or where the terms and measures DHS used to define the problem could not be seen or shared by the magistrate. It occurred also when legal representatives for parents suggested to the magistrate that legal process was not being observed by DHS and their clients were therefore at a disadvantage. Magistrate challenges to DHS conduct of a case were observed particularly in cases where a grandparent was suggested by parents' legal counsel as the proposed caregiver of a child. In one case observed, an application by DHS to assess the suitability of that care was seen as obstructive by the magistrate, who held that the availability of grandparents to care for children was the ideal solution. DHS claims that assessment was necessary particularly as the child's parent had in the past a troubled relationship with the grandparent were not viewed sympathetically by the court. Where however the grandparent was in dispute with their child, and caring for their grandchildren without the support of the parents, then the court usually returned the children to the mother's care.

The majority of protection applications are decided by consent between the parties. The magistrate oversees the negotiations about orders, access to children etc. in the court. Magistrates appeared not to intervene in straightforward cases although they would ask if parents were present, and if not why not and, would ask if orders were understood by the parties. In the contested cases observed the magistrates appeared themselves to be observers. The legal representatives argued the facts of a case and challenged witnesses' assessments and recollections of events. This meant in contested hearings that court debate focused primarily on legal points, debate that appeared to do little to clarify protective concerns. Contested hearings are often lengthy and recriminatory and magistrates were observed on a number of occasions to voice concerns about children hearing testimony which was damaging to their family. Debate about the relevance of hearsay evidence, argument about facts, witnesses' assessments and recollections, is part of the adversarial process. Yet, this debate is both alienating and excluding for children and their parents, debate that to them seemed unrelated to the child protection concerns raised about their child.

This was evident in the hearing of a case of alleged sexual abuse of a young male child, his mother the alleged perpetrator. The case ran for eight days and was dominated by the mother's legal representative who spent days cross-examining child protection workers and doing this in a hostile manner. The magistrate had little input into the court process. Concerns about the child, the harm he had experienced, appeared to assume a very secondary importance and he was returned to his parents.

Fourteen magistrates described the main task of the Family Division as that of deciding whether a child does, or does not, remain with their family. Yet it is difficult, one magistrate notes, to achieve this aim if there are insufficient resources to assist families and for magistrates to be confident this aim can be achieved. Another magistrate described the legislation as fault-based and the aim in hearing a protection application is to establish fault with the caregiving of a child by their parents. The current legislation is perceived to be less rehabilitative in its aims than previous legislation. This magistrate preferred legislation to act more as a circuit-breaker and pre-empt problems in families and allow magistrates more flexibility in dealing with cases where the parents may not necessarily be at fault.

Magistrates said there were some family, or parent problems, such as substance abuse or psychiatric disorder, that did direct their attention to specific issues: for example, a parent's motivation to change and, what resources were available to facilitate rehabilitation. Yet magistrates reported that whilst these issues were important considerations, they used the same guidelines to assess all child abuse cases. This process involved hearing the evidence, the merit of the case, balancing the interests of the parties involved and the risk to the child:

> ... only by hearing, seeing the individuals concerned that you are able to assess whether or not there was a reasonable chance of that mother being able to care for the child (M 01).

> I'm not sure you can approach it any other way than prima facie looking at the issues that are raised by either side (M 03).

Whilst the individual nature of allegations might influence magistrates' decisions, these influences had to be congruent with the expectations of the legal process.

> You work along the same rules. Essentially we are sitting there listening to what the professionals have got to say about these particular problems. We are wanting to know what the risks are if the child remains with the parent, what the chances of rehabilitation of the parent is. Common themes run through these cases so I'm not sure that I do start off; OK this is a serious alcohol problem of the parent, what are the particular areas that I'm going to apply to this case ... I'm just looking to ... what the harm has been, what the likelihood of the harm is in the future, what the case planning is, what is hoped for the future of all this ... (M 02).

Magistrates said that while there could be enormous similarities in child protection cases they resisted looking for commonalities and making assumptions about cases:

> I don't think there are any particular groups or classes of people who are likely to end up being abusive (M 06).

> There can be enormous similarities and you have to resist thinking 'I have heard all this before' ... people's problems run through all levels of society, people with more money have more choices (M 08).

All magistrates said that they referred to their own family experiences when hearing cases and magistrates, who were parents themselves, felt they could be more flexible towards families because they were aware of the pressures on families:

> ... when I was hearing those sort of cases I probably was thinking in the back of my mind – look my house is chaotic – there are occasions when I yell at the kids.. (M 03).

> I often look at situations and think 'there but for the grace of God go I', I could have done a lot of the things that I see ... yes I use my own yardstick often (M 07).

It also confirmed for them that children needed to be with their families:

> ... the need for the child to be with their family which is his or hers and have that bond which is the most important thing he has for better or for worse (M 07).

It also meant that these magistrates were aware of what was necessary for family functioning and therefore what the parents of children before the court needed to do in order to retain their children:

> I was very conscious of how hard it is to be a parent, and I was very conscious of how hard it is to be a parent with every support in the world ... I was particularly conscious that most of the women – fathers don't feature prominently ... must have been struggling terribly ... Just realising how hard it was ... it also meant that at a certain point I was more willing to take children away because I was probably more conscious of the risks to children (M 14).

> I felt a lot more confident when children were being placed with people who were educated even though there had been demonstrated emotional abuse, because you felt these were capable of learning (M 12).

The Individualised Nature of the Court Process

Magistrates said their role is to hear a case 'in the here and now', to examine the case as it is presented to them on the day the matter is in court and decide the case based on the immediate situation of the child before them. This can mean other significant factors are not considered because they do not currently impinge on the case as it is presented in court. Moreover, while the decision meets the immediate needs of the child it may not provide for planning for the longer term even when a child's circumstances and history suggest a long-term decision would ultimately best meet the child's needs. Little attention is given to the consequences of the legal process on individuals once the hearing is finished.

This is particularly evident in cases involving family violence as the court tends to see an act of family violence as a single event which, as a consequence of court intervention, will hopefully not recur. Research about family violence indicates a very different view, that family violence has a serious and long-term impact on children (Dale, Davies and Morrison 1986). The need to take a long term view of problems such as these is not readily accommodated by the legal process. This was evident in a case bought by DHS to seek a protection order for a three week old infant of parents with an intellectual disability. The infant had already experienced significant neglect. The parents already had a three year old child permanently out of their care, yet the order made returned the infant to the parents' care. Planning for the infant was seen by the magistrate as a separate and individual event and was not to be confounded by the circumstances of her older sibling.

The issue of selectivity of information presented about a case was also evident in a case of alleged physical abuse of five female children by their father. The father was self-represented and to assist his case called his wife as a witness to attest to his reputation as a good father. The demeanour and speech of this witness conveyed the fear which is found in situations of spousal violence. This was not noted by the magistrate. The DHS counsel needed to convey a different picture of the husband, one which reflected the history of child protection contact. His sensitivity to the wife's situation and his concern about the consequences for the wife and her children after court, placed him in a predicament. His careful attempts to encourage the wife to give a more realistic picture of the family were unsuccessful. Her fear made her testimony more or less incoherent. The magistrate could not approach the case in any other way yet it was plain the truth of the children's circumstances could not be properly explored within the framework of the adversarial process.

As a consequence of this re-framing of problems, orders and conditions may be made which are difficult to negotiate with families. This was especially obvious where a parent had a psychiatric illness and was unable to negotiate and keep to arrangements for children. The difficulties parents with long-term psychiatric problems have with observing appropriate boundaries in situations was unacknowledged by legal representatives in orders sought from the court. A nine year old boy, settled with extended family, faced this situation when his mother sought greater supervised access to her son, at times when extended family were at work, rather than at times when they were available. In these and other situations pressures to comply with court orders, and negotiate with volatile parents, caused great difficulty for extended family, care-givers and foster parents and at times jeopardised children remaining in such care.

The need to conform to adversarial requirements caused considerable tension in magistrates' and legal representatives' dealings with protective workers in court. Child protection workers believed that the adversarial process allowed legal representatives to be selective about what information was presented about a case. They believed also that this process was less sensitive to the vulnerability of children and parents whose private affairs were the subject of public debate in court. This tension appeared to hamper negotiations between parents and DHS and hamper therefore the possibility of case resolution.

The Adversarial Process

Magistrates have to conform to the principles of the adversarial system and oversee whether or not DHS can demonstrate that a child is at risk and needs protection. Magistrates and legal representatives are familiar with the rules and procedures associated with evidence, and expect debate about the admission and relevance of evidence. The hearing and testing of evidence is part of the functioning of the adversarial system. However it assumes that witnesses are always able to testify in an open court and have the ability to clearly articulate their views about case issues. It assumes that witnesses can speak objectively, neutrally and openly about private, and perhaps painful, matters. Equally it assumes witnesses can cope with hearing their private concerns made public, and cope with being challenged by counsel about the validity of their experiences. It is questionable whether witnesses can stand back from their painful experiences and objectively respond to counsel and clarify for the court what are the important issues in a case. Cross-examination of the older stepdaughter in a matter of sexual abuse took place in court in full view of her three stepsisters- who were also the subject of the allegations. These children were clearly attached to their father and their older sister and anxious for their parents' approval. No assistance was provided for them at court to deal with this situation. There did not appear to be any 'debriefing' which would assist them to cope with the court process. There was no mechanism in the adversarial approach to acknowledge the uniqueness of Children's Court matters nor to help children and families manage the court hearing.

Magistrates have to observe the legislative mandate of family preservation and minimum intervention in families' lives. Yet the nature of the family problems typically presented to the court, and the intervention usually indicated, makes this problematic. This was evident in cases that involved very young infants presented to the court whose lives were already characterised by extreme disruption and neglect, if not abuse. It was also evident in a case involving two very young children of parents with an intellectual disability. The magistrate returned the children to the parents' care. He noted that the legislation obliged him: 'to give the parents a chance'. He noted also that 'if it was a contest between equals then Grandma wins but the Act requires the parents are given a chance' (M 09).

In a number of cases it was evident that the context of the child protection concerns was overlooked in order to dispute the existence of the specific behaviours said to constitute the protective concerns. The aunt of a two year old profoundly intellectually disabled child successfully won custody of him despite considerable child protection concerns about other household members, one of whom had a criminal conviction for sexual assault, and others who were low functioning. Determined legal representation asserted that the aunt should be viewed on her own merits and not as an adjunct of other household members. It appeared that it was this view, combined with the magistrate's beliefs about family fragmentation and a lack of trust in the child protection service's assessments, that persuaded the magistrate that the child was best placed with the aunt. The aunt's affection for the child was undoubted, yet the milieu in which the child would now live was of great concern to protective services and there was substantial proven evidence to support these concerns.

The legislation (CYPA 1989) presumes that all children do have a family. Whilst children may live with a biological parent, they may also be living with other adults to whom they are not related and have no real connection. In a number of cases before the court children lived with their parent and the parent's partner. The court would see the parent's partner as a party with an interest in the child's case. Yet the child may have little emotional attachment to this person and not want them to influence their situation. There were cases where the child no longer wanted to remain with their family and had little attachment to them. The court's view of the importance of family to a child could not readily accommodate cases such as these.

The legislation provides no grounds for problems created by very poor parenting of children which do not fit within the category of actual harm to a child. Yet this can be as destructive for a child in the long term as is physical or sexual abuse (Finkelhor and Korbin 1988). Such problems were presented to the court as emotional abuse but they were rarely found proven. Other cases observed which were based on physical abuse, neglect, even in some instances on sexual abuse, often contained allegations about very poor parenting. However the lack of such a category as very poor parenting in the legislation and the difficulty therefore of finding it proven, meant parenting issues could not be tackled by the child protection service and the real issues of family dysfunction were obscured.

The two year child in the following case example emphasised a number of the above features. Determined legal representation for his young mother, with whom he lived in conditions of extreme neglect, despite support, argued more services could be provided to assist the mother. The young mother had considerable psychiatric problems and was disruptive and distracting in court. However, the magistrate's beliefs that support services could positively change a family's circumstances, combined with the court's reluctance to separate young children from their mothers, ensured the child remained in his mother's care.

This case highlighted that magistrates refer primarily to legal factors to decide cases when there is an absence of other reliable information to assist them. In this case very little information about the mother's psychiatric disorder was available, nor was there available to the court information about the impact of the mother's psychiatric disorder on her parenting.

The need for magistrates to observe the legislative aim of family preservation appeared at times to constrain their decision-making. This was evident when permanency planning for a child was presented as the best option. Magistrates would remind DHS that they had to ensure support services were provided to a family until all possible assistance was exhausted. The emphasis on family reunion was noted by the magistrate in a mother's application to vary access to her children who were currently in foster care as the mother had significant drug addiction problems. The magistrate ordered the foster family to make the children available to the mother as she wished despite the foster parents' application that it was difficult for them to vary access in the way the mother sought. The magistrate held the view that alternative care arrangements were not to supplant a parent's access to a child. There appeared to be little sympathy for the demands on foster families despite the community's reliance on them to offer children stability and nurturing for the time they are away from their family, and to do this with very little government financial support.

Lack of Agreed Definitions of Child Abuse

Magistrates' personal views about child abuse, family rights, and state intervention in individuals' lives appeared to influence their court decisions.

While the influence of the legal framework was more readily observed magistrates expressed views about cases that clearly indicated other influences.

The lack of agreement about what constitutes child abuse created great difficulty for magistrates and meant they relied on their own views about child abuse when deciding cases. Mention has been made earlier that what is understood as child abuse is not defined in the Act nor are there criteria to assess physical, sexual, emotional abuse, or neglect, or to define what is meant by an 'incapacitated parent'. There are no legislative criteria for 'significant harm' and 'best interests of the child'. Consequently, definitions about what actions or situations constitute child abuse varied from magistrate to magistrate and from case to case. Furthermore, how a child's problems are made out in the protection application is how the court assesses them and other problems may be put aside if they do not fit the specific grounds of the application.

There was also, very often, considerable disagreement between legal and welfare professionals about what does need to be present in a child's life to constitute adequate care and parenting. The criteria protective workers use to indicate child neglect or developmental delay, or child abuse, are readily deconstructed by legal representatives so that they appear meaningless or exaggerated. This process was observed when there was no forensic evidence to support protective concerns. Magistrates' attitudes to the work practices of the child protection service appeared to be a significant influence on their decisions.

This process was observed in a case in which allegations of sexual and emotional abuse were made by a fourteen year old boy about his father. The police investigated the allegations and brought the matter to court. The young man subsequently retracted his disclosures and sought to live with his father and stepmother. He was estranged from his mother. The case was lengthy and evidence of the problems in the parents' marriage was considerable. The young man sat outside the court for most of the eleven days of the hearing. He appeared a very troubled boy who needed help. However, the court attention was on the grounds of the application; whatever other problems the young man had were put aside unless they clearly related to the allegations presented. One wonders if his problems might have been viewed differently, and more appropriate help offered, if other grounds were available in the legislation or the legislation was more flexible in its response to child abuse.

The context of child protection rather than the judicial process was a source of frustration for magistrates. The adversarial approach of gathering all the facts and exchanging information between counsel prior to the hearing is what happens in the adult court. In the Children's Court however, often all relevant information about a case was not available at court particularly if the case is a protection application by apprehension and little is known about the child and their situation except that an investigation is warranted to exclude harm or significant risk to a child. In situations such as these magistrates believed they were being asked to make decisions in a vacuum. Magistrates found it easier to support DHS recommendations in cases where concrete facts clearly demonstrated protective concerns. Yet adequate case information did not always provide ready solutions. Often there were no clear choices available for children and therefore few options available to magistrates when deciding cases. The limited availability of support programmes, magistrate concerns about the substitute care provided for children, and the court's commitment to family preservation constrained decision options in child protection matters.

The case of a four year old child injured by her mother and now out of her care exemplified the lack of clear options for the court. The child's father was alleged to have sexually abused her and the child now lived with her paternal grandmother. The child's mother sought the return of the child to her care as she now had a new partner and a young infant. The mother had a criminal conviction for her injury of the child, there was also forensic evidence that showed abrasions to the child whilst in her father's care. Neither parent could provide this child with a positive environment. The court atmosphere was tense, due in some part to the disruptive behaviour of the mother's partner. DHS supported the return of the child to her mother. However, the magistrate directed the child remain in her paternal grandmother's care although the father retained custody. The presence of the grandmother, her demeanour in court and her clear and frank evidence, clearly persuaded the magistrate her care was the best option for the child.

Magistrate concerns about the substitute care arrangements for children in need of protection limited the options they saw as appropriate for children. It is already noted that magistrates viewed the presence of a child's grandmother in court as a positive solution for substitute care. However extended family are not always available, or appropriate, to care for children at risk. The court is then dependent on foster families or small-group homes to provide care for children who cannot live with their families. This dependence on substitute care appeared to frustrate magistrates because they had little confidence in the alternative care arrangements provided and were concerned both about the quality of substitute care and about the disruption children experience when they have numerous substitute care arrangements.

One magistrate was particularly critical in court about multiple placements for children, and critical of DHS for their part in this. Yet the lack of willingness of the court, and DHS, to make longer-term decisions about children, at an earlier stage in the court process contributes to multiple placements for children. This was evident in the case of a three year old child who had experienced multiple placements for much of her life and DHS had not challenged the 'drift' of this case and this child. Her young mother had often abandoned her to foster care. However the court gave her another chance at parenting her daughter.

There appeared to be a piecemeal approach to making decisions about children, not only because there was often no ready solution for some cases, but also because both the court and the child protection service appeared to prefer to make a series of interim orders about a case hoping that over time the matter would sort itself out. The lack of a case plan for long-term care for children where there were significant, and unlikely to be resolved problems, meant cases returned to court on a number of occasions, delaying the resolution of the case and possibly prolonging abuse or harm to a child. Given that the legislation directs that parents are to be given every possible opportunity to retain their children, there can be considerable delays in the resolution of matters as interventions are tried with families. Delays in decisions about children are positive when their parents can make the changes required to retain their children. Such a process however pays little heed to parents who will not be able to make the necessary changes and provides no mechanism to short-circuit the delays such children experience.

Magistrates, however, were reluctant to make long-term orders even when there was serious and long-standing harm to a child. The child protection service sought a guardianship order for a three month old infant whose mother was significantly cognitively impaired and medical and forensic evidence stated that the child could not ever be in the mother's care. The mother's appearance in court suggested she was unable to give rational instruction. However her legal representative was successful in obtaining an interim order so that the mother could explore what other services she could engage as neither she, nor her representative, conceded her incapacity to care for her child.

Delays can also occur when vexatious parents continue to bring cases back to court even when they have been out of their children's lives for some time. The court is obliged to allow parents to continue to dispute DHS intervention in their children's lives. This however intensifies the disadvantage the children already experience and hinders the planning and supports necessary for such children. Table 3.7 sets out the number of court applications per child protection cases (n=89).

Table 3.7 Number of court appearances per protection application

Number of appearances	N	%
1	17	19.1
2-5	25	28.1
6-10	21	23.6
11-16	20	22.5
17 or more	6	6.7
Total	89	100.0

The implementation of court orders was another source of frustration for magistrates. In some cases whilst the orders were entirely appropriate they were difficult to implement. Cases of sexual abuse in which the perpetrator is ordered to move out of the family home exemplify this. In the four cases observed, where the perpetrators were a stepbrother and uncle, this order was more readily accepted than when it was the child's father. In the latter cases a secondary victimisation occurred as child victims had considerable family hostility directed at them.

There appeared to be few mechanisms for dealing with parents who would not comply with court orders. One case has already been mentioned in which a child remained at home, without recommended medical treatment, while the legal process unfolded and the court waited for her stepfather to exhaust all possible appeal processes. In other cases, a parent would agree to comply with court orders whilst remaining unconvinced that the conditions imposed were necessary and so unwilling to actively cooperate with the order. In a case involving a three year old child injured by his mother's boyfriend, the court ordered the child returned to his mother on the condition that the perpetrator move out of the child's home. The mother clearly stated she would resume her relationship with this man when the court order lapsed. The lack of acknowledgment by the mother of the seriousness of the child's injuries or of her boyfriend's capacity for violence had little impact and the court appeared optimistic that maternal bonding would take priority over the adult relationship.

Court decisions that require parents to modify behaviours are difficult to monitor. Furthermore, such conditions might ask parents to use different behaviours with their children that they simply may have no ability for. Some orders contain conditions that are difficult to achieve: cases in which one family member is expected to supervise the other parent's access to their children not only create an unrealistic burden on the supervising parent but also means the child protection workers can neither facilitate supervision nor support the supervising parent. This was evident in a case about an 18 month old child, physically abused by his father (who was charged by police for these injuries). The magistrate ordered the child be returned to his parents' care but the father was not to be left unsupervised with the child. The history of spousal violence presented to the court, and the court appearance of a timid and vulnerable mother, clearly indicated to an observer that she would not be able protect her child from her husband whilst he remained living with them. The child protection service sought the exclusion of the father from the family home but the magistrate did not support this recommendation. How the mother could realistically monitor her husband's behaviour with the child was not addressed by the court order. Nor was it addressed how the mother could protect the child when she needed to be absent from the family home to attend work.

Violence between parents appeared not to be acknowledged by the court as a threat to the child. In a number of cases of spousal violence the children were returned to the care of their mother with court orders about cessation of the violence. This did little to address the impact of the violence on the child nor ensure the violence did cease. It was apparent that the intimidation by a father of his family in a case observed made the situation unworkable for the court and so there was no censure of the father's treatment of his children.

In reality, magistrates appeared to have few mechanisms for responding effectively to children and women who were fearful of violent parents and partners. In a case of two girls of 11 and five years their mother had left the family home to escape her husband's violence. She was now seeking access to her daughters. Her fear of her husband made it difficult for her to establish contact with her children and this fear also made it difficult for her to speak about her situation in the courtroom. There appeared to be little assistance for such women when they attended court.

Yet, if the magistrate does not impose conditions that relate to the child protection concerns, such as requiring parents to attend parent education courses, even when such conditions may appear to be unenforceable, then the magistrate may signal to the child and family that they do not have the problems the child protection service suggests they have.

Personal Frameworks

Children's Court work challenges the personal beliefs and values of magistrates in a way the adult jurisdiction does not, and a number of magistrates said they were mindful of their own values and how such cases challenged these.

> All of us have to be careful working with families, what it is that is driving us and what goes on in our own families – have to be careful not to get biases and blocks (M 06).

Magistrates emphasised it was important to separate out one's own experience from those of the child before them in court and, to be as non-judgemental as possible. Magistrates noted it was impossible not to hold particular beliefs and values, the issue was, however, to keep them in check:

> Whilst you can't help but have preconceived ideas, you are a product of your own environment ... I tried to be as non-judgemental as I could in the families that presented. Some of them were pretty ghastly (M 15).

> ... you couldn't possibly not have them ... to say that any of us come to the courts as blank sheets of glass with no preconceptions or values is absurd, it's a question of trying to recognise what your values and biases might be, so you keep them in check or you are conscious that they are in the equation when you are doing the cases (M 14).

However 'you have to make a difference between what happens to you and the rest of society' (M 05).

Whilst professional advice and evidence about a child's situation assisted magistrates, they also relied on:

> Applying my personal life experience and just being a human being ... what is reasonable and appropriate given our human experience and understanding (M 01).

Magistrates commented on how different were their own family experiences from those of the families who appeared in the Family Division. Nine magistrates commented that sometimes in seeking to contextualise a child's experience in their family they referred to their own family style, their parenting, to get a sense of significance or impact, on the child, of the event that brought the case to court. Ten magistrates commented that their own family background and family values influence their work:

> My family environment is entirely different to those who come to court. I wouldn't place the same values on them as I would on my own children ... you couldn't have the same expectations (M 01).

Several magistrates noted that there were cases in which they thought 'there but for the grace of God go I' (M 07). They understood from their own parenting experiences how hard it is to be a parent, and what supports and resources families need. M 14 said '... I realised how precarious it must be for someone without those supports', when exploring the reasons why a child had come to the attention of the child protection service. M 08 believed that 'it's a pretty powerful thing to take a child from its mother, albeit an inadequate mother. Who is perfect? It's very easy to be critical.'

Magistrates said that a child's right to their family is a paramount principle. They commented that when considering a case they looked for the bonds between the child and their family. Magistrates were distressed by the lack of constancy and affection they found in many children's lives:

> Always the issue was whether or not the person was capable of adequately caring and tending the child in their care and the nature of the bond that was in existence (M 15).

Generally the measures magistrates used to determine risk or harm were case specific. However, views about the importance of family were both a general and personal influence; so too was what their individual understanding of child abuse:

> What order to make in a particular case depending on a whole range of reasons, including of course, a magistrates own particular values about child protection (M 02).

Very rarely was there any censure of parents' ill-treatment of their children. The child protection service required parents to admit responsibility for what had occurred to their child in order for intervention/treatment work with the family to be effective. Magistrates and legal representatives believed this was unnecessary and that work with a family could take place regardless of an admission of responsibility. Magistrates also believed this stance failed to acknowledge the reality of some cases, for example, in which there is a likelihood of criminal charges if a parent admits to sexual or physical abuse.

DHS were insistent that the grandmother of a 10 day old infant needed to acknowledge the psychiatric problems of her low-functioning daughter prior to taking over the care of the infant. DHS contended it was essential that the mother had a full understanding that her daughter could not safely care for the infant. The magistrate believed DHS were being intransigent about the need for such acknowledgment and the court order reflected this.

Yet, where children have been subject to physical injury and there remains a concerning level of violence in the family, the return of a child without court censure of such harm may not convey to parents the seriousness of their situation and the precariousness of the child's situation. This may also minimise further risk for such children. Where children are in court and hear their experiences normalised, what message must children receive about their veracity, their safety, and their right to a less threatening family life. One wonders also about children's confidence in seeking help from adults after this experience.

The case of a two year old child physically injured by her mother and in the care of her grandmother exemplified this. The child was returned to her mother with a requirement they attend a residential parenting programme. The child's injuries appeared not to be the central concern in this case; the central concern appeared to be attention to the mother's rights. When children are returned to their parents in these circumstances, the lack of censure appears more obvious. Parents whose actions are not checked by the court feel vindicated. The parents of two young boys who had experienced severe maltreatment refused to participate in court-ordered anger management programs. The boys remained with their parents despite the father's criminal conviction for assault. Whilst the court was abhorring of the treatment of the two boys, the court applied no stronger sanctions to the parents than the disapproval of the magistrate.

The lack of court censure of abusing parents creates difficulty for the non-abusing parent and for the children. When child abuse is constructed as a family problem it can overlook the fact that one person is creating the problem. It suggests that all family members are responsible for making the situation better when in fact only one person may need to change their behaviour. It stigmatises a family even more than it already is, if the whole family is held responsible for, for example, physical injuries to a child when in fact other family members may have attempted to prevent the abuse. It may also place undue pressure on children to cope with the parent problems, such as substance abuse, psychiatric illness and intellectual disability, that are out of their control. Yet:

> The need for the child to be in the family, which is his or hers, and have that bond which is the most important thing he has for better or for worse (M 07).

> I think it is heartbreaking to see what happens to some children (M 13).

Professional Assistance for the Court

> I rely on professional social workers, psychiatrists, to give me advice, to give evidence about why the situation is. Depending on the qualifications and the expertise of that particular worker, that's a tremendous assistance (M 01).

Magistrates relied on professionals to give insight into the issues in a case and to either support or negate the child protection concerns. There was considerable variation in the availability of expert assistance for the court. Magistrates valued evidence from experts: paediatricians, child psychiatrists, psychologists, teachers, maternal and child health nurses. Welfare practitioners are the predominant suppliers of case information to the court, however magistrates' doubts about state intervention in family life, about how information on families is gathered, about the expertise of protective workers, appeared to reduce their inclinations to rely on DHS evidence. Furthermore, since protective workers are bringing the application before the court and are, in traditional terms the prosecution, magistrates did not accept that the protective workers could both be objective witnesses and bring a child protection application at the same time.

There was negligible use by the child protection services of expert witnesses who could explain the developmental and familial needs of children and therefore the deficits the children before them were experiencing in their lives. Negligible information about research into child abuse was presented. The lack of information about the developmental or behavioural norms of children meant magistrates focused more on the possibilities for family preservation when deciding case outcome. In only one of the cases observed for this study was an expert witness called by DHS to explain research findings about the sexual abuse of children. The magistrate said this greatly helped his understanding of the case, and the DHS recommendations. Where magistrates were confident in the expertise of witnesses it was apparent that this directly influenced the case decision.

This was evident in a case involving allegations of sexual abuse of a child by his mother. In the absence of explanation about why the boy's behaviour was atypical and problematic, the magistrate preferred the testimony of the psychologist provided by the mother's legal counsel. He explained the child's problems in terms of the mother's inadequate parenting which could be remedied, but not if the child was removed from his mother. Since this view was consistent with the magistrate's views on family preservation the child was returned to his mother.

Magistrates reported they greatly valued professionals who offered them independent, objective information. These professionals provide the court with theoretical or contextual information about children's best interests. Six magistrates referred to the Children's Court Clinic as an excellent source of objective information. The Children's Court Clinic is an independent unit of the Department of Justice to which magistrates can refer cases for assessment, though parties need to agree to the assessment:

> We relied very heavily on the Children's Court Clinic ... you'd look a lot to the Clinic ... (M 03).

> The people from the Children's Hospital were usually terrific. Children's Court Clinic were very good. I drew a lot of comfort in the most difficult emotional abuse cases if there was a senior social worker from the Children's Hospital and a good child psychiatrist. I would feel greatly comforted and put considerable emphasis on the evidence, they knew what they were taking about (M 14).

Where cases involve a number of professionals, there is often a range of views about what is in a child's best interests. Yet, while:

> All professionals are helpful, but it's up to you to eventually take from that information ... in a way you have a reaction towards a situation ... that reaction is either backed up by one professional or totally destroyed by one (M 07).

What is problematic is that, in child protection cases, professionals see people at different times during problem situations and the parents may have changed circumstances or present differently to the various professionals. There are no guidelines for magistrates to balance such different sources of information. One magistrate referred to a very complex and lengthy case he heard in which the experts were in disagreement as to whether or not sexual abuse had occurred:

> That was one of the difficulties of fact-finding. You simply had cases where the experts would be in heated disagreement. Remarkable disagreement ... people's mental state changes and it depends when the person was seen what trauma they were under at the time (M 12).

Magistrates had difficulty with the way child protection workers prepared and presented their cases for court. Much of the difficulty appeared to be with the nature of the evidence protective workers gathered to support these claims. Magistrates generally acknowledged the complexities of child protection work.

Yet the dichotomy between the gathering of evidence for child protection purposes and the legal principles which govern evidence was especially noticeable and magistrates often expressed frustration with what they saw as the inattention of DHS to court procedures, which they believed might disadvantage children and their families.

Yet, many cases do not have the conventional evidence: the photographs, the eyewitness accounts, the 'hard' evidence favoured by the adversarial system, for child protection cases. Protective workers are often reliant on children's disclosures of abuse or on the accounts of teachers, child carers, and other family members to substantiate allegations of risk of harm, or actual harm, to a child. Preparation of reports for court is difficult when, for example, families decline to cooperate with child protection, or when children are very young and cannot disclose information, or when a range of professionals are involved in a case. So, evidence can appear incomplete, be substantially based on hearsay or the worker's impressions, and it may be presented in a way which is not legally coherent. Moreover, the decision by the child protection service to seek a child protection order may not be taken until an assessment is completed and so the information about a case that is presented to the court is what has been gathered for the purposes of a child protection assessment, not necessarily with a court appearance in mind.

Reports are the basis of much of the evidence tendered to the court by child protection workers. Both magistrates and legal practitioners viewed the preparation of these reports and preparing for court as a major emphasis in child protection work. Yet, when protection applications were based on the apprehension of a child, there could be gaps in preparation for court, such as delays in reports being provided. This, again, was a source of frustration for magistrates, and given the adversarial system's reliance on evidence, at times invited critical responses from magistrates and perhaps punitive measures. The magistrate, in a case of the mother's injury of her two year old child awarded costs against the child protection service as the mother's legal representative had not been supplied with the court report. Yet, in a case involving a three month old infant, the magistrate declined to release a clinical report about the mother's impairment and low functioning as it would be detrimental to the mother's request to reclaim her child. The mother of the infant was not long out of prison, was profoundly brain damaged, and had serious addiction problems. DHS counsel subsequently successfully applied for the release of the report as its contents were essential to the understanding of the case.

Another apparent source of frustration was that in child protection matters the protective worker who brings the application to court may not be the same practitioner who assessed the merit of the child protection notification. The child protection worker at court therefore often needed to refer to case records to explain the child protection concerns. This could give a fragmented case presentation that created difficulties for magistrates, and legal representatives, in arriving at the facts of the case. One magistrate said he was unhappy with the typed summaries of interviews that were prepared by child protection workers and placed on the case record. It was his opinion, and one he noted he had previously mentioned in court, that child protection workers should keep their handwritten notes on file to ensure the evidence can be verified. Explanations by child protection workers that it is inappropriate to take notes when interviewing children, particularly when they are disclosing highly personal and frightening information, was not well accepted. Legal representatives also found this explanation difficult to accept as it was their view that the court's need to have available all the information relevant to a case is of greater importance than other considerations.

Legal practitioners were highly critical of welfare assessment techniques; legal counsel suggested that the working practices of protective workers, in one case, were calculated attempts to gather evidence. An example raised in court was that the suggestion by the child protection worker, that one of the younger children might like to do a drawing to distract the child from a difficult situation during an interview with the parents, was not a distraction but rather: 'you asked [the child] to draw to gather evidence, didn't you?'. Legal counsel, when appearing for parents in contested hearings, regularly challenged child protection assessments by dismantling the context of the assessment into small, often meaningless parts, so that the conceptual foundations on which the assessments are made, appeared nonsensical.

Giving evidence about parents and children was not straightforward for child protection workers. They were mindful that, after court, they would still have to work with the family and believed there was little appreciation of this by the court. They were mindful that the disclosure of private and sensitive information could threaten this relationship, as could legal representatives' attempts to discredit the testimony of protective workers. Magistrates believed, however, that welfare practitioners did not always respect the autonomy of the court and magistrates' antipathy to bureaucratic processes was apparent. The lack of autonomy of, and lines of authority for, protective workers contributed to this view. The need for the child protection worker to consult with their supervisor before they could respond to magistrate proposals to vary recommended courses of action for a child and family greatly frustrated magistrates, and was viewed by some as an example of the interference of the bureaucracy with the running of the court.

Magistrates Views about the Family

The *Children and Young Persons Act* emphasises the importance of family preservation and magistrates' decisions reflected this. The desire to maintain the child in their family is shared both by magistrates and the child protection service, and the court appears to go to considerable lengths to ensure orders assist this. Five magistrates reinforced the importance of family to a child and the need to acknowledge the diversity of family approaches to child care:

> ... the family is the fundamental unit in society if you can have it and everyone is entitled to the opportunity to have a family. But a lot of the children we see don't have families and you would like to give them more of an opportunity (M 13).

> Families are very diverse. You have to be aware that the social textbook family isn't the only family, you have to be aware of the incredible diversity and possibility of care. The basic tenet is that there is love and support and stimulation – that's crucial (M 05).

Magistrates said it was their statutory duty to ensure family preservation:

> The important principle that the state doesn't intervene in the rights of individuals (M 05).

> To return a child to a family with no outside interference, as much as possible (M 11).

However, in a number of cases before the court there was already a considerable history of disruption, and perhaps damage to a child, and little sense of family for the child. Yet the need to maintain a family appeared to exert a powerful hold over magistrates, both from a legislative and personal point of view. Magistrates' less than positive views about state intervention in family life, combined with their unfavourable views about foster care, supported their desire to maintain children in their families. This commitment to family preservation appeared at times to be given greater weight by the court than the welfare of the child. Magistrates therefore found it difficult when confronted with cases in which family reunion was not in the best interests of the child: there was a general reluctance to accept that some adults may be unsuitable parents. Unsuitable perhaps because their personal problems interfere with their capacity to parent even though they genuinely love their children.

Where there appears to be a family unit or the promise of a family unit with two parent figures, the court is more hopeful for children and so more likely to return children to families. This was mentioned by the magistrate when deciding to give three children of four, three and one years, who had suffered significant neglect when in the care of their mother, to their father, recently released from prison, and his girlfriend, so that they could have 'a go' as a family, despite the inadequacies of both biological parents because of their drug addiction.

The fixed notions of what constitutes a family which appeared to be held by the majority of magistrates led to outcomes such as those just outlined. The view that two adults and children constituted a family for court purposes did not always match the reality of the relationship away from court. This was apparent in a case involving two children of four and two and a half years whose mother and father/stepfather had significant drug addiction and domestic violence problems. The children were in separate care: the child of both parents with his paternal grandmother, the mother's other child in foster care. The paternal grandmother was prepared to care for her grandchild but not the child with whom she had no biological connection. Yet both children were very attached to each other and wanted to be together. Neither parent could care for the children. The court preferred a family member cared for the children together but a grandparent was available for only one child. There were very few family alternatives for these children.

The primacy of importance of the care of children by their family made it difficult for the court to accommodate the limitations of some families. Magistrates remained hopeful that the offer of support services would improve family functioning. Where parents attended court magistrates appeared more likely to be sympathetic to their circumstances. Certainly magistrates appeared more willing to return children to families where there were two parent figures even though only one may be the biological parent. Where parents admitted there were problems, where parents agreed to seek help, where parents had steady employment, then magistrates appeared more hopeful about their children. Even where there were other problems, for example, family violence, psychiatric disability, parents agreeing to accept help suggested to magistrates that they were willing to change. Counselling appeared to be highly valued by magistrates. A legal representative's mention of agreement for counselling was an effective strategy for parents to win concessions from the court no matter how inappropriate for the child this strategy might be. Yet seeing counselling as a 'cure all' is problematic; it certainly imbues therapists with far greater power and responsibility than they would wish to accept.

The magistrate's positive view of parent attendance, together with the parents' agreement to participate in counselling and anger management programs, and strong legal representation, appeared to be deciding factors in a case involving a three month old male child physically abused by his father. The child was returned to his parents (from the care of grandparents) because the father now had employment, had admitted to his alcohol problems and agreed to attend an anger management program.

The court appeared reluctant to intervene in families because of particular parent problems, for example parents with an intellectual disability, parents with substance abuse problems, where their children may not yet be significantly harmed, but their environment undermined normal childhood development and perhaps also personal safety. This was so, it appeared, in part because there were no agreed baseline characteristics for being a parent to which the court could refer to assist decision-making, together with magistrates' natural preference for a child to remain with their family. The mother of a young boy was genuine in her desire to retain the care of her son. However her alcohol problems made it difficult for her to get herself to court. The case was regularly adjourned in the hope that the mother would come to court, involve herself in decisions about her son and undertake treatment for alcoholism. The young boy experienced regular changes in short-term care arrangements as he moved between home and placement, as his mother both failed to come to court and to enter a treatment programme.

The idea of the family supported by magistrates, the community and the legislation, did not however always match magistrates' experiences of families at court:

> There are certain prejudices which aren't in the Act which are set down as social mores: that children are best raised with aware, conscientious parents. That seemed to be the basis of all cases, ultimately that one had to try and achieve that situation as often as possible. In a lot of cases it was utterly futile but that seemed to be the underlying rationale ... there was a bias in favour of the nuclear family. There was a bias in favour of people in the middle class ... (M 12).

Magistrates and legal representatives referred frequently to their beliefs about bonding and attachment and objected to child protection arrangements which separated a child from their parent. There is a substantial literature about disrupted attachment and the damage of the orphanage care of the past on children. These concerns appeared to exert a powerful influence on magistrates. However magistrates' knowledge about what constitutes attachment or bonding appeared limited. Magistrates appeared to strongly believe that all parents can bond with their children and that this attachment is powerful enough to overcome parent/child difficulties. Magistrates appeared also to believe that children who live with their parents are attached to their parents, and that generally children can move beyond the harm they may have experienced in their family. Yet, the child's perceptions of who they saw as family was rarely sought or referred to. Children have great difficulty expressing their dismay at what has happened to them. Indeed many children in this situation express a wish to return home as they most often see their choices as their family or residential care. A child's need for a family appeared to be always interpreted by the court as the need for their family rather than their need for a family, which might be provided by extended family or others who have may provided care to the children over a period of time.

Cases varied in terms of parental involvement and their presence in court. Where there was a lack of parental interest and involvement in cases it was difficult for magistrates to implement the legislative aims of family reunification. In approximately one in five cases presented in the Mention Court, during the study, no parent appeared; in a number of cases the child's mother had disappeared, in nine cases a parent was absent because of imprisonment. There were cases in which parents refused to come to court, and/or refused to assist the court in decisions about their children.

The two magistrates who had training in child related areas found knowledge of child development gave them a framework to assess children's needs and to assess a child's particular situation. They believed that such training in children's issues gave magistrates an objective view about child protection matters. This was important because the individual experiences of magistrates greatly varied and reference to one's own family experiences was not necessarily the best measure of a child's needs.

Magistrates were ambivalent about alternative care for children; six magistrates expressed concern about the poor organisation of foster care for children and said this concern might incline them to leave a child in their family's care albeit with support services:

For me there is a real issue with foster care, the numerous places children are sent, it is not unusual for kids to have numbers of placements. Kids need stability with one adult, when they don't have that I see them ending up in the Criminal Division. CSV [DHS] has to get this sorted out before magistrates will trust them in regards to substitute care (M 04).

... all I could really order was that the child would be placed in the Department's [DHS] care ... but I would know very little about it. I knew from other information that often the foster placement left much to be desired ... (M 01).

The dilemma for me was that I always thought the options were pretty awful. No matter how good a system you have the options will always be awful, so what you are really talking about is will I allow the child to be damaged in this way or will I allow it to be damaged in that way ... what am I going to offer him to save him from his mum not handling him properly. I am going to offer him an institutional life or a life moving between foster parents and it's not really an option (M 14).

Magistrates always preferred extended family care for children, to avoid foster care arrangements, and where grandparents (mostly the grandmother) could offer substitute care for a child then that was always viewed as the most appropriate option for a child. The importance of grandparents is imprinted on our cultural consciousness. Grandparents symbolise powerful emotions desired by parents for their children: unconditional love, security, time available to concentrate on the child, people who had successfully negotiated their way through adulthood, and who were wise. Adults who have enjoyed the affection of their grandparents generalise this to all other grandparents. It was apparent that magistrates took this view. Furthermore, assumptions were made that all grandparents are adequate parents, have the resources to parent young children and want to alter their lives to again parent very young children. Yet a number of grandmothers were the salvation of their grandchildren, very often sibling groups of two or three, and in one case, five children. They (the grandmothers) attended court and assisted the child protection service. This was often at great cost to themselves, most particularly in terms of ongoing relationships with their own children – the mothers and fathers of the grandchildren.

One magistrate emphasised that although it was always preferable to keep a family together, the child's interests must predominate. This magistrate's very clear distinction between parent and child issues was not typical; his view that the court's commitment to family preservation must always be tempered with what is in a child's best interests was mentioned only by two other magistrates. This magistrate's view that, in some cases, a child's best interests might lie outside their family was not a view with which magistrates were comfortable. One magistrate suggested there was:

> [a] 'Madonna' complex of you know, mothers and babies, they belong together and mothers love babies and there is no problem (M 14).

However, five magistrates said that whilst they regarded the child's right to their family as paramount, and that this was consistent with their beliefs and experience, they had to focus on a child's situation as it was presented in court and the magistrate was:

> ... governed to a large extent by your own assessment of those people in the courtroom (M 11).

The legislative commitment to family preservation and community concern about children being removed from their families meant that those magistrates who did not oppose statutory intervention in child welfare might not be sympathetically viewed by their peers. Yet, five magistrates mentioned that the underlying rationale of family preservation was at times unrealistic:

> A lot of magistrates ... were very concerned about the fact that they perhaps were going against what seemed to be the tide of legal opinion at that time, that yes, you just never make those orders (M 15).

It was apparent that child sexual abuse cases confronted magistrates and legal practitioners beliefs about families and parent-child relationships. Magistrates' views about the primacy of the family made it difficult for them to accept that membership of a family may be permanently destroyed for a child who experiences significant harm at the hands of parent. In other cases, children appeared at times to remain in their families because there was no real agreement about time limits on parents' attempts to improve their family's situation.

Magistrate Views about Families before the Court

Magistrates all conveyed a sense that it is struggling families who find their way to the Children's Court. These were families who had few personal and material resources to resolve their problems. They were often the children of parents with a history of welfare involvement. Eight magistrates said that poverty was a common characteristic of families before the court:

> The population is substantially from people who don't have much education, lower socioeconomic class and abuse backgrounds themselves, but I'm also noticing a number of different cultures appearing in court and that's very different from 10 years ago ... (M 13).

> ... [families] coming up for contested supervision or guardianship, were those very poor families, struggling families, single mothers, single parents with de-facto husbands, with drug taking, criminal activity by the de-facto and a long history of involvement with welfare and the department (M 03).

> I get the impression a significant number of parents before the Court are impoverished single parents, mainly females (M 10).

> The issues are always the same, it's always some sort of abuse or neglect or abandonment or matters of that type (M 02).

Magistrates believed that families with the resources to pay for help could avoid coming to court:

> ... wealthy families can afford to pay for intervention from the outside to come in an support them if there is a problem in the family (M 09).

> It's fashionable to say that we see everybody here at the Children's Court. It's not just poor people but rich people too. It's absolute nonsense ... for a start if you are ... in a more privileged family everyone will get the school counsellor and psychologist and psychiatrist (M 14).

The better access to services and the greater financial resources of middle class families meant they could sort out their problems privately:

> The richer you are the more you can afford to buy services and the less likely the young social workers are to interfere. And if you have family they might step in and help you out ... although there is a substantial weighting to lower socioeconomic families, it's not confined to them (M 05).

> People who are better off financially can be diverted (M 08).

> The ones who get before the courts are the ones who have no funds to protect themselves (M 15).

Three magistrates suggested that perhaps in middle class areas child maltreatment is more noticeable and therefore more likely to be acted on, rather than in poorer, lower socioeconomic areas, where family problems might be greater and more complex. Two magistrates also suggested that the introduction of mandatory reporting of child abuse in Victoria had led to an increase in the presentation of trivial cases:

> You are more likely to get an allegation of bruising on a child in Camberwell [comfortable middle-class suburb in Melbourne] than you are from the Footscray office (M 10).

Various parent problems and family constellations were seen as commonplace before the court. Problems such as family violence, drug abuse, alcohol abuse, psychiatric problems, parents with very little income and poor employment prospects, with little education and who had children at a very young age were regularly presented:

> Women choosing violent males, violent males choosing submissive compliant women ... and the parents came from broken families themselves ... (M 05).

> Lack of finances is a major issue. Problems with drug abuse and alcohol abuse are regular matters in our courts (M 02).

> The broad categories in protection are teenage girls who are having trouble at home, tiny babies born to heroin addicted mothers – that's one of the saddest ... a small percentage of physical abuse ... cases of youngish mothers not coping with difficult toddlers (M 14).

> Struggling to make ends meet, often producing children at a very young age without any particular skills, without any employment prospects and so the pressure is on (M 02).

Table 3.8 shows that the sole income of half of the families in the study was social security payments.

Table 3.8 Parent income

	Are parents in receipt of benefits?	
	N	%
Yes	31	68.9
No	2	4.4
Not known	12	26.7
Total	45	100.0

Magistrates referred to particular parenting practices coming to the attention of the court, most often in regard to physical abuse or excessive discipline of children. Different parental attitudes to obedience, or the right to discipline children physically, emerged in particular sociocultural contexts in some cases of physical abuse. Four magistrates suggested ethnic considerations might explain the appearance of particular ethnic groups before the court for excessive punishment of their children: '... some are ethnic based. They may believe they should punish the children in a certain way' (M 07).

Adolescent freedom was at times the issue in these cases, because of different parental sociocultural attitudes to independence: one magistrate referred to this as adolescents having a 'foot in both worlds' (M 08).

Ten of the magistrates commented that a significant number of the children in child protection matters came from single parent families, mostly mother-only families. They also commented on the absence of fathers in children's lives. Six magistrates expressed concern about the number of de-facto fathers in the lives of children. The majority of magistrates commented on the high level of family violence in many of the families; one magistrate referred to mothers who attract violent partners who then abuse her children, another referred to a ping-pong effect in some families where parents serially break-up and reunite. Magistrates also commented on the number of merged families who featured in child protection matters, usually where a child's mother had re-partnered, borne another child and included a partner's child or children into their unit:

> Nearly all families were either a single parent or de-facto, families with foster children, lots of families, married couples but they were not normally the more serious cases (M 03).

> Lack of a father, very common. Lack of a constant father, maybe a series of fathers. Irresponsibility, fathers not taking responsibility (M 01).

> Lots of children, all from different fathers, different named children, all living in the same house, children with stepfathers, children without fathers (M 13).

> A lot are polyglot families with children from a number of relationships – his/her and ours – people who are stressed because they do not have enough money (M 07).

Tables 3.9, 3.10 and 3.11 show that the children involved in child protection matters in this study generally lived with their mother (41.9 per cent), and in just under one third of the cases in the study (n=89), the children had siblings who lived away from them, often with other relatives or in long-term foster care. Table 3.12 shows that since children in child protection cases very often came from mother-only families, it was the mother who was either putting the child at risk of harm or who had actually harmed the child.

Dysfunctional families, families in which there is a cycle of neglect, parents with a history of involvement with welfare, either with their own children or from their family of origin, as noted in Table 3.13; all were visible groups to magistrates. They were parents:

> ... [who] are expected to raise a child with hardly any experience, usually coming from a similar sort of family themselves (M 12).

> Families who are fairly impoverished who come from backgrounds of generational abuse and neglect where there has been no emphasis on parenting skills (M 02).

and who:

> ... had no expectations of self worth (M 05).

> ... you see the absolute underbelly of society – the underprivileged people in the community who never had a chance (M 08).

Magistrates also suggested that parents who were not cooperating with the child protection service were likely to be brought to court to compel parents to deal with the child protection concerns. Another group of parents sought to use the Children's Court as a second Family Court (the matrimonial matters court), to deal with child access problems. Where a matter was before the Family Court of Australia, and a dispute arose, or a decision about custody was made and the other parent disputed it, they might allege child protection concerns to have the case reassessed. Whilst a case is being dealt with in the Children's Court, its orders take precedence over Family Court involvement. A cross-jurisdiction protocol is in place in an attempt to alleviate some of this difficulty but when child protection concerns are alleged the statutory child protection service is obliged to investigate.

Table 3.9 Parent relationship status compared with sex of child

	Sex of child					
	Male		Female		Total	
	N	%	N	%	N	%
Children's parents						
Married and together	10	33	13	32	23	32
Separated	7	23	8	20	15	21
Divorced	6	20	13	32	19	27
Never in partnership	1	3	1	2	2	3
Mother whereabouts unknown			3	7	3	4
Father whereabouts unknown	3	10	7	17	10	14
Other	3	10	4	10	7	10
Total	30	100	41	100	71	100

Table 3.10 Child's place of residence at the time of the protection matter

At the time of the PA, who was the child residing with?		
	N	%
Both parents	22	27.2
Single mother	24	29.6
Single father	4	4.9
Mother and partner	10	12.3
Father and partner	3	3.7
Relatives	5	6.2
Foster parents	5	6.2
Community service	6	7.4
Other	2	2.5
Total	81	100.0

Note: PA refers to Protection Application.

Table 3.11 Child's siblings' place of residence

Other children?		
	N	%
Living away from child subject	15	53.6
In care	7	25.0
Other relative	3	10.7
Other	2	7.1
At home	1	3.6
Total	28	100.0

Table 3.12 The relationship of the perpetrator to the child

	Sex of child					
	Male		Female		Total	
	N	%	N	%	N	%
Relationship of alleged perpetrator						
Parents	8	22	14	32	22	28
Mother	16	44	14	32	30	38
Father	5	14	8	18	13	16
Mother's partner	1	3	1	2	2	3
Male sibling	1	3	4	9	5	6
Mother and partner	2	6	3	7	5	6
Father and partner	1	3			1	1
Other family member	1	3			1	1
Other	2	6	1	2	3	4
Total	36	100	44	100	80	100

Note: parents refers to both parents as perpetrators.

Table 3.13 Family history of welfare contact (no. of cases for which information was available, n=56)

	Child's family had previous contact?	
	N	%
Yes	53	94.6
No	3	5.4
Total	56	100.0

Parents' Rights and Children's Rights

Magistrates were clear about the importance of the family for the child and that parents' rights had to be observed when the child protection service was seeking to intervene in a family's life. However, court activity centred around adult participants and children often appeared left out of a process that was essentially about them. This meant at times that the right of a parent to retain their child was more strongly defended than the right of the child to have their interests treated as the court's primary consideration. The often vague and inconclusive evidence of child abuse provided in court by child protection workers, combined with the requirement to find cases proven 'on the balance of probabilities', meant decisions appeared to favour parents. Our contemporary Australian shame about the forced separation of indigenous Australian

(Aboriginal) children from their families, together with community views about the impact of orphanages on children who now as adults attest to the misery of their upbringing, has created a powerful ideology about the harm caused by state intervention in family life. The lack of success of such intervention is regularly seen by magistrates in the Criminal Division of the Children's Court. Concern about state intervention in family life and the importance of family autonomy therefore appeared to make magistrates more sympathetic to parents' viewpoints than to those of the child protection service.

The strong belief shared by all about a child's need for parents meant magistrates appeared sensitive to community criticism that they too readily contribute to the fragmentation of family relationships. This was particularly evident where the parents had problems with, for example, intellectual disability, substance abuse, or psychiatric problems. The court appeared to have a belief that these parents could be as inherently good as any other parent, it was just that they had a particular problem which diminished their parenting capacities. Consequently very young children tended to remain with their parents until it was overwhelmingly proven that they needed alternative care, which could have unfortunate consequences for the children. It appeared difficult to convey to the court how great is the damage to children from such parental problems. Whilst the legal argument for the parents may be won in these circumstances, the children have certainly lost.

The apparent primacy of the rights of parents was seen in cases where vexatious parents sought numerous adjournments in cases, or returned cases to court, to challenge the court's right to intervene in their family. The court seemed to have little power to deal with the difficult life of children who were the subject of child protection matters. It appeared to be more straightforward for magistrates to keep children with their parents and to order that families receive support services that could improve the situation and achieve the legislative aim of family preservation.

The next chapter examines the factors that shape magistrate decision-making and links these comments and observations to broader issues with the adversarial approach to resolution of child abuse cases. It also notes the similarities between the findings about magistrates in this study and what the judiciary in other studies, and in other jurisdictions, say about child welfare decision-making. Reference is also made to the tension which exists between welfare and legal practitioners and the impact of this on the courtroom process and court outcome. Again, examples of cases observed or comments made by magistrates and practitioners are quoted to explain how magistrates approach their work.

Chapter Four

Magistrate Decision-Making

> The issues are much the same in terms of the way in which we approach things. You weigh up the evidence. You weigh up the risks. You look at all the alternative propositions and try to do something which fits the requirement of the legislation and at the same time protects the children (M 02).

Magistrates, as qualified lawyers, described their decision-making approaches in legal terms and were highly individualised and case-specific in these descriptions. How magistrates weighted case factors, and information in child protection matters, appeared to involve four reference points. Magistrates said they looked first and foremost to legal factors to decide child protection matters. They examined the grounds of the allegations to ensure they complied with legislative requirements, the evidence to support these, the merit of the case, and the attitudes and demeanour of the parties. The best interests of the child were therefore established in a 'judicial manner' (M 11):

> you start off ... with the provisions [CYPA 1986 s.87] which set out those matters we have to take into account, making an assessment of all the evidence ... is the child protected from harm, and having resolved that, then what you are doing is following section 87, trying as much as possible keeping the family together (M 02).

Second, magistrates referred to the individual decision frameworks they developed to measure harm and risk to a child. Magistrates said they needed to be personally satisfied that 'what is alleged has happened' (M 03). Magistrates did not talk in terms of a specific framework but rather in terms of the issues they looked for in a case to guide their considerations; issues such as parental competence and motivation to change. The nature of the child abuse allegations would also direct magistrate thinking about what needed to change in a family in order for a child's situation to improve:

> If you have severe psychiatric disturbance in the mother who is schizophrenic or [has an] intellectual disability severely, then that pinpoints certain issues and makes me look down a certain pathway (M 13).

The third reference point magistrates used to assess the merit of child protection concerns was their personal frameworks and their personal family experiences, particularly in the absence of clear measures and legal certainty. Their views about their role in the jurisdiction, their beliefs about families, and about intervention in families, were important elements of this framework. Magistrates believed firmly in the importance of family life for children and that every endeavour must be made to maintain children in their family:

> To try and preserve families intact as much as possible and to try and intervene to ensure that problems with families didn't become so severe that the children were taken from the family (M 09).

> I suppose your starting point and the law reflects this, the commonsense starting point is initially, it's in the best interests of any child to be within the family. So that was always my own personal starting point ... it's a balance. When does damage become so damaging that it's more in the child's interests to be away (M 14).

Magistrates' less than positive views about the expertise of child protection workers and the merit of their intervention were also part of this framework. Magistrates were concerned by the extent to which state intervention was required in families to address child protection concerns. Some magistrates expressed concern about too hasty intervention despite the legislative aim of minimum intervention. They were concerned also by what they perceived as uncertainty and ambiguity about claims made by child protection. Craft, Epley and Clarkson (1980) found in their study of child protection decisions that the individual biases of the worker were a more important influence on decisions than the characteristics of the case. It was apparent in the current study that individual magistrate's views were influential although the case characteristics did modify a magistrate's response.

The fourth reference point for magistrates was what they considered were the available options for a case. Magistrates when assigning weight to the options for a case considered 'where I think the right comes down' (M 03), to deciding 'on the material that is before us' (M 05), and, 'what the harm has been, what the likelihood of the harm is in the future, what is the case planning ... [in a case]' (M 02), as well as 'am I satisfied the claims made by CSV (the child protection service) are borne out' (M 03). These measures appeared to have the same uncertainty and ambiguity that magistrates ascribed to the claims made by child protection services, as noted above. Magistrates' concerns about substitute care for children and their beliefs about hasty intervention into family lives strongly influenced them to retain children in their family when the child protection service believed the best option for a child was to be placed away from their parents. Firmly held beliefs about the unsuitability of foster care made many magistrates prefer that extended family cared for children. It was not an option always favoured by the child protection service, particularly when there was no assessment of grandparent capacity to care for the children:

> The child wants to go home. The parents want the child to go home ... I just take notice of that and I send the child home. One of the chief considerations in the Act is that families should be kept together. I think the Department [the child protection service] tends to ignore that often (M 07).

However, achieving the legislative aim of family preservation was seriously hampered by shrinking resources:

> That [family preservation] might be a good ideal, but it's not going to work unless there are proper resources so in the end you are constantly having to be aware of the ability of CSV [DHS] to implement the policy of keeping families together. Did they have the resources to do this (M 09).

Magistrates acknowledged that the child protection service viewed harm and risk to children differently from that of legal professionals. However, it was the task of the magistrate to attend first to what is legally and legislatively permissible in child protection matters. In reality, the legal framework was the only clearly articulated framework that magistrates had to assist in their decision-making. The evidence in a case, the legislative merit and legal appropriateness of the child protection application and the matters raised within it, were part of this primary consideration. Magistrates all referred to the need to decide matters on the balance of probabilities. Douglas and Laster (1992) found that magistrates indeed viewed legal considerations as their primary concern in the resolution of disputes. Court outcomes had to be legally justifiable and this included determining disputes about social problems.

Magistrates placed great emphasis on the protection of the rights of the parties and the need to respect family, and therefore, parent autonomy. They accorded great importance to the principles that every individual has the right to their day in court, that the court needs to find the truth in order to resolve a dispute, and that each case is to be seen as unique and is to be judged on its merits. Douglas and Laster (1992) found that magistrates believed it was their role to stand between the individual and the government to ensure that individuals received just and fair treatment in the eyes of society. Magistrates in this study certainly placed great importance on ensuring that parents were heard by the court and that welfare intervention was justified. Magistrates were also concerned to ensure that parents were viewed by the court in the most positive way possible.

The dominance of the legal framework also meant that legal representation played a significant part in court decision-making. Norris (1993) found, in her study of child abuse matters in the Family Court of Australia, that legal representation directly influenced outcomes. Lawyers' understanding of the legal system and magistrates' greater familiarity with legal rather than welfare frameworks was more favourable to the court in the running of a case than was the approach of welfare professionals. The adversarial approach ensured that legal factors were brought first to the court's attention, and this meant that legal practitioners were very influential in how cases proceeded. Certainly, magistrates emphasised the importance of legal practitioners to the court. Scott (1989), Schon (1988), and Douglas and Laster (1992) all referred to the influence of professional socialisation on how professionals select information and the decision frameworks they construct for decision-making. The inherent difficulty in reducing broad welfare concerns to issues of fact and the lack of complementarity between legal and welfare concerns made magistrates more receptive to cases that made legal sense, and more attentive to factors in cases which conformed to their individual views about children and families. Given this, it is not surprising that energetic legal representation and parental attendance at court by both parents were often more persuasive factors to magistrates than child protection service recommendations.

Magistrates' views that family matters are essentially private and their reluctance to permit intrusion into family life are different from the principles on which welfare practitioners operate and the conflict between these principles was clearly a source of tension between legal and welfare professionals (King and Trowell 1992; Swain 1989; Smart 1989).

The Individuality of Magistrate Decision-making

> I'm not sure that I do, start off, OK this is a serious alcohol problem of the parent, what are the particular areas that I am going to apply to this case..maybe in some subconscious way there are certain elements, things I'm looking for, but I think basically I am just looking to see what the witnesses are going to say about the particular case, what the harm has been, what the likelihood of the harm is in the future, what the case planning is, what is hoped for for the future of all this, that generally applies to all of the cases and not just some (M 02).

The studies of judicial decision-making reported in the literature found that it was a combination of legal rules, discretion, and the behaviour of court participants which influenced decision-making (Konecni and Ebbeson 1982; Hogarth 1987). Lawrence (1981 et al.) found also that magistrates' personal experiences, legal factors and the actual court proceedings- especially, the number of parties present in court, and the strength of their views- influenced decision-making. Fitzmaurice and Pease (1986) suggested the disparity in decisions arose because judicial decision-makers tend to overvalue individual case-specific information and overlook information available about other similar cases. Certainly in this study magistrates did not find it easy to explicate the factors that influenced their decision-making. There was no shared common decision-making model across magistrates although it was clear that there were factors common to their decision-making. The magistrates most comfortable with decision-making in the Family Division and who could articulate a clearer approach to deciding child protection matters were the few who had spent more time at the Children's Court or who had considerable experience in family law. Bond and Lemon (1981) found, as did Lawrence and Homel (1987), that experienced magistrates did indeed develop their own decision strategies. They also developed individual ways of selecting significant facts and weighting them. Ashworth (1984) and Asquith (1983) had also found that judges emphasised the individuality of decision-making. This highlights why there is such variability in court outcomes even when cases are similar in nature.

Yet magistrates did respond to particular issues which arose in cases, such as their concern about placing children in foster care. It was apparent therefore that magistrates developed individual mind-sets, or individual knowledge frameworks, as suggested by Lawrence (1981 et al.), to process the cases which came before them. Lawrence (1981 et al.) and Scott (1989) found that the schema or frameworks magistrates constructed were influenced by a combination of personal, social and environmental factors. The magistrates in the current study were required to consider not only the statutory requirements but also to be aware of bureaucratic pressures, and community expectations, as well as the case details. The lack of guidelines, and often lack of case information meant magistrates referred to their individual frameworks, or 'cognitive image' (Dhir and Markham 1986) about an event or behaviour to extract the information needed to decide case outcomes.

The *Children and Young Persons Act* offered little definitive assistance to magistrates in deciding child protection matters. Magistrates therefore referred to their individual decision frameworks to assess risk to a child or significant harm to a child:

> Does that strike me as serious harm, would I, is that something that ought to be tolerated within a family for a child? (M 03).

And:

> Am I persuaded, am I satisfied that these things exist or these things have happened? (M 03).

However, six magistrates commented that the lack of key definitions of child abuse and the ambiguity about appropriate parenting practices was a fundamental problem for them:

> It is the problem in those child abuse things, what's the standard? How do you know? It may be that you never know (M 08).

The legislation fails to accommodate the multifaceted nature of child protection concerns. It fails to provide grounds that adequately deal with the very poor parenting of children. Child protection cases based on such concerns were often unsuccessful at court because on legislative grounds there was no case to answer. This created particular tension between magistrates and child protection workers.

The factors magistrates looked for in cases were not always clear to them, as Corbett (1987) had found when the magistrates in his study could not clearly identify the reasons why they selected a particular decision as the appropriate case outcome. It was difficult 'to articulate outside a given case what factors come into play in a decision' (M 03). They all referred to the need to first assess the evidence and the merit and legislative appropriateness of a child protection application. They also looked for a family history of welfare contact, to see what were the parent problems, to understand the family structure, and to clarify whether other jurisdictions had been involved with the family. Magistrates also considered whether what was presented at court was a repeated problem and whether there was an immediate possibility of change in the child's situation. Magistrates stated that they preferred to avoid the idea of a 'check list' (M 14) as matters were best decided on a case by case, and evidentiary, basis. They conceded however that particular parent problems and the particular nature of the case did often suggest issues for consideration.

Magistrates relied on the case material presented to them and approached the case from that material. A number of magistrates wished they could inquire independently into cases but accepted that they were dependent on the child protection service to present the necessary information. Magistrates suggested that they took the same approach in deciding all child protection matters but the observation and interviews found there were differences in their approach according to the nature of the case. Yet they acknowledged that a specific child abuse problem generated specific questions for consideration and acknowledged also that there was a hierarchy of difficulty across cases; more straightforward matters were readily resolved while other cases demanded greater levels of proof. Cases that appeared to be straightforward, and were described by magistrates in these terms, were cases which were more amenable to a legal resolution. Cases which made sense to magistrates, that is cases in which the child protection concerns were justified and the child protection service proposals were congruent with magistrate assessment, were also considered straightforward. Cases which challenged magistrate beliefs, or which were not legally well supported, or were about matters which were unfamiliar to magistrates, were considered more difficult to resolve. All magistrates referred to the conflicting aims of the Children's Court work: the court was required to ensure the continuity of the family as well as ensuring the safety of the children. These aims were contradictory in some child abuse matters.

The vagueness of the notion of 'significant harm' was a difficulty for magistrates. 'It is a very unscientific thing' (M 01), and the criteria used to decide it varied across magistrates and welfare practitioners alike. This provided little certainty and consistency for decision-makers. It also provided for inconsistent intervention in families. One magistrate suggested that:

> Significant harm just seems to me to be one of those catch calls that you use to put on as a criterion in a situation (M 07).

Nine magistrates did refer to long-term risk and significant damage to a child to decide significant harm:

> Significant damage ... which may have some lasting or permanent effect unless resolved by the intervention of counselling and treatment (M 02).

Another magistrate commented that:

> I can't say that I applied some definition of 'significant' – it seemed to me to mean serious harm, the risk of serious harm (M 09).

However, in deciding about significant harm:

It was a matter of just listening to the evidence and coming to a view about how serious – in the place of physical harm – how serious the injury was, how likely you thought that the harm would be repeated and how successful you thought that some sort of intervention in the family life would be with the child remaining at home ... in the end there is no line you can draw in the sand, you have to hear the evidence (M 09).

The safety of the child in all aspects of that child's development is the central thing for me (M 06).

Decisions about significant harm, three magistrates said, had to be:

reasonable and applicable ... feeling a reasonable satisfaction with your decision (M01).

Magistrates also considered:

It was important to consider the best interests of the child were being preserved according to the legislation by remaining in the family as much as possible, but in the end if the harm was significant or the risk of harm was significant, you had to make some other order ... it all depended on the evidence and what came out in the hearing (M 09).

Decisions however, are ultimately made by considering:

Where I think the right comes down (M 03).

Magistrates were asked if the nature of the allegations made about a case influenced their decision-making. How might it make a difference to the factors they look for in deciding child protection matters if the case involved physical, sexual or emotional abuse, or parent problems of substance abuse, psychiatric disorder, intellectual disability? When magistrates spoke about individual cases, it was apparent that the nature of the case and the evidence presented did affect decision-making. Cases where the parent's problems were straightforward or were long-standing and no longer amenable to counselling, or where it was clear a parent had a good chance of rehabilitation, were easier to decide. Cases in which there is sufficient evidence available, for example, forensic evidence in a physical abuse case, are also more straightforward:

If you are making the decision, if you have to be a decision-maker, you are looking to grasp onto things. Things like physical abuse. Things that you can see, that you can be satisfied about quite easily – they are easier to grasp (M 03).

I think if there is drug-taking or drinking to the extent where ... where you can't be sure of the child's safety, then I would take the child away. Or if there were severe abuse, like fractures, if there was severe abuse like fractures or other injuries, I would take a child away (M 07).

The uncertainty about what constitutes child abuse and their unfamiliarity with how child protection judgements are made, created difficulties for magistrates in their assessments of information about the impact of the alleged abuse on the child. Behaviours now defined as child abuse have only recently come within the legal domain. Boss (1995:134) notes there are varying legal definitions of child maltreatment and varying protocols for dealing with it. There is a lack of consensus amongst legal professionals and social workers: on what constitutes child abuse, the best interests of a child and on what is appropriate intervention to ameliorate child abuse (King and Trowell 1992, Ronnau and Poertner 1989; Parker, Summer and Jarvis 1989). Moreover, Clark (1995) determined that community ambivalence about state intervention in family life which, combined with an uncertainty about what constitutes child abuse, makes courts reluctant to support child protection interventions. Certainly, the lack of legislative definition of what is meant by the best interests of the child, or what is significant harm, and the lack of scientific established criteria, made these decisions difficult for magistrates. They were reliant on evidence and reports to the court yet the often ambiguous nature of these provided magistrates with few cues for assessment. This ambiguity appeared to be understood by some magistrates as evidence that child protection workers lacked competence rather than as the consequence of the inherent difficulties in substantiating child abuse. Garbarino (1986) argued however that the variability of family functioning makes it very difficult to provide such fixed criteria.

Parent problems such as psychiatric disorder, intellectual disability, and substance abuse appeared to direct magistrates to consider particular issues. They were issues such as parental ability to care for the child, the intensity and duration of the parent problems, the likelihood of rehabilitation for a parent, the degree to which a parent's impairment interfered with their personal functioning, and a parent's apparent motivation to change. Magistrates also considered the extent to which the impairment in a parent constituted a risk to the child.

Cases of physical abuse were considered by magistrates to be more straightforward because evidence and proof was usually available. However this was not often the situation in cases of emotional abuse:

> If it's physical, and a broken limb, then that's easy. But how can you tell psychological harm? (M 07).

They were cases which were not straightforward because there was a lack of agreement about what actions constituted emotional abuse, and the assessment of emotional abuse involved value judgements that were a concern to magistrates. Magistrates were reluctant to make decisions which could not be supported by hard evidence.

Magistrates said they needed to think differently about cases of sexual abuse. Evidence in these matters is very often based on disclosures made by children, and on child protection workers' assessments. The lack of evidence created great uncertainty about such decisions most particularly when the child protection application sought the removal of the perpetrator from the family:

> They are different because if you are talking about sexual abuse or physical abuse it's a more forensic exercise so you are dealing with more points of proof ... the emotional abuse is much harder because there are so many value-laden judgements on the part of the social workers and on my part too. I think they are very different fact-finding exercises (M 14).

Two-thirds of the magistrates referred to the different standard of proof required to prove sexual and physical abuse allegations. Magistrates had to ensure these cases were properly proven:

> If you say we have a principle here of the presumption of innocence on criminal matters it's got to be established, you have got to prove before you can invoke the sanction of the law (M 08).

Nine magistrates confirmed that the best interests of the child was the central issue they had to decide in child protection matters. Magistrates varied however in the ways they defined and decided the best interests of the child:

> I try to see what's been happening for that child in the evidence that's before me, and what it has meant for that child to be living in that particular environment (M 06).

> I basically did it on the evidence before me, what was alleged and verbalised. What can I say, it was then a question – does that strike me as serious harm? Would I, is that something that ought to be tolerated within a family for a child? (M 03).

Some magistrates did refer to very child-specific factors to assess best interests. What a child's wishes might be, how parents speak about a child, whether a child's situation ought to be tolerated, were matters raised by seven magistrates when considering the child's best interests. Parents' wishes were an important influence:

> It's often very difficult to not take into account the parents' wishes as well because obviously the parents are very emotional and often there are situations where parents are genuinely involved and desire ... their children (M 02).

Magistrates were also mindful that their decisions ought to reflect community standards about child care and unacceptable risk to a child, and asked themselves if a decision was reasonable or appropriate given the family circumstances and the parent's motivation for change:

> What one would expect from your general knowledge of society (M 12).

> What you think is reasonable or appropriate given human experience and understanding (M 01).

The options available for a child, the parent's capacity and willingness to change, and the origin of the current problem, were also important considerations:

> Is the child going to be at risk of abuse – it must be given high priority. Overall capacity to care, is there some psychiatric disturbance and they are the difficult cases; it's very difficult to know whether it was just at that point in time the person could not care for the child or whether it was a longer term process ... (M 13).

One magistrate noted that the age of a child was important in determining a child's best interests:

> It might be a little toddler, you are saying I don't want to give up yet, I want to try and keep it with its mother. So sometimes if it's younger you might be trying harder to keep it with its mother (M 14).

Another magistrate looked for whether the parent could guarantee their child's safety, whether there were sufficient resources to support the family and whether the parent would cooperate with the child protection service. This magistrate also paid particular attention to what were the child's wishes and to how the child presented in court.

The pull between the continuity of family on the one hand, and the safety of the child on the other, was a constant concern: the dilemma of protecting a child from harm and yet keeping a family together as much as possible was mentioned by five magistrates. The legislative imperative of family preservation was a powerful influence on magistrates who relied also on their own judgements about, and experiences of, family life and parental roles in their decision-making. Magistrates in this study appeared to always look for ways in which a child could remain with their family and to incorporate this into their decision.

However, one magistrate was concerned that the aim of keeping a family together as much as possible and complying with legislative requirements may mean sending a child back home when it may not be the best option (M 02). Yet, another magistrate suggested that since there was mandatory reporting of child abuse there was a sufficient safety net for children, so that if their return home was unsuccessful, they could get help.

Magistrates said another important consideration was the circumstances of the alleged child abuse. Magistrates wanted to know whether the abuse was the result of one action which happened at one point in time or had occurred over a greater period of time. Where the child abuse appeared uncharacteristic of a parent and the parent was accepting of help, then magistrates accepted that a child's best interests clearly remained with their parents. However:

> Always the issue was whether or not the person was capable of adequately caring and tending the child in their care and the nature of the bond that was in existence (M 15).

Magistrates emphasised the importance of involving families and children to decide their best interests in an attempt to preserve children's bonds with their families:

> We try very hard not to say anything that a parent will go away feeling they have been very much personally judged ... [it is] important for the children to feel part of the process because they do have an awareness that we are making decisions about their lives (M 06).

Magistrates found it a challenge to reconcile their considerable legal training and expertise with the decision-making demands of the Children's Court:

> Actual fact-finding was extraordinarily difficult given the competing versions of the facts emerging especially when you had to deal with the hearsay evidence of very young children (M 12).

The case-specific approach meant magistrates were unaware of court outcomes in the other courts. Yet it was not unusual for one child protection matter with similar presenting problems to follow another with different outcomes for seemingly similar problems. Magistrates clearly varied in how they weighed case factors, or case information, to assist their decisions. However, professionals who offered the court independent objective information were greatly valued. However, one magistrate noted that the worth of such evidence was dependent on 'the standard of the person who made the statement' (M 12).

The Availability and Utility of Case Information

Parker, Sumner and Jarvis (1989) and Brown (1991) found that the information available to magistrates about a case was a significant influence on decision-making. The magistrates in their study found difficulty in obtaining enough, and appropriate, information to assist decision-making. Brown (1991) in her study also found that magistrates were frustrated by the variability of information contained in social reports, and the variability in its utility to magistrates. Reports prepared by social workers were singled out for comment by magistrates in the Parker, Sumner and Jarvis (1989) study. They commented that they needed to 're-code the content to objectively assist them' (1989:101). Magistrates in the Brown (1991) study believed that the welfare professionals viewed social information about a case as of greater importance to the court decision than legal considerations. Magistrates in the Children's Court study commented that it was their role to look first to the legal possibilities for the case rather than assume a welfare orientation.

Schon (1983:42) also found that magistrates were often critical of child protection workers' competence; they referred to the 'confusing messes' of child welfare practice. Judges in the study by Martinez (1980) found social workers' evidence and child protection court reports often failed to convey the importance of welfare concerns or explain the clinical reasons why the concerns represented significant risk to a child.

Magistrates in the Children's Court study were critical of the child protection court reports. They emphasised they had to rely on the information the child protection service supplies the court; they looked to the reports to find clear information about why there are child protection concerns, and the facts that support these concerns, and the facts that justify intervention in a family. Magistrates expressed frustration about the utility of this information and by their inability to obtain more, and more useful, information about a case. Yet often in child protection cases the facts about a child's situation were not completely known and might have been impossible to obtain. Furthermore, the facts about the child protection concerns may have been based on the social worker's interpretation of events rather than on actual accounts as there may have been no physical or forensic evidence available to support the allegations.

Magistrates were particularly critical of what they believed were judgmental accounts and the selective use of information about a family to provide less than objective reports for the court. The frustrations of magistrates with the provision of information to the court at times coloured their assessment of the validity of welfare concerns. This had implications for how child protection workers were viewed as witnesses in court particularly when their court reports were unfavourable to a family.

However, in reality the experimental studies noted in the literature found that the particular factors that influenced judicial decisions factors were not always entirely located in case material and might in fact be external to the court reports (Hood and Sparks 1972; Kapardis and Farrington 1981; Lovegrove 1988 and MacKnight (1989). This was certainly typical of the child protection matters in this study. They were cases which were subject to numerous external influences because they required the court to hear the opinion of other professionals and to negotiate with other agencies to assist the work of the court. It was apparent in this study that a significant amount of decision-making in child protection cases did occur prior to the court appearance to ensure the family support services could be provided and the case recommendations be implemented. The reality that decision-making in child protection cases could not be determined by legal factors alone, and that it involved parties outside the courtroom, was noted by magistrates as a considerable source of frustration for them. Ballenden, Laster and Lawrence (1992:3) had also found that in cases involving welfare and social issues, a substantial amount of decision-making may in fact be made prior to court: 'the real gatekeeper is the step prior to the law-maker or law-keeper'.

Decision Influences

The social and psychological nature of Children's Court matters, and the lack of acknowledgement of these issues within the legal framework, meant magistrates relied on their discretion, and therefore on personal frameworks and individual life experience both to comprehend welfare concerns and to formulate appropriate responses to them. These personal frameworks varied across the individual magistrates although their views on the needs of the child for stability of care and responsible parenting were generally shared. It was the degree to which these views were pursued which varied across magistrates as they exercised their discretion when making child protection decisions. Whilst magistrates therefore first ensured that their decisions were in accordance with legal principles, they then referred, as Hogarth (1987) suggested magistrates do, to their views and intuition about cases before they formed their decision.

Bond and Lemon (1981) and Lawrence and Homel (1987) found that legal decision-makers did develop specific schemas to process case information. It was apparent in this study that magistrates developed such schema to assess the information provided about a case and to direct their thinking about case outcome. The problem of parental substance abuse was one example of this.. A number of magistrates believed that with substance abusing parents there was 'nothing intrinsically wrong with them as parents other than their own difficulties' (M 11). Magistrates who held this view were more willing to maintain children with their parents in the hope that the parents would have treatment and improve their parenting. Other magistrates saw substance abuse as very serious and as an indicator of the need to remove a child from their parents' care.

Saks and Kidd (1980) confirmed the influence of intuitive judgements, and stereotypes, when decision-makers are confronted by problems about which they have limited knowledge and little experience. Magistrates in this study all spoke about their unfamiliarity with child protection cases and the lack of assistance they are given with information about these issues. Therefore they relied on other sources of information, such as past experience and memory, to assist their decision-making. Relying on memory can also be misleading as it might be based on flawed associations of events or ideas. Moreover, Nisbett and Ross (1980) found that an individual's initial judgement can be resistant to further information about a situation if they have to discard information they value. Particular cues about an event or a person evoked specific responses in magistrates. One such stereotype was the 'granny factor', that is to say the positive view about the importance of grandparents, which influenced magistrates to accept a substitute care plan for children by their grandparents regardless of child protection requests to assess their capacity to care for the grandchild:

> Why is the Department involved ... the child is with a grandparent ... why is it a problem to be with Grandma and mum ... does it matter if Grandma won't accept [the mother's psychiatric problems]? (M 05).

McKnight (1981) found that magistrates' sentencing behaviour did reflect their world view. This has particular implications for the selection and value of information used to decide a case. Magistrates in this study, for example, gave more credence to information which conformed to legal principles. Magistrates' commitment to the principles of personal and family autonomy, which emerged in this study, meant they could not always accommodate the different circumstances of child abuse cases. This was particularly difficult when the case circumstances required intervention in families and suggested the separation of children from their parents. The culture of magistrate decision-making is that it is a legal process and so legal interests must predominate and these receive priority over welfare concerns. While child protection concerns must be viewed seriously this was to be done within the legal framework. Where welfare and justice interests conflicted, as for example in cases where the separation of very young children from their mothers was recommended, magistrates insisted that legal principles must prevail, in the absence of anything which suggested otherwise. One magistrate noted that decisions which separated children from their families were judicially unpopular and a magistrate who was seen to make them too readily or too often might be criticised by their peers.

Knowledge of, and ideas about, childhood development varied considerably across magistrates. The majority of magistrates referred to adult-oriented or parent-oriented factors to assist decisions and referred to a parent's chances for rehabilitation, their motivation to change, their willingness to engage in counselling, as assessment factors. Only two magistrates referred to child developmental needs as a factor to consider. Both these magistrates were themselves the parents of younger children. A number of the magistrates were parents and referred to the need to know the child's point of view about what has happened, and referred to their personal beliefs about the needs for nurturing and stability in a child's life. However, magistrates found it difficult to deny determined parents the right to retain their children even when they had few parenting skills. Parental determination to retain their children was also viewed by magistrates as a positive sign about a family. In reality there was often little available information at court about the range of welfare concerns that were part of child protection cases. There was little information available, for example, to assist magistrates in understanding the impact of parental psychiatric disorder on their children and hence to make the most appropriate decision in these circumstances.

Hogarth (1981) also found that the decision strategies used by decision-makers were influenced by how an individual conceptualised the world which in turn influenced the importance they attached to information and what information they selected to make sense of decision situations. Magistrates said they referred to their own life experience to assess the social factors in child protection cases. This may explain the different emphases magistrates give to particular aspects in a case and the variability in their decision-making. Magistrates clearly varied in how they defined child abuse and differed on what behaviours constituted abuse and how seriously they were to be taken.

Magistrate reliance on the legal framework and the adversarial approach meant the availability of case information was of particular importance to the court. Magistrates could act only on the case material presented to them at court. Cases were more readily resolved if evidence was available. In the absence of good evidence, or if legal representatives negated the child protection concerns, magistrates return to the heuristics, the cognitive schema they develop (e.g. that it is best for children to remain with their parents), and on the presumptions derived from their legal training (e.g. the inadmissibility of hearsay evidence). The problem of family violence was an example of this issue. A court decision might be made about, for example parents' access to a child, without reference to the broader context of family violence and to the inability of parents to cooperate about access.

The factors that magistrates selected as influences on their decisions were linked to their perceptions about the cases which came before them. All the magistrates agreed that generally the families who were before the court were more female single parent families, with little income. The majority of magistrates expressed concern about the lack of fathers in these children's lives. They referred also to the increasing number of merged families appearing before the court. Many of the magistrates noted intergenerational child abuse as a factor in these families, and also a history of welfare contact.

The analysis of court records revealed that cases most typically presented to the court involved children between birth and four years of age. They were usually before the court because of physical abuse or the risk of physical harm to the child, or concerns about the child's physical development or neglect of the child. Emotional abuse was often included as a coexisting ground of the application. Family violence figured prominently in the grounds for protection applications. Poor parenting practices accounted for the majority of problems bringing the cases to court. Parents typically had drug and alcohol abuse problems, psychiatric disorders, little income, little education, were very young, and often had few employment prospects.

Four magistrates were concerned about the extent of emotional abuse which appeared in cases before the court. Parental problems with substance abuse and psychiatric problems were the most common problems in applications based on emotional abuse. Emotional abuse as the primary ground of a protection application predominated among children aged five to ten years. It was of great concern to magistrates as it is an allegation that is difficult to prove. The emergence of sexual abuse of children was noted by most of the magistrates as a growing problem for the court, and the difficulties magistrates experienced with sexual abuse cases have already been documented. These cases provoked powerful personal reactions in magistrates. They were cases that were nearly always contested, with both parents energetically legally represented, and they were cases that required high levels of proof. The survey data showed that the perpetrators in child sexual cases were as likely to be the mother's partner or male sibling as the child's father.

Magistrates did refer to particular knowledge to justify their decisions. All magistrates referred to knowledge about infant-mother bonding and attachment and were unsympathetic to child protection recommendations that the protection of a child might require separation of the child from their parents even for a short time. However each magistrate individually defined attachment and bonding behaviours. The majority of magistrates operationalised attachment as the physical co-location of a child with their mother. Therefore the desire to preserve attachment was cited as the reason for the court's emphasis that parents must have access to their children, even when the child had been out of the parent's care for some time.

This influence of idiosyncratic views was apparent also in magistrates' attitudes to counselling. Parents who agreed to have counselling were favourably viewed by many magistrates as it suggested the possibility for change in a family's situation. Yet not all situations were amenable to family counselling, most particularly cases of child sexual abuse where counselling for the perpetrator was not necessarily of benefit to the child. However, because counselling was viewed so favourably, the court depended on the existence of treatment programs and family support programs to effect change in families.

Information or research which suggested that counselling was not always appropriate was likely to be ignored by the court.

Brown (1991) raised the issue of cultural appropriateness of measures applied to defendants before the court. A similar view could be taken of the interventions most favoured by magistrates in child protection matters in this study. The majority of the magistrates took a 'pathology' oriented view that all behaviours were amenable to change, if the right treatment was available. They also took the view that child abuse is a problem which can be ameliorated because parents have a natural propensity to love their children and are aware of, and conscientious about, resolving their problems, what Dingwall, Eekelaar and Murray (1983) describe as the rule of optimism. This view might get in the way of the magistrate considering the child protection concerns from the child's point of view or from considering what child abuse research might suggest about the possibility of change with certain families and certain behaviours. It also fails to account for the limits on resources that are available to assist families.

Another persuasive view amongst magistrates, which was both personally and legally congruent with their principles, was that families found their way into the Children's Court because they lacked the resources to seek alternative help. Magistrates believed also that it was prevailing social conditions that significantly contributed to child abuse. They therefore placed great emphasis on the provision of support services to facilitate changes, rather than embrace alternative propositions put by child protection workers. Magistrates therefore explained the causes of child maltreatment in the social-situational and sociological terms as described by Boss (1995). Despite a preference for treatment programmes as a resolution for child maltreatment cases, and the individual pathology orientation this might suggest, as the explanation of child abuse, magistrates in this study preferred societal explanations.

As well as relying on individual frameworks to decide cases a magistrate's personal satisfaction with a decision was an important test of decision-making in this study. Decision theory confirms that individual decision-makers select information about situations which conforms to their experience and personal biases so that decision outcomes are both familiar and comfortable. The mind-sets or cognitive schema developed by judicial decision-makers need to be understood in order to understand what factors are important to the case decision (Ashworth 1984; Asquith 1983). It was clear from the court observations that individual magistrates reacted differently to the range of child abuse issues. Cases of child sexual abuse evoked particular responses from magistrates. Several magistrates noted in interview that child sexual abuse allegations were too readily made without regard to their significant consequences. There was a view amongst magistrates that children's disclosures may not be always entirely accurate, in contrast to child protection workers who always responded to such disclosures. The views of welfare professionals could not always disabuse magistrates of ideas or experiences salient to them and evoked by cases of child sexual abuse.

Magistrates were influenced by their attitudes to the welfare bureaucracy, and their views about the work practices of child protection workers and the way in which they presented matters at court. As mentioned earlier child protection court reports were very often based on the child protection worker's assessment of the child's problems. Whilst the assessment often included the accounts of other relevant professionals such as teachers, nurses, and other welfare practitioners, it was not usual to have any forensic evidence, photographs or eyewitness accounts. The view that cases were based more on welfare than legal fact, combined with uncertainty about the professional expertise of child protection workers, did at times bias magistrates' views about the validity of child protection concerns and the recommendations about these. Yet analysis of the court records shows that magistrates' decisions generally agreed with the statutory welfare authority recommendations. Where there was disagreement, it usually centred on the magistrate's preference for lesser orders.

The Magistrate Role

The role of the Children's Court magistrate is a specialist one. All magistrates described the role as substantially different from their role in any other jurisdiction. The work of the court was perceived to be more difficult, and the pressures on magistrate were greater, than in other jurisdictions. All the magistrates commented that the work of the court was not so much legally as socially and psychologically complex. It was technically frustrating because of the different rules about the admission of hearsay evidence and the conduct of hearings. Three magistrates who did not find the role of the Children's Court magistrate as personally difficult as the others believed that the Children's Court allowed greater creativity in decision-making. Whilst it might not test the magistrate as a lawyer it allowed them to draw on other skills and life experiences.

Given the complexity and difficulty of child protection matters, the way in which magistrates saw their role had an important bearing on their management of the court process. Magistrates are trained to be objective and to adjudicate disputes between parties. Their objectivity requires them to not be unduly influenced by issues other than those which are directly related to the case in hand. How magistrates viewed their role was also an important component of the decision frameworks they developed to respond to child protection matters. Magistrates who work in children's and family courts are increasingly being asked to resolve problems of family dysfunction (Edwards 1992:1; Swain 1989:229). This requires them to work with professional groups who have practice interests which are different from their own. Moreover they are required to decide about social problems, problems which are not readily addressed by court process and about which there is considerable ambiguity. Magistrates suggested that their legal training did not equip them for this role. However, magistrates said it was their role to ensure that child protection workers were accountable to the court for their interventions in families. In so doing, they believed they were acting as community representatives who ensured state intervention was warranted and children were not separated from their parents without just cause. Parker, Sumner and Jarvis (1989) found that magistrates in their study believed that their judgements were more in common with community thinking than say the welfare workers' judgements about the young people who were before the court. Fitzmaurice and Pease (1986) also found that magistrates believed that their views were relatively common and represented those of the community, what is referred to as the false consensus bias. In reality the community might not share magistrates' views or judgements about child abuse matters.

Magistrates were, in general, committed to family maintenance. This at times meant that magistrates would give parents 'a chance', thereby prolonging decisions about children. The court was at times unrealistic about a parent's capacity to change and this prolonged the length of time children were left in less than satisfactory family situations. A few magistrates believed that this approach may fail to acknowledge the difficulties parents experience with their children. It also meant that what magistrates perceived as the 'real issues' in a case might not be the same as those that concerned the child protection service. Certainly, the observational findings supported this minority view. The court appeared to have fixed notions about what constituted a 'family'. The presence of parents at court, and the presence of grandparents at court as possible care-givers for children, were both viewed favourably by magistrates. There appeared to be a belief that if the child resided with their family this would secure parent/child attachment and would be powerful enough to overcome parent/child difficulties. Magistrates did not acknowledge this influence in interviews but observations and court records confirmed that when a child's parents lived together the child was more likely to be placed on an Interim Protection Order or a Supervision Order than on a higher order. Equally, a parent's stated preparedness to comply with court conditions about counselling and treatment programs was favoured by magistrates even when there had been numerous, and unsuccessful attempts, to achieve necessary changes in families.

The observational findings suggested that while magistrates generally agreed about the characteristics of their role, their behaviour in court varied. Some magistrates did not intervene and allowed cases to be run by the legal representatives. Others were considerably interventionist, most particularly when one of their valued beliefs was challenged, or the child protection worker's evidence was unhelpful. Magistrates very often advocated for the child by asking questions of the children, and by reminding parents of the seriousness of the allegations before the court. However, all magistrates saw themselves as making the child protection service accountable for their intervention in a family's life. It was the magistrate's role to balance the competing interests of children, families, and the statutory authority.

Magistrates did not regard themselves as having any role in case planning. Yet the court decision clearly directed the role, and the actions, of the child protection service. The court appearance of a case was only one aspect of the child protection service's work with a family and was undertaken to secure change in a child's circumstances. The court decision had a significant impact on how a family worked with the child protection service after court. Yet magistrates did not believe that they should consider the court appearance and decision as part of an overall plan for a child.

Child Abuse Research

All magistrates acknowledged the need for information about those issues which typically confront a children's court magistrate. Whilst they acknowledged there was some literature available to them at court and a considerable amount of material had been circulated by the senior magistrate at the time, magistrates said they needed direction about what they needed to know. Eight magistrates said they sought out material to prepare themselves and to improve their understanding of the jurisdiction. One magistrate prepared himself for his appointment to the Children's Court by obtaining and reading relevant material which was supplied by the statutory welfare authority.

One magistrate commented that whilst magistrates do need to know more about child abuse, and child abuse research, magistrates also needed to know how to apply such knowledge to decision-making. This magistrate was concerned that child abuse cases might be processed according to favoured frameworks developed by the literature, and that this might influence welfare professionals to adopt particular positions about cases and seek out case information which substantiates their protective concerns:

> But then how do you know that this case fits in the pattern ... in these [difficult] cases it's a common trap to fall into to make a decision in a difficult case and then seek to substantiate it (M 05).

Magistrates expressed concern about looking at cases in terms of categories or patterns given the legal system's emphasis on the individuality of a case. A number of legal counsel who appeared regularly at the court were interviewed by the researcher who sought their views of the Children's Court. They commented on the specialist nature of the jurisdiction and its highly individualised nature. They commented on the importance of knowing about the individual decision-making characteristics of magistrates to best present a case in court. It was their belief that a magistrate's personal philosophies shaped their understanding of case issues and that in some instances a magistrate formed a view of a case beforehand and approached the hearing in a way which reinforced that particular view.

Children's Court Decision-making

The fourth reference point for magistrates was what they considered were the available options in a case. Children's Court decisions were difficult for magistrates not only because there were few guidelines about the assessment of child abuse but also because there were limited choices for decision-makers and uncertain outcomes for children and families. They were cases in which: 'social awareness is just as important as technical competence' (Richardson 1984:547). They were difficult because child protection decision-making involves magistrates in decisions about competing social values as much as in deciding a specific dispute between individuals. They were difficult also because decision-making in child protection is decision-making in a context of uncertainty and the decisions are what Jabes (1982) described as 'non-programmed' decisions. There were no guidelines to assist magistrates with these decisions and no clear definitions of what behaviours constituted child abuse. There were no transcripts of Family Division hearings because the Children's Court is not a court of public record. There was no record made of reasons for a particular decision and hence no body of decisions to which magistrates could refer.

Magistrates' views about particular issues such as substitute care were observed to influence case decisions. Moreover, magistrates in their interviews took particular stands on issues which were personally and legally important. Magistrates' views about foster care, and about the removal of children from families were clearly linked to the contemporary accounts of children, presented in Australian media, who suffered such separations in the 1950s, 1960s, and 1970s. In the hearings in which these issues arose magistrates referred to the trauma of foster care and to media reports about these. Child protection workers were unable to dispute these claims or assure the magistrate that arrangements for a child in the particular case were entirely different from the global view the magistrate held about substitute care.

The 'one off' nature of court matters was a limitation on magistrate decision-making; they had to deal with the case as it was presented on the day of the hearing:

> people put on all sorts of fronts for the court ... one of the problems in any court, you don't know the half of it ... (M 03).

The observations suggested that magistrates had little knowledge of the professional practice of child protection workers and therefore had little sympathy with the difficulties they experienced in the investigation of child protection notifications and in the organisation of cases for court. Magistrates failed to see that if a protection application was by apprehension little may be known about a child. The apparently large number of welfare workers involved in a case, the need to assess family members before they could provide substitute care for a child before the court, and the dearth of information provided to magistrates, entrenched their beliefs that the welfare bureaucracy frustrated the court and delayed the resolution of child protection matters.

Yet, often there were no clear choices available for children and therefore few options available to magistrates when deciding cases. Although, magistrates said they found it easier to support child protection recommendations when concrete facts clearly demonstrated child protection concerns, adequate case information did not always provide ready solutions. The limited availability of support programmes and magistrate concerns about the substitute care provided for children, constrained their decision options.

Magistrate concerns about the substitute care arrangements for children have already been noted. However extended family are not always available, or appropriate, to care for children at risk. The court is then dependent on foster families or small-group homes to provide care for children who cannot live with their families. This dependence on substitute care frustrated magistrates as they had little confidence in the alternative care arrangements provided. They expressed concern about the quality of substitute care and about the disruption children experience when they have numerous, and different, care arrangements.

Numerous returns of a case to court as perhaps orders are tested means children may have numerous placements between short-term units, parents, and foster care. The same foster care arrangements may not be available to children each time they are needed. One magistrate was particularly critical in court about the issue of multiple placements for children, and critical of the child protection service for their part in this. Yet the lack of willingness of the court, and the child protection service, to decide on permanent care for children much earlier in the court process directly contributes to multiple placements for children.

The need for magistrates to observe the legislative aim of family preservation appeared at times to constrain their decision-making. This was evident when permanency planning for a child was presented as the best option. Keeping a child with their family is the primary focus of the court and magistrates reminded the child protection service they had to ensure support services were provided to a family until all possible assistance was exhausted.

Magistrates and the Welfare Interface

Magistrates expressed considerable frustration with what they perceived as child protection workers' lack of knowledge about the legal system and their lack of sympathy for its procedures. They were also less than certain about the professionalism and investigative competency of the child protection service:

> You do start to wonder about 24 year olds who have never had a family and are telling people in their 40s and 50s who have three or four kids how a family should be organised. I saw a lot of families bristling ... most of the witnesses are always going to be young because when they are senior they stay at the office (M 12).

What the law might establish as truth might be very different from what the child protection worker has experienced in their intervention in a family (Smart 1989). The system of opposites which operates at court, which requires parties to present opposing accounts, does little to give validity to child abuse concerns. It was in contested matters that the variance between legal and welfare practice was most apparent. The mistrust of the knowledge frameworks child protection workers use to verify child protection concerns was obvious in these hearings. A dismissive attitude towards child protection workers' testimony, the level of personal denigration and discrediting of such testimony, and the trivialising of the concerns they raised in their reports, created an oppositional environment in court that was unhelpful for practitioners and children alike:

> Magistrates are used to having to decide cases on the best evidence, decide on the quality of the evidence and then be confronted with evidence here which often is very ordinary and which often is not supported very well by the supervisor either (M 02).

Magistrates had difficulty with the way child protection workers prepared and presented their cases for court and this appeared to make them unsympathetic to child protection workers' claims. Much of the difficulty appeared to be with the nature of the evidence the child protection service gathered to support their claims about cases:

> [Child protection workers] have no legal training – and in my view they present as fearful, arrogant, give often one-sided reports and that can be very difficult when you are trying to assess evidence. Social workers don't understand the concept of 'hearsay'. In the Children's Court while there are not rules of evidence, yet social workers don't understand they have to report what they observe (M 05).

The evidence child protection workers present to the court is very often hearsay evidence and the facts of a case are the child protection workers' assessments of child and family functioning, together with information from other family, teachers, welfare workers, nurses etc. Whilst the legislation allows for the admission of hearsay evidence, magistrates and legal representatives have some difficulty accepting this. Child protection workers are often reliant on children's disclosures of abuse or on the accounts of teachers, child carers, and other family members to substantiate allegations of abuse. Preparation for court is difficult when, for example, families decline to cooperate with the child protection service, or when children are very young and cannot disclose information, or when numerous other professionals are involved in a case. Child protection workers believed the court was unsympathetic to these difficulties.

Magistrates acknowledged that child protection workers were more familiar with the family problems in the case before them. However, their view that they could not always rely on the accuracy of child protection information frustrated them. So too, did their difficulty as lawyers in accepting hearsay evidence. Magistrates mistrusted such evidence because they believed it was often one-sided, biased, and focused only on a family's weaknesses. Magistrates also expressed frustration at being confined by the material which was put before them as they could not carry out their own investigation.

However, child protection workers believed that the legislation was used in a more adversarial way than was required and hearsay evidence could be used, although magistrates would still want evidence to be relevant. Child protection workers were often unprepared for this process and did not have the benefit of legal advice, especially in the early stages of cases, when it looked likely that the case might be contested. Child protection workers also expressed concern about the magistrate's lack of control over the court process, over the length of hearings, over how legal practitioners conducted their cases in court and over how child protection workers are often treated by the court.

Many child protection cases do not have the forensic evidence, photographs, eyewitness accounts – the definite, confirming ('hard') evidence that is central to the adversarial system. Seven magistrates believed the child protection service:

> Social workers select out the information that suits them (M 05).

And one magistrate believed that social workers':

> desire to include pointless details about the things and the necessity to put them into reports, gratuitously put the boot in..parents would read the reports ... and ... get cheesed off (M 12).

And, further:

> go into the witness box, throw a report at you which would run the whole gamut from day one with every minor detail (M 12).

The lack of conventional evidence frustrated both magistrates and child protection workers alike. Yet, proof of harm or risk to a child is often difficult to produce except in some cases of physical abuse and sexual abuse. Therefore child protection workers commented that they felt they had to be very convincing as to why the actions of a particular family were abnormal.

Twelve magistrates believed the quality of evidence provided by child protection workers at times hampered the hearing of a case. One magistrate noted that when the child protection worker presents only one side of a case they fail to provide magistrates with decision options (M 02):

> A very important part of our task is to be aware of situations in which you lose objectivity and make sure you retain your objectivity (M 13).

Magistrates commented that they could not consistently rely on child protection evidence as this evidence as it was often incomplete, not sufficiently objective, perhaps quite nebulous and that it was presented by inexperienced workers:

> Some of the social workers were wonderful, particularly the senior ones ... some of the younger ones, it's a terrible thing to say, but the more life experience I have the more I think you need ... I think some of the inexperienced social workers are a little bit guilty of interpreting children's behaviours and events without a lot of knowledge (M 14).

Yet, child protection workers commented that it was often impossible to reduce what were broad and difficult problems of child abuse down to the court's preference for more narrowly focused family problems. For example it was easier to convey concerns for a child if they could be described in terms of a specific parenting problem, or a parent's chronic illness, rather than as pervasive child neglect. The child protection service had difficulty persuading the court that their views about the significance of particular events in a child's physical, cognitive, and emotional state were well founded. What is acceptable parenting is a vexed question throughout the community and the court was mindful that it needed to be flexible in its judgments about this.

The dichotomy between the gathering of evidence for child protection purposes and the legal principles which govern evidence contributed to the difficulties magistrates experienced with child protection matters. The decision to seek a child protection application may not be made until the investigation is completed and so the case is presented as it was gathered – for the child protection investigation – not necessarily with a court appearance in mind. Therefore, evidence to support child protection concerns may appear incomplete, be substantially based on hearsay or the child protection worker's impressions; it may be presented in a way which is not legally coherent:

> [evidence that is] like a patch work quilt made up of notes taken by other people, conversations with other people. They take it out of an enormous file. Often they haven't been directly involved in the matters they are discussing (M 05).

This frustrates magistrates and legal representatives alike who believe that where there is a likelihood of court action, cases ought to be conducted with legal principles in mind, with child protection workers having:

> training about the courtroom, about writing reports and about how to handle evidence in court (M 14).

A further frustration was with the language used by child protection workers in their descriptions and definitions of 'at risk' behaviours, information that when presented in court reports and testimony often did not make much sense to magistrates:

> I get frustrated with the terminology and lack of experience (M 01).

Giving evidence about parents and children was not straightforward for child protection workers. The need to present the court with facts about a family's problems had to balanced with the reality that the child protection service had to preserve a relationship with the child and family, after the court appearance. There appeared to be little appreciation by the court of this pressure on child protection workers: that the disclosure of private and sensitive information may threaten the relationship families have with the welfare authority, on whom they often rely for support so that they can retain the care of their children:

> The same social workers who would bring the cases before the court in an adversarial setting claiming that this parent wasn't appropriate, might be the same social workers who were supervising that parent and that's an enormous constraint because it's an absolute no-win situation for the parent (M 14).

> That was a constant difficulty. You would have a mother with resentment for the social worker with whom she previously got on really well when she was helping her, but when the social worker saw things getting out of hand she would bring an application and then they were adversaries (M 11).

Magistrates generally acknowledged the difficulties and complexities of child protection work. There did appear to be a limited understanding that at the end of the hearing welfare practitioners still have to work with a family:

[Even if] the case isn't presented as lawyers would like it, but that's a minor point. It shouldn't affect the running, I don't have a lot of disagreement with the social workers. I don't always agree with their recommendations but it's my job to decide that, that's not a problem, they've got their job and I've got mine. It was only niggling things about presentation, by and large I found their work acceptable (M 12).

Four magistrates believed child protection workers are competent, if perhaps a bit judgmental at times. They acknowledged their genuine desire to assist children and their families:

I think on the whole workers, their knowledge is very good and they are doing a good job (M 06).

Three magistrates referred to the relative youth and lack of work experience of some child protection workers. Whilst magistrates believed child protection workers generally acted in good faith, their inexperience undermined their capacity to be helpful to the court:

We don't provide the community with experienced well-paid welfare workers who are able to maintain the job and come up with the best recommendation (M 15).

It's always been an issue that you are dealing with very young social workers who might be overzealous and can't substantiate their position, but I just think they're green and I don't see the point in alienating them or attacking them (M 13).

The adversarial system assumes there is a contest between equals, yet in child protection matters there are few examples of contests between equal parties. The need to dispute the validity of child protection concerns, which often involved discrediting parents or child protection workers, did little to encourage cooperation between welfare and legal practitioners and did little to encourage parents to accept the need to modify family behaviour to retain their children. Magistrates did, however, prefer as much as possible to encourage agreement between parties and referred cases for pre-hearing conferences to assist this.

Magistrates expressed particular frustration with the bureaucratic nature of the child protection service and their antipathy to bureaucratic processes appeared to influence court decisions. Magistrates believed that welfare bureaucracy did not always respect the autonomy of the court and, at times, sought to exert control over court proceedings. The lack of autonomy of, and lines of authority for, child protection workers contributed to this view:

> One of the problems with the social worker is that she was also carrying a torch for the Department. She was the policeman, the prosecutor, as well as the witness. That made it difficult. She was out there to win her case. If I decide this child is to be put into care – 'What's your objective opinion in this situation?' I say, and that often got mixed up. That's a failing in the system (M 01).

Magistrate requests that a protective worker vary a child protection service recommendation or propose an alternative course of action generally needed to be authorised by a more senior child protection worker away from the court. The need for the worker to consult with their supervisor before they could respond greatly frustrated magistrates. The lack of immediacy of response from DHS to a magistrate request was viewed as an example of the interference of the bureaucracy with the running of the court.

Two magistrates commented on what they believed to be the fixed criteria child protection workers used to arrive at their recommendations for a case at court. They believed these criteria were frequently overly judgmental and their expectations of parents too high. Magistrates suggested child protection workers are black and white about what is acceptable parenting. Four magistrates expressed a view that this inflexibility may stem not just from a lack of experience but also from a particular culture that existed within the welfare bureaucracy. It was suggested that the bureaucratic nature of the child protection service contributed to such difficulties. One magistrate believed there was a culture of compliance within the statutory welfare authority, that it was a hierarchical structure which curtailed the independence of its workers:

> A culture which pervades the bureaucracy ... of people not wanting to make mistakes ... (M 08).

Magistrates said they decided cases as 'a case by case thing' (M 11). Three magistrates believed the child protection service adopted particular positions on specific child abuse issues and expected the court to support these positions. They referred to these as 'ideological positions' which they believed were particularly evident in cases of family violence and child sexual abuse. Two magistrates expressed a view that the welfare bureaucracy selected out specific classes of cases for particular child protection attention. Magistrates were concerned that cases might be brought to court because the concern about them was based on such fixed, or preconceived positions, rather than focused on case-specific concerns:

> There is a lack of quality in the workers evidence ... often you find what they've done is extremely one-sided, biased, they fix on a particular position ... (M 02).

> Their reports are full of a totally one-sided story. Everything that helps their case they put in, everything that doesn't, they leave out, they are not professional (M 07).

A number of magistrates noted resistance from child protection workers when questioned about their recommendations. One magistrate suggested that when the court sought information about the basis on which a case was presented at court, or questioned recommendations, the child protection workers viewed this as unnecessarily intrusive:

> One of the problems that arises is that somehow or other the courts are intruding, obstructing good management (M 08).

However, the legislation provides limited decision options. Both magistrates and child protection workers viewed each other as inflexible and not pragmatic in their decisions and recommendations.

Six magistrates expressed concern about what they perceived as the too swift intervention of the child protection service. These magistrates believed that child protection intervention should remain an action of last resort. One magistrate suggested it was the inexperience of many child protection workers that led to unnecessary interference in family lives, they looked:

> At things much more seriously than I would (M 03).

Four magistrates suggested child protection workers too readily removed children:

> In the short term they [DHS] often seem to be separating children and they have a lot of difficulty persuading me that children are better off in foster care than they are with their own parents (M 07).

Magistrates also suggested that child protection workers were not consistent in their responses to children and families. One magistrate believed that families who cooperated with DHS were more likely to be positively viewed and assisted by the child protection services who:

... work really well with people who are pliable (M 02).

Difficult clients received different treatment from DHS and were perhaps not offered the same options. Two magistrates commented that where clients are perceived as difficult, child protection workers asked for different, stronger orders:

> Which reflect their inability to relate to the parents as much as the fact that they really believe this is the right order of the moment (M 02).

Two magistrates believed children are too readily removed in times of family crisis, and were more likely to be removed when their parents were not cooperating with DHS:

> I sometimes think if you confess, you will achieve whatever you like as a parent, but if you say 'No, I'm not interested, go away, or it never happened' then you will have terrible trouble in the short term (M 10).

The genuineness of protective workers and their desire to assist children was not in question; it was the welfare approach to child protection matters that frustrated magistrates. Parents could be difficult, they were often not easy to work with and this was reflected in the case presentation:

> ... workers are making recommendations on things which reflect the inability to relate to the parents as much as the fact that they really believe this is the right order at the moment (M 02).

Yet five magistrates firmly acknowledged the good work of child protection workers. While one magistrate noted that at times the child protection service was too quick to intervene, caution was important and:

> ... generally many of the workers make sensible decisions and resolve things (M 09).

One magistrate acknowledged it is the child protection workers who see the family situation outside the court and who are more familiar with the families' problems than is the magistrate. The court environment is an artificial one and the magistrate very often has a good deal less information available to them than they would like, information which is available to the welfare professionals although they may not be able to present it at court. One magistrate acknowledged that welfare professionals who know families away from the court and who have training in child welfare greatly assist the court:

> You would have an officer of CSV [now DHS, the statutory welfare authority] who would most likely be more experienced than myself in the area of child welfare who clearly knew the family and who worked day by day with the family away from a court atmosphere because people put on all sorts of fronts for court ... one of the problems in any court, you don't know the half of it, and I often felt that in a Children's Court that in some cases you really ought to spend a week with the family (M 03).

This particular magistrate also acknowledged the court's need to clarify the child protection service's aims and case plan when deciding cases. This magistrate's acknowledgment of case planning as a consideration in decision-making was not typical in magistrate responses. In general, magistrates saw their independence from welfare authorities as essential. Only three magistrates referred to the case planning process of the child protection service, or the future expectations for a case. References to case management and case planning consequences were expressed primarily in relation to concerns about substitute care. Only nine of the 15 magistrates referred to the court hearing as a part of the welfare system process.

Another magistrate commented that whilst he did not always agree with DHS recommendations, it was his job to question case issues, just as protective workers had their job to intervene when child protection concerns are substantiated:

> They've got their job and I've got mine ... but by and large I found their work acceptable (M 12).

The tension between the need to observe the legal process yet be mindful of welfare concerns was referred to by most magistrates. They felt burdened by the kinds of decisions they were required to make, often in the absence of the independent objective case material that would be available to them in the adult jurisdiction.

The Child Welfare Jurisdiction

Parker, Sumner and Jarvis' (1989) study of judicial decision-making about young people illustrated the tension between the welfare and justice approaches which is characteristic of child protection decision-making. The contradictory views of magistrates and child protection workers are well canvassed in the study findings and magistrates commented at length in their interviews about their frustration with the welfare bureaucracy and child protection workers' practice. Magistrates' frustrations were more likely to be explained as due to the incompetence of child protection workers or their unfamiliarity with legal process rather than the consequence of the complexity of the child abuse matters.

King and Trowell (1992) referred to the dominance of the legal discourse in contemporary child protection matters and the study findings confirm this. Magistrates turned first to legal factors to interpret the welfare and child protection concerns into legally relevant issues for the court to tackle. However, the lack of guidelines, and often lack of case information meant magistrates referred to their individual frameworks, or views about an event, to extract the information needed to decide case outcome. As Lawrence (1981 et al.) and Scott (1989) had found, the mind-set of the decision-maker was an important influence on decisions. Certainly, the magistrates in this study developed individual strategies to assess the merit of cases. The substitute care schema, and the 'granny factor', that is to say the positive view about the importance of grandparents, is one that has already been referred to in this study. Another example was the 'drug habit schema' where a magistrate, when confronted by a case involving parents with drug problems would seek particular information and ask specific questions, based on the framework or schema s/he derived to decide such cases. A magistrate who held a more optimistic view about parents with drug abuse problems may focus more on parent rehabilitation and be less inclined to remove a child from their parent's care.

Decision theory confirms that individual decision-makers select information about situations which conforms to their experience and personal biases so that decision outcomes are both familiar and comfortable (Saks and Kidd 1980). Magistrates in this study all spoke about their unfamiliarity with child protection cases and the lack of assistance they are given with information about these issues. Therefore they relied on other sources of information, such as past experience and memory, to assist their decision-making. Magistrates did not readily absorb unfamiliar and empirical information about child abuse particularly when it did not fit with their personal view about what was the appropriate outcome for a case or when the information presented was at variance with what was the legally indicated resolution. Schaffer confirmed these implications in his study of child welfare decisions. He found that:

empirical knowledge about the nature of parenting plays little part in arriving at a decision, instead preoccupations are guidelines and [they] override the requirements of particular cases (1990:5).

Magistrates in this study emphasised that it was important to consider cases on their merits, and on a case by case basis. Ashworth (1984) and Asquith (1983) had also found that judges emphasised the individuality of decision-making. This individualistic approach did much to explain, Fitzmaurice and Pease (1986) suggested, the disparity in judicial decisions. It also meant that there was no predictability to judicial decision-making. In this study, magistrates did respond to particular issues which arose in cases but there were no apparent patterns in decision-making.

McKnight (1981) found that magistrates' sentencing behaviour did reflect their world view. Magistrates' commitment to the principles of personal and family autonomy, which emerged in this study, meant they could not always accommodate the different circumstances of child abuse cases. Yet magistrates needed to work with the welfare bureaucracy to process child protection matters. Their reluctance to do this was based on views such as those just noted as well as a belief that welfare professionals attempt to interfere with the autonomy of judicial decision-making in the welfare jurisdictions.

Summary

The study identified a range of factors that influenced magistrate decision-making. Magistrates looked first to legal factors, which is not unexpected given their professional training. Magistrates said they decided cases on their merits and on legislative grounds. However, what the study could not achieve was to identify the clearly defined decision-making process magistrates used in child protection cases. Magistrates resisted the idea that this was possible, or even appropriate, because of the individualised approach to the resolution of legal disputes. Yet, the study does give an insight into a previously unresearched area. It also reveals the dichotomy between legal and welfare aims in child protection and the considerable tension which therefore arises out of efforts to resolve child protection concerns at court.

The findings are especially valuable to the field of social work as they identified the role and approach of the Children's Court in child protection matters, and identify the criteria magistrates used to decide these matters. The study also identified a number of issues that confront the child protection service when bringing applications before the court. The emphasis magistrates placed on the legal character of their work and the importance of the adversarial approach to deciding cases has implications for how child protection workers prepare and present court matters. Magistrates, as qualified lawyers, operated within a legal framework and were accustomed to adversarial procedures as the way to make decisions. Cases were only readily resolved if evidence was available and legal representation organised.

The study findings emphasised the significance not only of legal, but also personal and situational factors to magistrate decision-making, although these are generally under-acknowledged by legal decision-makers. In the absence of firm evidence magistrates said they referred to personal frameworks to assist decision-making. It was apparent that magistrates did fall back on heuristics, on cognitive schema, as the literature suggests decision-makers do, in order to make decisions. Presumptions derived from their legal training such as a dislike of hearsay evidence, personal experiences such as their own parenting, or media reports such as those about the problems of foster care, were mentioned by magistrates, and observed by the researcher, as the personal frameworks and cues magistrates used.

There was a number of schema, or presumptions, which appeared particularly influential. Among them was the presumption that it is best for children to stay with their parents, and the beliefs that intact families are 'good risks', as are parents who want to keep their children and are prepared to go into treatment or counselling programmes. Another powerful belief was that failing parental acceptability, the extended family and grandmothers in particular, are preferable to foster care. The beliefs that allegations of sexual abuse are often poorly founded, and the disclosures of young children not reliable, were also influential. Magistrates responded to particular cues in cases; they responded more favourably to cases in which both parents were present at court, and were more sympathetic to parents whose substance problems were related to alcohol rather than to illegal substances such as heroin.

Magistrates emphasised the importance of their work in the Family Division and went to considerable lengths to ensure matters and parties were dealt with in the legally appropriate way. However, it was difficult work because it was not straightforward legal decision-making but rather social and psychological decision-making. They were qualified legal practitioners and, as magistrates, were clear about the role of the magistrate as the adjudicator in legal disputes. However, the role of the magistrate in the Family Division, and their control over information about the matter before the court, varied significantly. They were reliant on child protection workers to assist them yet magistrates believed the information available to them about cases was often poor. There might not be enough information, or the case issues were complex, or magistrates had to rely on hearsay evidence, or magistrates believed the information was poor because of the different approach taken by welfare practitioners to legal practitioners. Moreover, there was no body of knowledge at the court, in terms of reasons for decisions, to which they could refer for assistance. Magistrates, however, were resistant to steps which might make them more consistent and less arbitrary in their decision-making, such as the use of checklists about, say, indicators of emotional abuse, or receiving feedback about court outcomes etc.

Magistrates' decisions were therefore unpredictable and variable. Their less than positive views about child protection workers meant they could not comfortably rely on their assessments about cases. Magistrates did not view the court appearance as part of the welfare plan for a child and family. The professional culture clash between the legal/adversarial approach of lawyers and magistrates and the social welfare approach of child protection workers had significant implications for the management of child abuse matters.

Magistrates believed they had an important role in making the child protection service accountable to the court for their intervention in a family. They believed they also had a role in reminding protective workers of the need to protect parents', and children's, rights in disputes about welfare concerns. The outcome of this was that parents' rights appeared to be more protected than children's rights, and the court rarely censured parents over the treatment of their child even when a child may have sustained significant injury. The legislation created difficulty for magistrates and child protection workers alike. Whilst it set out the grounds for a protection application, it did not clearly define what was evidence of abuse, risk to a child, or a child's best interests. The legislation emphasised the importance of family preservation and the desirability of minimum state intervention in family life. In reality, this meant that family preservation appeared a higher priority than child protection and a preference for child protection orders which provided for the least intervention in a family. It meant that even when it was clear that a child needed long-term, or permanent, care this could neither be proposed by the child protection service nor considered by the court. This, combined with Clark's (1995) comments on community ambivalence about welfare interference in family life, and uncertainty about what constitutes child abuse, emerged as important themes in this study. Magistrates were often reluctant to support child protection interventions, not only because they might not conform to legislative guidelines and were not well justified, but because the interventions challenged legal principles. Child protection workers could do more however to provide information, and theoretical frameworks, to inform magistrates about child abuse and provide them with a decision framework for use in their work.

Child protection needs predictability to provide a more coherent approach to intervention in child abuse. There also needs to be more agreement between professionals about what constitutes child abuse and what constitutes appropriate intervention. Whilst magistrates remain without assistance in deciding these difficult matters this cooperative effort in child protection is not possible. Judicial decision-makers' resistance to scrutiny of their decisions, however, makes it difficult to obtain information about their decisions.

Magistrates approached their work in the Family Division with care and competence. They believed however that the difficulty of this work was unacknowledged by others. They commented that this work did not enjoy a high status in the legal system and that magistrates might prefer not to be assigned to the court because of this, and because of the emotional difficulty of the work.

The next chapter looks at approaches to child welfare dispute resolution other than within the court system. It discusses, in particular, the introduction of pre-hearing conferences and family group conferences into the child welfare jurisdictions in Australia and the success of pre-hearing conferences in the Children's Court, Victoria. It notes that such alternative processes make a very real attempt to address the marginalisation of children by the legal process.

Chapter Five

Alternative Dispute Resolution

> It's difficult in a different way. It's difficult, it's very emotional, it's not really law. You are not using legal training other than training for magistrates to make decisions. There is not much case law to know about so it's not testing you as a lawyer which the criminal jurisdiction does – its using your experience of life, trying to be objective as you can. It uses different skills altogether (M 11).

The way magistrates describe child protection decision-making in this book suggests it is not simply legal decision-making but is also social and psychological decision-making and therefore more amenable to a less adversarial approach. The specialist nature of the Children's Court jurisdiction presents magistrates with particular difficulties, a number of which have already been noted. For example, the gathering, presentation and testing of evidence to support or negate a case and the rules that govern this, are central to the adversarial system and do not easily accommodate welfare issues.

However, the court system is the system Australia has for the resolution of disputes. The Constitution provides for the judicial determination of contested matters to assure individual parties that due process is observed. Care and protection applications are heard at first instance in all Australian jurisdictions in magistrates' courts. Most jurisdictions in the last decade or so have, however, introduced some form of alternate dispute resolution either as an alternative to court proceedings or to complement the court process (Charlesworth et al. 1990; Bagshaw 1995). These other approaches to dispute resolution have been sponsored by the legal system to avoid the difficulties presented by the adversarial nature of court resolved disputes.

Hallett and Hazel (1998:16) note that fundamental questions have been raised about the appropriateness of adversarial hearings and legal discourse for decision-making in civil proceedings concerning care and protection. Considerable attention has been given to the cross-national differences in child protection systems and one of the most significant has been the comparisons between adversarial and inquisitorial systems. A comparison of these systems is canvassed in the next chapter. However, what does emerge when the comparisons are made is that the inquisitorial approach, as it operates in Europe, appears to offer a more therapeutic or rehabilitative response to child abuse as it focuses on family functioning and the amelioration of family difficulties. The adversarial system with its emphasis on legalistic, coercive and proceduralised responses both fails to provide the flexibility that child protection matters need and requires a forensic approach to investigate risk to a child and assess adult culpability whilst gathering proof of child maltreatment or neglect.

The growing use of mediation in courts and in children's matters is based on the belief that active participation by families, which might include extended family, in discussions about welfare concerns for the safety and well-being of their child can help the family and the welfare authority come to a solution that avoids litigation (Campbell 1997). It also observes the United Nations Convention on the Rights of the Child, to which Australia is a signatory nation, which sets out a child's right to be cared for, and protected by, their parents. The state is allowed to intervene only when children are being neglected or abused. Australian child welfare legislation therefore supports parents' rights to maintain their family relationships, unless these are harming the child, and to receive assistance from the community to do so.

The tensions which exist when the legal process is required to resolve welfare concerns have been well documented. Some of the issues which arise in family law disputes before the court are not readily resolved in the traditional manner of adjudicating between competing rights. Kieran McGrath (Temple Street Children's Hospital, Dublin), at the Joint European Regional Seminar on 'Social Work in a Changing Europe' (Dublin, 22–24 August 1997), commented that the conflict inherent in the adversarial approach, in which parents and the welfare authority argue their case via their legal representatives, is stressful and, one could infer, not conducive to encourage parents to change the care of their children in order to reduce risk of harm or maltreatment. The Hon. Justice Alistair Nicholson, Chief Justice, Family Court of Australia has noted that:

> research has consistently shown that litigation exacerbates hostilities and the capacity for ongoing co-operative parenting, and that early settlement has the converse effect (The Law Reform Commission, Ireland, *Report on Family Courts* 1996:54).

The pattern of increasingly costly and acrimonious child protection proceedings has led to the introduction in Australian jurisdictions of other approaches such as family group conferencing and pre-hearing conferences to avoid the difficulties presented by court-resolved disputes (Lagay et al.

1994; Swain 1996). Moreover, these approaches involve families in making significant decisions about their children that are more likely to last. The contemporary discourse about working with families in statutory settings suggests that focusing on a child's extended family, and the family's capacity to care for the child within their family, provides both a more effective response and a more effective outcome, to child abuse cases.

Hallett and Hazel (1998) suggest that the introduction of mediation schemes, and similar administrative processes, into child protection is also a response to increased representation for children and parents. They note, as do others, that it is easier for parents and children to express their views in a mediation-type forum and that the emphasis on cooperation assists families and welfare agencies to work more positively to achieve change. Pearson et al. (1986) reported that social workers, parents, lawyers and children participating in a mediation scheme in Denver, USA, in an attempt to agree on child protection case plans, found this process a useful addition to the system. Hallett and Hazel (1998:28) also report that the Flemish community in Belgium set up a mediation committee within the administrative system as an alternative to judicial intervention, to try and achieve agreement between children, parents and welfare services who are unable to reach agreement about child protection matters.

Hetherington et al. (1997:91) suggest that a mediation or alternative dispute decision process can act as a buffer between the administrative and legal domains. Pre-Hearing Conferences that were introduced in 1993 into the *Children and Young Persons Act 1989* provide such a buffer within the legal domain. Pre-Hearing Conferences were established to provide alternative dispute resolution in the Family Division of the Children's Court, Victoria. It was hoped that the use of a mediation process could avoid the difficulties inherent in court-resolved disputes. It also acknowledged the movement to encourage families to participate in discussions about child protection concerns for the safety and well-being of their children.

Pre-Hearing Conferences in the Children's Court

The Family Division of the Children's Court, Victoria, hears all child protection matters. Magistrates direct families and the child protection service to attend a pre-hearing conference when the welfare authority believes there is a need for a child protection order and the need for this is contested by the family. The conferences are held 'with a view to achieving a conciliated solution'

(Campbell 1997:5). Whilst the primary focus is to resolve welfare concerns, legal requirements must be observed, and any options negotiated at a conference are referred back to a magistrate to ratify any agreement reached. The full range of child protection matters is referred to a pre-hearing conference, from applications for interim orders to permanent care orders.

Pre-hearing Conference Convenors, who are Governor-in-Council appointments, lead the conferences that are conducted in an informal manner away from the main court offices and courtrooms. The participation of the family is fundamental to pre-hearings and in the two to three hours that are set aside for each conference, the convenor ensures parents have the opportunity to hear what the welfare authority wants them to change about the care of their children. The discussions must be in a manner that can be understood by a family and not in legal and professional language. The convenor aims to facilitate negotiation and settlement by introducing facts or opinions that could be considered by the parties, identifies for the parties the issues the court might consider if hearing the case, and outlines the consequences if they do not settle at the conference. The convenor has to ensure the interests of the child are not harmed by any agreements made. This discussion is confidential for all participants; only an attendance record and outcome is reported to the court.

As well as family members and the welfare authority professionals – their caseworker and supervisor, legal representatives attend to represent parents. Children aged seven years and over are always represented by Legal Aid: the legislation requires this separate representation. Children and their parents are seen as separate parties at the pre-hearing conference although the court sees the maintenance of the family unit as of central importance to the child. Not all parents elect to be represented; some choose to self-represent. Legal representatives do not act as formal legal advocates: they attend to present their client's instructions and advise the parents or children they represent. Families may also have friends, relatives or professionals to support them. The legislation does not provide for participation by professionals such as doctors and teachers so it can be difficult to obtain information from them although the child protection worker usually includes this in the application report prepared for court.

The Victorian government funded an evaluation of pre-hearing conferences in 1994. Lagay et al. (1994) found that of the 180 conferences held for 149 families in the first 11 months of the programme, 60 per cent of the cases achieved a settlement (Campbell 1997:6). Magistrates and families reported that they found the process a helpful one. Conferences observed for the study confirmed that parents valued the opportunity to be heard and to speak for themselves. Legal and welfare professionals, and parents, interviewed for the evaluation study believed pre-hearing conferences were an acceptable alternative to court. They found them more participatory than a court hearing, which they found formal and alienating. Parents interviewed during the evaluation commented that it was better to discuss issues informally than fight in court where cases can get bogged down and be expensive for those who do not have legal aid. Cases in which no agreement was reached tended to be matters that involved allegations of physical and sexual abuse where to settle might be incriminating and involve legal consequences for the perpetrator.

The Effectiveness of Pre-hearing Conferences

Sheehan, Rechtman and Ban (1998) undertook a study of pre-hearing conferences undertaken within the Family Division of the Melbourne Children's Court (Victoria). The study aimed to gather information about the effectiveness of conferences and the factors that assisted or hindered settlement. A questionnaire was completed by the pre-hearing conference convenors for every case heard at a pre-hearing conference during the months January–July 1998. Information was gathered about the nature of the child protection application to the Court, about the child and their family, about who attended the pre-hearing and about the conference outcome; a subjective assessment by convenors about the success of the conference and what factors contributed to the settlement – or lack of settlement – of the dispute was also recorded.

The study findings were drawn from 228 conferences: the total number of pre-hearing conferences held during the study period. What was found was that 98 conferences achieved a settlement, 41 were adjourned (a significant number can be expected to settle without further court hearing), and 89 conferences did not achieve a settlement.

New child protection applications (n=91 out of 138) were generally brought on the grounds of physical harm and emotional abuse (*Children and Young Persons Act* section 63 (c) and (e)). Table 6.2 indicates that the child protection applications brought on the grounds of physical harm (s63c) and emotional (s63e) abuse were more likely to achieve a settlement. Table 6.3 indicates that the age of the child did not influence whether a settlement was achieved. The large number of adjournments in emotional harm cases indicates that often parents were given a period of time in which to address child protection concerns before further court action.

Table 6.1 Types and outcomes of pre-hearing conferences held (n=228)

Outcomes:	New protection applications	Further orders, extensions	Breaches	Total
Settled	60	28	10	98 (43%)
Adjourned	26	11	4	41 (18%)
Not settled	51	25	13	89 (39%)

Table 6.2 The grounds of new child protection applications brought by the child protection service

Section 63	Settled	Not settled	Adjourned
(a) and (b)	6	4	4
(c)	49	37	17
(d)	4	4	1
(e)	56	41	21
(f)	7	14	4
Total	121	100	47

Table 6.3 The ages of the children involved in the new child protection applications brought by the child protection service

Age	Settled			Not settled			Adjourned			Total children
	New protection application	Ext.	Brch	New protection application	Ext.	Brch	New protection application	Ext.	Brch	
0–3	41	11	5	14	5	4	41	5	10	136
4–8	27	12	2	15	2	1	24	13	15	111
9–12	21	9	1	6	2	0	20	8	2	69
13–14	7	3	2	1	1	0	2	5	0	21
15–17	2	3	0	1	3	0	4	6	1	20
Total	98	38	10	37	13	5	91	37	28	357

Table 6.4 Decisions about new child protection applications (n=60); settlements achieved at pre-hearing conference

Interim protection order	17
Supervision order	21
Custody to secretary order	10
No order proven	2
Long interim accommodation order	5
Withdrawal of application	4
Undertaking	1
TOTAL	60

It was clear that in order to achieve a settlement there had to be a reasonable level of agreement between parties around the facts leading to the involvement of the statutory welfare authority. Also, when the child protection service was clear about how and why a child was at risk of harm, and also clear about how a parent can address that risk, then that directly assisted the settlement of the matter. The quality of legal advice provided to family members also significantly affected the outcome of the pre-hearing conference. Legal representatives, who were able to recognise the usefulness of mediation principles and a negotiation framework, were more able to assist their client to respond to child protection concerns. Likewise, representatives who were able to work with welfare professionals and recognise the significance of child welfare matters were also better able to realistically advise their clients.

The quality of the child protection service representation also affected the outcome of the conference. Whilst the DHS representatives who attend are not legally trained, they are trained child protection workers. Whilst they come to the conference with a specific recommendation about a child protection order in mind, if they are able to negotiate this with parents, hear the parents' responses to the child protection concerns, and argue the significance of risk to a child with parents and legal representatives, then settlement is more readily achieved. Therefore, flexibility on the part of legal representatives, parents and the child protection service, was a significant influence on achieving a settlement at the conference. Moreover, where the conference participants focused their discussion on clarifying issues and when family members accepted the child protection concerns, and there was a high level of negotiation skills by one or more participants, then a settlement was more readily achieved.

However, when there were factual disputes around issues leading to the child protection application and parents, legal representatives and the child protection service could not agree, then settlement was unlikely. The quality of legal representation was a significant influence when there was such a dispute. In the cases in the study, unsatisfactory legal representation, whether it was due to a lack of knowledge of legislation and procedures, or to not understanding the child protection service's concerns, an inability to negotiate, or inexperience, and intransigence, inhibited settlement in cases in which a representative more sympathetic to mediation might have achieved a more positive outcome.

When the child protection service proposed plans for the family that the family did not accept, such as time limits in which certain goals were to be achieved or the family did not wish to accept the support services the child protection service nominated as conditions for an order, parents were reluctant to accept a child care order. It was clear that a number of families lacked trust in the child protection service following its long involvement with their children and/or the parents themselves, and the parents feared any more involvement with the child protection service. Where the child protection staff appeared to be inflexible in their approach to the family, had poor negotiation skills, or were perhaps inexperienced either in their job or in the legal process, settlement could not be achieved. Other reasons cases did not settle were because an essential participant failed to attend or because a family member could not understand the proceedings as a consequence of intellectual disability or psychiatric illness or was drug affected.

One of the great difficulties for the statutory welfare authority is that generally parents and legal representatives do not support statutory involvement in families and find it hard to agree on the facts that have brought the family to statutory attention. To assist settlement in child welfare matters, parents need to be encouraged to alter aspects of their parenting; defensive legal representation and a perception that a stigma is attached to parents involved with the statutory authority do not encourage parents to cooperate with welfare practitioners. The role of the legal representative is therefore crucial in advising a parent that their actions have brought them to the attention of the welfare authority, that parents must take responsibility for their actions, and why these actions fit within the child welfare legislation. The role for the legal representative can also be crucial in advising parents this should be a starting point for further action. The pre-hearing conference demands a different role for the legal representative; their role is one of adviser, it is not to test evidence, not to be adversarial. They are to encourage their client to speak on their own behalf.

The Child's Voice

Alternative dispute resolution processes, like pre-hearing conferences, attempt to take into account the particular needs of children by giving them a voice in decisions that affect them. Their rights are properly protected via separate representation at pre-hearing conferences. However, the children are still dependent on adults to act on their behalf and the problems they face are decided by their parents or other adults. Debates about the child's best interests, that are the focus of child protection proceedings, revolve around what are the participating adults' views. The legislative mandate of family preservation, combined with the generally held view of legal representatives, that a child's interests lie within their family and that all parents are generally capable, encouraged legal professionals to very often view a child's, and their family's interests, as the same.

This means in practice that a child could have difficulty having their separate interests heard. The view that child abuse ought to be seen as a family problem encouraged legal representatives to see a child's problems as best dealt with within the family context. It was an approach that failed to acknowledge those cases in which it is one member of a family who is the perpetrator, and failed to acknowledge the vulnerability of the non-abusing parent. In order to achieve a resolution the significance of what has happened to a child might be minimised, and a child encouraged to accept the outcome to preserve the family.

Hunt and McLeod (1997) comment that the responses of the legal and welfare professionals involved in mediation are pivotal to its success. The increasing legalisation of welfare issues has on the one hand been effective in giving parents more rights in contesting the need for statutory intervention in their family. On the other hand, it has led to an often more combative relationship between parents and statutory welfare agencies that has thwarted cooperative efforts to address child protection concerns. The Victorian child welfare legislation provides for legal representation of children aged seven years and over in care and protection matters, and this includes pre-hearing conferences. However, legal representatives are not required to have specific training in such representation, despite the importance of their role and the need for different responses in a mediation process from those of the court hearing.

The quality of legal representation in pre-hearings in the Melbourne Children's Court, depended on the familiarity of the representative with children's matters and on their sensitivity to the particular needs of children. Many representatives developed considerable skill in this area, although they are not specifically accredited for this work, as is the case in England. What was apparent, in the Children's Court, Family Division (probably representative of any adversarial system), was that it was assumed that children are able to give instructions to their legal representative, and are confident enough to question or dispute how the legal representative might interpret their experiences to other adults. It is questionable how effectively a child is able to instruct their legal representative, for example, when they are attending a pre-hearing conference with their parents, and might want to give a different account to the one being given by the parents. A child might be anxious for their parents' approval, or perhaps fearful of the consequences of their disclosures. Children who have experienced family violence are particularly vulnerable in this regard. Certainly, little account appeared to be taken of how a child made sense of the debate between professionals and family members about their family problems.

Alternative dispute resolution aims to find solutions to problems through informal discussion, away from court formality. Yet, for children attending a pre-hearing conference it is still a daunting experience. The language used by professionals they need to talk to is often unfamiliar. The professionals involved in their case may be unknown to them, especially legal representatives who may meet the child for the first time just prior to the pre-hearing. Yet the child has to rely on this representative to present their views.

Whilst alternative dispute resolution is set up to provide individuals with the opportunity to participate in finding solutions for their family difficulties, when parties are legally represented the discussions can too readily be dominated by representatives using legal frameworks to direct the discussions. Attention to due process and individual rights must not be put aside because it is alternative dispute resolution. However, careful attention needs to be paid to the roles of professionals who attend alternative decision fora. So too must there be clear agreement about the aims of these fora and about the balance between protecting the rights of participants and providing a venue for proper discussion about welfare issues.

Family group conferences are another form of alternative dispute resolution, introduced in Victoria, as in other Australian states and in other countries, as a process that gives families primary responsibility to make plans for a child family member when there are proven child abuse concerns, and to plan who is to care for the child. It is a framework that best meets what Campbell (1997:5) describes as the child-in-family-in network-in community orientation of current child care policy. They are attended by family members and professionals and, in Victoria, are not attended by legal representatives.

They are perceived as a case planning framework rather than a forum within the legal process, unlike the pre-hearing conference.

Family Group Conferences

Family Group Conferencing (FGC) has its origins in New Zealand and has been introduced in varying ways into the United Kingdom and Canada, in both the juvenile justice and child protection services, as it has in Victoria (Ban 1995). Swain and Ban (1997) found in their preliminary evaluation of FGC in protection and care in Victoria, that 80 per cent of the 128 family group conference participants they interviewed were satisfied with their involvement in the FGC, and the process and outcome of the FGC. The favourable findings of this preliminary evaluation of FGC led to the its implementation throughout the child protection service in Victoria.

Bullock, Millham, Mount and Scott (1995) in their study of FGC in England found that the 'working in partnership' characteristic of FGC, of family and professionals working together, was a significant factor in achieving positive outcomes for children on child protection orders. It was the approach of working on family strengths, so that children could have 'their' family, that achieved better results than more traditional family interventions. Hassall (1996) and Marsh and Crow (1998) both found that family group conferences promoted lasting solutions for families whose children were in the child protection system, because it was a process that promoted better communication between family members, gave them a sense of independence in terms of making child care plans, and therefore seemed to produce a greater commitment by family members to make such plans work. Marsh and Crow (1998) found in their study in England that out of the 80 FGC they examined, 83 per cent of the case plans produced by the conferences were successfully implemented. Furthermore, the social workers involved believed that the children in two-thirds of the families in the study were better protected as result of the FGC. Trotter (1999) found in his study about working with involuntary clients, that more effective work is achieved when families are involved in decision-making processes about their children and that this can directly contribute to less child abuse and better case planning.

The need for child-centred, family-focused practice in child protection is well established in the statutory welfare service in Victoria (DHS) and in other parts of Australia. South Australia has family care meetings that are mandated under the *Children's Protection Act 1993* (ss27–36). These are convened and conducted by a care and protection coordinator appointed by the Senior Judge of the Children's Court. As with pre-hearing conferences in Victoria, these meetings are conducted under the auspices of the court. Tasmania and the Australian Capital Territory provide for family group conferences within their child welfare legislation. New South Wales, like Victoria and Western Australia undertake family group conferences as a family decision-making and case-planning framework; they are variously run by or auspiced by the statutory welfare authority.

However, family group conferencing requires statutory decision-makers to forgo their control over decision-making about children under the care of the child protection service. A study undertaken by Trotter, Liddell, Sheehan et al. (1997–98) set out to find whether FGC was effectively established in the child protection and care system. The study also set out to look at the commitment of families to implement the case plans that came out of FGC. The study compared the experiences of professionals and family members, involved in 30 FGC, with the experiences of professionals who were involved in 30 cases that went through the usual child protection planning process.

Families were found to be generally happy with FGC and less happy with experiences of other case planning meetings (Evaluation of Statewide Implementation of FGC 1999:27). They commented that they had opportunities to speak for themselves, to work cooperatively with child protection staff and to make decisions about what was to happen to their child family member. It was however, the extended family members who were most enthusiastic; parents of the child subject of the FGC were less enthusiastic, as they had been investigated by child protection and their child now subject to care orders. However, they were more positive about FGC than other case planning meetings but the FGC process did not incline them to now feel more positive towards the child protection service.

Child protection staff were also positive because the process involves families and gets families to commit to case plans in a way other case planning does not. However, professional staff who came from external agencies, and who had been involved in FGC, did not believe that FGC provided better decision-making about children although they acknowledged that it was an opportunity for families to hear what were the concerns about a child and what options, and statutory limits, there were for the child. They were not convinced that FGC led to better case plans being developed. They were the group that flagged the potential for victimisation of children within FGC and commented that whilst FGC improved family relations, the protection of children's rights within family rights needed to be addressed.

However, it was generally agreed that FGC made an impressive contribution to planning for children in need of care and that strengthening families was preferable to statutory control over children within the child protection system.

Mediation in Family Disputes

The Family Court of Australia is the court that deals with matrimonial matters, residence and contact decisions and adoption and guardianship decisions about children. The Family Court has placed great emphasis on dispute resolution services and conciliation counselling for children as part of determining residence and contact arrangements for children whose parents are no longer living together (*Mediation and Arbitration Act 1991* amended the *Family Law Act 1975*). The Court has a dedicated counselling service and refers also to social workers and psychologists to assess the implications for a child's welfare when their parents are in dispute. The Court's mediation service approaches dispute resolution in much the same way as FGC and pre-hearing conferences. The Court emphasises that individuals take responsibility for making decisions that affect their lives (Fehlberg and Taylor 1984, in Gibson's *Mediation of Family Disputes in the Family Court of Australia*). The Court also prefers that parties consider alternatives and possibilities for settlement away from judicial determination. Mediators do not offer legal opinion. They set out to identify disputed issues and possible solutions and draw up an agreement that may or may not be registered with the Court. Individuals attend with legal representatives who have an advisory rather than adversarial role.

This process, known as family mediation, has achieved significant success when parties feel they have been able to make their own decisions rather than have decisions imposed on them. However, individuals who may feel at a disadvantage in such processes, or who would prefer an independent arbiter, may not feel they have had an equal role in the outcome. Women who have experienced domestic violence have certainly raised this concern (Graycar 1992). However, the Court is mindful of the need for there to be a reasonable power balance between parties and recognised that family mediation cannot be considered for all cases. However, the Family Court finds, as do other courts, that over 90 per cent of people settle their disputes before the final hearing of a case. The Court actively supports mediation as a way of best resolving family relationship problems and has found that there is generally better compliance with court orders when parties have drawn up their own agreements.

Mediation in Juvenile Justice

Mediation and reparation schemes have also been used in juvenile justice systems as a way of both providing for rehabilitation of the young offender and compensation for the victim. Braithwaite (1989) has proposed the notion of restorative justice as a way of dealing with young offenders away from the courts. Certainly, in Victoria, family group conferencing has been used within the juvenile justice system in an attempt to involve families and communities in strengthening the sense of responsibility of young offenders for their crimes. These schemes have spread to numerous countries: from its origins in New Zealand, to European countries (Belgium, Germany, Netherlands, Portugal and Italy), to Scandinavian countries (Denmark, Finland, Sweden), to Ireland and the USA. The meetings aim to get the young person to take responsibility for their offence and agree to undertake alternative activities, to in part, make good the damage they have done (Hallett and Hazel 1998:27). Some schemes may require the young person to meet their victim or a representative of the victim. The meetings may also involve the young person's family so that they will also share responsibility for the rehabilitation of the young person.

These schemes have met with a mixed response. In New Zealand, young offenders are dealt with by a family group conference. The conferences are seen as successful in diverting young people away from court and custodial sentences (Maxwell and Morris 1994). Families, and victims, welcomed the opportunity to be involved. However, Wundersitz (1992) is concerned that such diversionary processes may not protect a child's legal rights. Certainly these individualised efforts may mean less attention is paid to the broader social and structural contexts of crime. Furthermore, they might also overlook a young person's need for help.

However, children who enter the juvenile justice system and the care and protection system are often amongst the most vulnerable children in the community. The various schemes mentioned offer opportunities for conciliation and mediation, either within or away from, the legal system. These schemes offer young people and their families a voice in changing behaviours that put them at risk of further offending, and offer parents in care and protection proceedings the opportunity to amend behaviours that put their children at risk.

Summary

Conventional systems for decision-making in child welfare, when they operate on adversarial principles, aim to narrow what are often broad child welfare concerns down to specific issues for the court to tackle. This reductionist approach 'where each side presents a case before the court, the function of which is limited to deciding who has won' (McGrath 1997:32 citing Spencer and Flin 1973:75), diminishes the importance of the context in which child abuse occurs and fails to provide resolution for the problems of family malfunctioning that characterise child abuse cases. Mediation schemes that avoid litigation and include family members in discussions about child protection concerns can help the family and the welfare authority come to a solution to resolve these concerns. Such schemes also reflect that work in child protection must be a partnership between welfare and justice approaches and ensure children and their families are heard and noticed by professionals in our community. In Victoria, pre-hearing conferences were established to provide alternative dispute resolution in child protection cases in the Children's Court. Family Group Conferences were initiated by the child protection service, the Department of Human Services, in 1996, to provide opportunities for families and children and young people to make case planning decisions. Although the child protection service sets a 'bottom line' about what must be in place to protect a child from harm, families are encouraged to decide about the care of their children and what courses of action are to be undertaken to address child protection concerns. Both schemes have met with considerable support.

In 1995–96, 91,000 cases of child abuse or neglect were reported to state and territory welfare departments in Australia; almost one-third of these were substantiated (Australia has a population of around 18 million). Whilst only around 6.5 per cent of notifications in Victoria resulted in court proceedings, the child protection and legal systems need to find ways to support these children and as much as possible maintain them in family care. The justice and individual rights perspectives that shape how statutory agencies respond to such children need to be re-conceptualised to include alternative dispute resolution as an approach that can be effective in deciding the best interests of children. The legal system needs to relinquish some of these functions and work in partnership with appropriate professionals, and respond to families wanting to participate in decisions about its members.

The next chapter canvasses how other jurisdictions responded to child protection decision-making, specifically England and Scotland, and some description is given about the inquisitorial approach of some European countries (Holland, Germany and France) in comparison to the adversarial approach of the Australian child welfare jurisdiction.

Chapter Six

Future Directions

> Some magistrates say that they don't want to know what happened afterwards because we just have to make our decision on the evidence before us and then forget about it. But I think in the Children's Court it's different. We are talking about the whole system, the adversarial versus the inquisitorial system ... we are talking about a completely different system where you make decisions and follow them up and you get reports to say what's been happening (M 01).

The appropriateness of adversarial hearings and the legal process for making decisions in child protection matters has been widely debated and the development of alternative dispute resolution schemes (discussed in the preceding chapter), is an important outcome of this debate. The difference between inquisitorial and adversarial systems is, perhaps, the most significant difference in the legal framework of child protection systems in Australia, New Zealand, the UK, and Western Europe. Professionals, both legal and welfare, who operate within an adversarial context, look towards the inquisitorial system as offering more flexibility, as it functions more 'on the basis of an inquiry rather than a contest' (McGrath 1997:37). Certainly, the frustrations magistrates have reported, in this book, with child protection decision-making, are reflected in the above quote. Although magistrates emphasised the importance of due process, attention to individual rights and legislative obligation, they were hampered by their inability to get all the information they wanted about a case.

Hallet and Hazel (1998:15) found that the differing national systems of child protection also reflected national views about the right of the state 'to intervene authoritatively in matters of child welfare'. In Australia, whilst there is acceptance that there ought to be intervention in families to provide essential child welfare services or protect children from abuse or neglect, such intervention has to be legally justified rather than based on social work discretion. The introduction of mandatory reporting of suspicions of child abuse, in most Australian states and territories, has meant a greater use of legal measures in child protection. It has also meant there is emphasis on the need to establish fault with parents, to permit the involvement of welfare services, rather than propose that need is the basis for the involvement of the child protection service in a family's life. Australian child welfare legislation states that the best interests of the child is the paramount principle in decisions made about the child and that partnership with families is central to working within child protection work. Yet when child protection services can only be implemented by way of a court order, the legal challenges that often accompany applications for orders promote conflict and discourage collaboration between parents and child protection. McGrath (1997:68) suggests that 'the best interests of the child is a concept referred to but not necessarily adhered to, given the conflictual nature of the (adversarial) proceedings'. However, the way the law is implemented is just as important as the content of the law itself, and so Victorian legislation has introduced the pre-hearing conferences, described in the previous chapter, to provide for a more conciliatory approach within the legal context.

The *Children and Young Persons Act (Victoria) 1989* was considerably influenced by the *Children Act 1989* with its provisions for providing positive help for children in need and such services for families that would both improve children's circumstances and avoid, if possible, their removal from their families. The Act also obliges local authorities to consult parents about their children, even when compulsory measures of care are taken, as the local authority has a duty to promote contact between the child and their parents. The English legal system is based on the same Westminster, and adversarial, principles as the Australian system. Yet while the same issues that confound legal decision-making in child protection in Victoria are found in the English system, there are significant differences in the nonjudicial elements of the child protection process, developed to manage the competing interests of family autonomy and statutory intervention.

The Child Welfare Legislation Framework in England

The *Children Act 1989* established that the one jurisdiction hears all child welfare matters whether they are applications for care and protection and are public law matters, or whether they are child care issues arising in private law (matrimonial) matters. The Act aimed to provide a coherent philosophy about the relationship between the state and the family. Whilst the Act confirms that children are best cared for by their family of origin, it provides a framework for responding to children whose care by their families falls below what is acceptable. A number of deaths of children known to local authorities in England during the 1980s had focused government and community attention on the inaction of child protection agencies. The Act therefore provided for the child protection register: the registration of children about whom there are confirmed child protection concerns, children who remain with their families and receive services, but their situation is supervised by the local authority.

The *Children Act* defines a child as being in need if they do not have the opportunity to achieve or maintain a reasonable standard of health or development unless they receive services from the local authority and that their health or development is likely to be impaired unless these services are provided (White, Carr and Lowe 1995:11). The local authority is obliged to provide services that will prevent children from suffering ill-treatment or neglect, and so reduce the need for the local authority to seek child care or supervision orders from the court.

The Act provides for the child assessment order; this allows the local authority to investigate a child's circumstances to determine whether or not the child is suffering or likely to suffer significant harm. If necessary, the child can be assessed away from the home for a period not exceeding seven days and the court can make an interim care or supervision order. An emergency protection order allows the local authority to remove a child to safe accommodation if a child is likely to suffer significant harm. It also enables the local authority to have access to a child. The police can also seek an emergency protection order, or use police orders to remove a child to safety. A guardian ad litem (for the child) and a solicitor are always present at an emergency protection order application. The local authority can seek a care or supervision order when they believe there is a likelihood of significant harm to a child and that this is because the child is not receiving the appropriate care for a child in their circumstances.

Where the child abuse allegations concern physical or sexual abuse or serious cruelty or unusual circumstances, for example, Munchausen's syndrome by proxy, the police and the local authority undertake a joint investigation, so that the one process meets civil and criminal law requirements. Other matters, where the allegations about physical abuse are minor or less visible or where the allegations of sexual harm are based on the indirect concern of others, or when allegations are about neglect or emotional abuse, these are investigated by the Social Services Department of the local authority.

Before seeking a child care order from the court, the local authority must consider whether specific threshold criteria have been met. The *Children Act 1989* s31(2) requires the court to be satisfied that the following criteria have been met before making a care order or supervision order:

(a) that the child is suffering or is likely to suffer significant harm and,
(b) that the harm or likelihood of the harm is attributed to:
   (i) the care given to the child or likely to be given to the child if the order is not made not being what it would be reasonable to expect a parent to give or,
   (ii) the child is beyond parent control.

However, the local authority must always consider whether satisfactory arrangements for the welfare of the child can be achieved without a court order at all, and if the authority is pursuing an order then it has to be sure that this is in the best interests of the child and they are required to present the court with a clear plan for the child.

Whether or not harm is significant for the child is decided by comparing the child's health or development with what could be reasonably be expected of a similar child or a similar age child who is not in a situation deemed to be at risk (s 31(10)). *Harm* is generally defined by the Act (s31(9)) as ill-treatment of a child or the impairment of the child's health or development. *Development* refers to the physical, intellectual, emotional, social and behavioural development of the child; *health* means the physical or mental health of a child. *Ill-treatment* refers to sexual abuse and other forms of ill-treatment that are not physical. The comparison with the similar child, and consideration of whether the child is suffering, or is likely to suffer, are pivotal considerations. What is the care of the reasonable parent compared with the care by the adult/parent of the child in question, is also significant.

The Children Act (s1(I)) emphasises that 'the child's welfare shall be the court's paramount consideration'. The Law Commission recommended therefore that the following factors should be taken into account when determining the welfare of the child (White, Carr and Lowe 1995:11):

(a) the wishes and feelings of the child (in light of their age and understanding);
(b) physical emotional and educational needs;
(c) the likely effect on the child of any change in circumstances;
(d) age, sex, background and any characteristics of the child which the court considers relevant;
(e) any harm the child has suffered or is at risk of suffering;
(f) how capable each of the child's parents is in meeting the child's needs.

The Act considers that delay in determining questions about a child's upbringing is detrimental to the welfare of the child and so aims for matters to be finalised within three months. The court is expected to set a timetable for proceedings, to ensure any delay is the minimum possible. The Act also directs that family proceedings matters (child protection cases) must be heard when they are ready and not postponed until the outcome of criminal proceedings, unless there is a real benefit to the child to wait for that outcome. However, the average amount of time taken before there is a final decision in a contested matter is reported by professionals as more like seven months, with some cases taking up to 12 months (Sheehan 1998).

Family Proceedings

The High Court, County Courts and Magistrates' Courts have jurisdiction over proceedings under the *Children Act 1989*. However, cases generally commence in the family proceedings courts which are Magistrates' Courts. Approximately 20 per cent of matters commence in the County Court; they are cases that are unduly complex or are expected to last more than five days. Approximately 5 per cent of cases commence in the High Court when decisions on law are required. The family proceedings courts can hear both property and private law matters as well as child welfare public law matters. They also hear cases which involve allegations of domestic violence and in which there is an application for an exclusion order.

A specialist panel of three Magistrates appointed to the Family Panel hears cases in the family proceedings courts. Magistrates are lay justices although they undertake basic training before they commence sitting and specific training which makes them eligible for appointment to the Family Panel. They are appointed to serve for three years and can be reappointed. The justice's clerk of each Magistrates' Court provides legal advice to the lay justices and conducts the ordinary business of the court. The family proceedings courts can hear cases lasting up to five days including the time taken to reach a decision and the time taken to present the reasons for this decision. The justice's clerk records the reason for the court's decision in writing prior to the delivery of the decision and very often assists with the structure of the reasons. An appeal against a decision made by the family proceedings court goes to a single judge in the Family Division at the County Court.

Family proceedings are private and there are no transcripts of proceedings. The individuals entitled to be present in family proceedings are the officers of the court, the parties and their legal representatives, representatives of newspapers and any other person that the court allows to be present. Although the child is a party in the family proceedings court, the child is not present in the court unless the court considers it is in the child's interest to be present, having considered what evidence is likely to be given and so long as the child is accompanied by a guardian ad litem or a solicitor.

The court appoints a guardian ad litem in all child care and adoption proceedings to represent and safeguard the interests of children. The role of the guardian ad litem is to provide the court with an independent report on the child's own wishes and feelings and to assess the local authority's plans for the child. The guardian also chairs any meetings that might be held prior to the hearing, in order to identify areas of agreement and dispute (s1(2) of the *Children Act*). The guardian has the right to examine and take copies of any records held by the local authority, in order to prepare their report. The guardian might provide interim reports setting out what are the issues for the court to decide or might ask for a review of whether the threshold criteria have been met. The guardian ad litem however has no automatic right of audience at the court. Local authorities are legally obliged to set up and administer guardian ad litem panels from which the courts can appoint. Guardians ad litem are usually very experienced social workers who are self-employed and work independently.

The guardian is involved in decisions about the child: such as where a child should live, the school they attend, and any decisions that need to be made about a child during the course of proceedings. The guardian also ensures that the child understands what is happening to them and how the legal and welfare issues and decisions might be explained to them. The strength of the guardian ad litem system is that there is somebody who is there for the child and only for the child.

The guardian may also instruct experts to assist in an investigation of the child protection concerns. It is now the practice in the English courts that all parties instruct the one expert to respond to instructions both from the parents and the local authority. There are cases however, for example in child physical abuse, where the parents and the guardian ad litem might want the opinion of different experts. The reports prepared by the experts, and provided to the court, must be available to all the parties and unfavourable reports can no longer be withheld. This inquisitorial or information gathering process is of great benefit to the court. However once proceedings are commenced the adversarial process takes over.

A solicitor for the child is also appointed either by the court or by the guardian if one has not already been appointed. The guardian ad litem instructs the solicitor on the matters that relate to the interests of the child, unless the child is considered competent enough to instruct the solicitor themselves. The guardian ad litem and solicitor partnership provides the courts with a unique synthesis of social work and legal skills. Solicitors who represent children in family proceedings matters are selected from the family practice register, a list set up by the Law Society Child Care Panel, for lawyers who have trained in, and have a special interest in, family proceedings matters. The Law Society established the children's panel because it recognised that 'children's work is a specialised area which should only be undertaken by advocates with appropriate knowledge, experience and personal qualities' (Children Act Advisory Committee: Final Report 1997:3). The Committee remained concerned however about the inappropriately adversarial approach to family proceedings taken by advocates appearing in cases in the higher courts. The Committee suggested in its report that funded legal representation should be available to parties prior to proceedings, rather than waiting for the issuing of proceedings, to facilitate opportunities for settlement.

The Welfare-Legal Interface in Practice

The *Children Act* provides a framework within the English system for considerable interagency and interprofessional work. Whilst there is no mandatory reporting of child abuse system there are established protocols for collaborative work between the police and local authority social services departments, teachers and other health professionals. Great energy goes into pre-court work with families, to case conferences and interagency consultation to avoid the generally acknowledged tensions associated with the adversarial system. *The Best Practice Handbook In Children Act Cases* (1997) emphasises the utility of pre-trial mediation to see whether litigation can be avoided and a settlement negotiated. However when a case does go to court, particularly the higher courts, there is a marked shift from collaborative work to an adversarial approach. There are few opportunities for mediation to deal with disagreement; once parents contest the need for an order; once proceedings commence, parties are polarised and agreement is more difficult, if not impossible, to achieve.

The protection of children in England, Wales and Northern Ireland involves a working relationship between the social services departments, the police, medical practitioners, community health workers, schools, voluntary agencies and others. However professionals comment that the community is still ambivalent about what constitutes child abuse and equally what constitutes normal behaviour within families. As in Australia, making sense of child emotional abuse presents the judicial system with its greatest challenge. The challenge for child protection workers is to provide the courts with sufficient evidence of harm to a child for the case to survive the adversarial process

Child protection professionals describe contemporary English child protection as a series of complex bureaucratic procedures and as a service in which there is a pervasive culture of blame that is directed both at parents and at child protection workers (Cooper, Hetherington and Katz 1996). Child protection has shifted from being a professional concern to a political issue: the need to not make mistakes, to be sure that due process is observed and individual rights protected, and to ensure there is always sufficient evidence to persuade the court of the merit of child abuse concerns. This has lead to what Hunt and McLeod (1997), in their study of *Child Protection, the Courts and the 1989 Children Act* describe as the emergence of a culture of defensive accountability in child protection: the construction of sufficient bureaucratic procedures to ensure that things will not go wrong.

The 'no order' principle and the priority of keeping cases out of court has also created an uncertainty about at what point child protection should cross from concentrating on family support to being about intervention to ensure child safety. It also meant that child protection became a crisis management service rather than a service to work with and support families. This was particularly so in child neglect cases, which are by nature often very different from, say physical and sexual abuse cases. Child neglect cases are most often cases in which there are long-term problems; there may be no one particular crisis which brings the case to the attention of the local authority but rather the culmination of years of neglect of a child. Even so there may be little concrete evidence to support the local authority's concerns. An application by notice in such circumstances may be difficult to support if, on the given day when the case finally comes to court, there is no crisis to report but rather long-term child protection concerns which do not readily translate into legal fact.

The emphasis on parental rights has also led to a legal presence in all child care matters. The success of child protection intervention is therefore dependent, to a large extent, on the quality of legal representation. Variation in the quality of legal representation can also contribute to great variation in court outcomes. However, the legal department of the local authority also has considerable influence on court outcomes. The local authority legal department has to decide whether the welfare concerns presented by social services are sufficiently legally grounded to support a care application. There can be considerable variation in how the legal practitioners interpret the threshold criteria for a case compared with the child protection service interpretation; moreover, they may dispute the social services' case, or disagree with social services about the readiness of a case for court.

Proof in child neglect matters has received particular attention from Stevenson (1997) who believes that courts have great difficulty in understanding what actions or circumstances constitute emotional harm and neglect. Establishing the existence of the threshold criteria which permits statutory intervention is particularly difficult to achieve in child neglect matters, although it is generally acknowledged that neglect is very damaging to children. They are cases that do not have disclosures about abuse in the same way as do cases of child sexual abuse. Moreover, emotional harm is not life-threatening in the same way as physical harm to a child and a child may be ill-treated without obvious impairment, which then leads to difficulty in proving that this is child abuse. Stephenson (1997) further suggests that in England, as in Australia, the courts and society are reluctant to stigmatise a parent and looks for ways in which this category of child abuse can be explained so that it does not require legal sanctions.

Cooper, Hetherington and Katz (1996) suggest that the culture of legal adversarialism, which so concerns Australian welfare practitioners, is also evident in the English system. However the structure of cooperation and heightened awareness of professional concern which surrounds child protection work, before court proceedings and to some extent in the family proceedings courts, is supported by the legislation and is in marked contrast to the Australian approach. The Australian system is viewed as over-reliant on procedures and on the courts to operate the child protection system. It is a system in marked contrast to the Scottish system; a legal system that resembles the systems of law in continental Europe rather than those of Westminster. Scots law relies on establishing broad principles from which decisions in individual cases are decided, as opposed to the common law system of England that relies heavily on previous decisions and on building up general principles from individual cases.

The Scottish Jurisdiction

The Children (Scotland) Act 1995 provides the legal framework within which the Children's Hearing system, established in Scotland for over 25 years, is central to the provision of child welfare and juvenile justice in Scotland. Scottish child care law does not differentiate between children and young people who might be in need of compulsory measures of supervision either as a consequence of child maltreatment or of offending behaviour. Child welfare cases are heard by lay tribunals, comprising representatives of local communities, in a non-adversarial and relatively informal setting (Hallett and Murray et al. 1998). Children's hearings, in principle, provide parents and children with the opportunity to talk about welfare concerns and contribute to possible solutions. However, whilst the children's hearing decides the outcome of a local authority application for compulsory measures, if parents or young people do not accept the grounds of the case, the Sheriff must decide whether the grounds are established and the case returns to the children's hearing to decide outcome. It is a system that is seen to be welfare focused, that addresses the needs and individual circumstances of a child, in a relatively unbureaucratic way. Lay panel members are unpaid; they come from a wide range of backgrounds, and are independent of welfare agencies and the justice system.

Lord Kilbrandon in his Report of 1968 recommended the one framework for children and young people who are in need, be they in public or private law matters. *The Social Work (Scotland) Act 1968* therefore set out child care law for Scotland and provided the framework for decision-making about children when their parents separate, for child welfare matters, including adoption, and for the operation of the children's hearing system. The Act also obliged the local authority to provide services for families and to respond to the needs of children in difficulty. It also obliged parents to cooperate with social services when there were established concerns about child abuse or neglect involving their children. Lord Kilbrandon believed that if the local authority was obliged to work with troubled families, and the community was involved in this through the Children's Hearings system then families were dealt with as members of the community, and that this contributes to the strength and social cohesion of the community. Panels of lay people from the community were to be appointed to conduct Children's Hearings; a panel would comprise three members chosen for their interest in, and knowledge about, children. They were to be appointed from each local authority area in order to represent the interests, the nature and the social groupings of that community. The Panel would meet to discuss in an informal manner the personal difficulties facing the child, consider relevant information about the child and decide whether compulsory measures of care for a child. The Committee took the view that court procedures were not appropriate to determine the needs of children whether they were troubled or troublesome, rather children's special requirements could be better met by providing education, treatment and social care services. Lord Kilbrandon also took the view that the best interests of the child was the paramount consideration and that individual rights could not supplant this.

The Kilbrandon Report recommended a clear division of responsibility between the courts and the Children's Hearings. However, in order to protect the legal rights of children and parents in contested cases, disputes about the facts in a child care matter or the grounds of the child protection case were to be decided by the Sheriff Court and not by the lay hearing. The Sheriff Court's role in child protection is twofold: to hear matters in the criminal jurisdiction in relation to adults accused of offending against children and in civil matters to hear cases that are referred from the Children's Panel for a proof hearing. If a parent does not accept the grounds or the reasons for their referral to a panel, for example that they have abused their child, the Children's Panel must either discharge the case, which is unlikely when child abuse is alleged, or the Panel refers the case to the Sheriff. After hearing the case for the parents, and after considering the evidence provided by social services, the Sheriff finds whether or not the grounds are established; if they are, the case is referred back to the Children's Panel to decide what is an appropriate decision about the care of the child. The standard of proof in children's matters is the balance of probabilities standard except where the criminal standard of beyond reasonable doubt is required. The Sheriff also hears appeals by the child or parents against decisions by the Panel but not in the open court. *The Social Work (Scotland) Act* required parents to play a much larger part in the hearing system than they would have in the courts to encourage their cooperation and more successful outcomes for their children.

Child Protection

The Children (Scotland) Act was introduced in 1995. This new legislation confirmed that parents should normally be responsible for the upbringing of their children and should share that responsibility with the community; local authorities are to make every effort to keep a child in their family home. Parents are expected to protect their child from abuse, neglect or exploitation. Their failure to do this permits statutory intervention although any intervention has to be properly justified and be supported by relevant services. The Act states that the welfare of the child is the paramount consideration when his or her needs are considered by courts and children's hearings. However, no order is to be made unless the court or the hearing considers that to do so would be better than making no order or supervision requirement at all. The child's views should be taken into account where decisions such as these are being made about their future.

Scotland does not have mandatory reporting of child abuse however the local authority is obliged to respond to children in need and at risk of harm, or to children who are actually harmed. Local authorities share responsibility for child protection in Scotland with the police, the health service, the Procurator Fiscal Service and with the Scottish Children's Reporter Administration. The procurator fiscal is a lawyer, a public appointment, not dissimilar to the position of the Director of Public Prosecutions in Australia; the procurator fiscal deals with criminal matters arising out of children's matters. Local authorities have child protection committees to facilitate interagency and interdisciplinary cooperation and this is recognised as essential for effective collaboration in child protection.

The legislation requires local authorities to safeguard and promote the welfare of children in their area who are in need. A child is deemed to be in need of care and attention if they do not have the opportunity to achieve or maintain a reasonable standard of health or development unless the local authority provides them with the services they need. A child is in need also if they have a disability or are affected by the disability of others or if their health is impaired and they are not receiving the services they need.

A child who is deemed to be in need of compulsory measures of supervision are set out in s52 of the Act:

(a) a child is beyond the control of any relevant person;
(b) that the child is falling into bad associations or is exposed to moral danger;
(c) the child is likely (i) to suffer unnecessarily, or (ii) be impaired seriously in their health or develop due to a lack of parental care;
(d) that the child who has had offences committed against them (including sexual offences, assault, ill-treatment, neglect, exposure, abandonment, and exposure to serious risk);
(e) that the child is, or is likely to become a member of the same household as a child in respect of whom a scheduled offence has been committed;
(f) that the child is, or is likely to become a member of the same household as a person who has committed a scheduled offence (any of the offences referred to above, a person commonly known as a Schedule 1 offender);
(g) that the child is, or is likely to become a member of the same household as a person who has committed incest;
(h) that the child has failed to attend school regularly without a reasonable excuse;

(i) that the child has committed an offence;
(j) the child has misused alcohol or any drug (whether or not it is a controlled drug), or has inhaled the vapours of a volatile substance other than for medicinal purposes;
(k)
(l) the child requires accommodation or is the subject of a parental responsibility order or their behaviour is such that they require supervision, requiring the local authority to act.

Children's Hearings

Anyone who has concerns about a child along the lines as set out above can contact local authority social services or the Authority Reporter. The Authority Reporter receives and considers information about children who might be in need of compulsory measures of care. If the Reporter considers there is sufficient evidence to prove that a child is in need of compulsory measures of care on at least one of the grounds as set out in the *Children (Scotland) Act*, then the Reporter refers the case to a children's hearing. Alternatively, the Reporter may decide it is in the child's best interests to be referred for voluntary assistance, or may decide to take no action at all. The Reporter has the authority to make enquiries to decide if there is sufficient evidence to support a referral to a children's hearing. The majority of referrals to the Reporter do not proceed to a hearing. However, if a child is referred to a children's hearing, the Reporter informs the child, their parents and other relevant people such as the local authority or police, if they have referred the child, about their decision and preferred course of action. The Reporter gives the Children's Panel members, the child and relevant persons, seven days in notice in writing of the time and place of the hearing. Parents have the right to attend a hearing and the right to appeal. The child also has the right to attend and the right to be heard. A Children's Hearing comprises the three panel members, the family, perhaps their representative (legal representatives can attend but in a voluntary capacity), the social worker and other professionals. The Reporter attends the children's hearing to record proceedings and advise the Panel on legal matters.

The Scottish Children's Reporter Administration administers the Children's Hearing system. Reporters are independent officials, appointed by the Secretary of State. There is a Principal Reporter for Scotland and seven reporter manager areas. There is an Authority Reporter in each area. The Reporter is generally a lawyer or social worker.

Children who come into the children's hearing system are referred to the Authority Reporter by social workers, the police, by education authorities, by the procurator fiscal, by friends and neighbours, by parents or the child itself. The local authority, and any police officer, must refer a child to the Reporter if they have received information that suggests compulsory measures of supervision may be necessary. A child is also referred when there are adoption proceedings, or where a parent has failed to ensure that their child attends school regularly. Reports are exchanged with the parents and the Panel prior to the Children's Hearing and the Panel can call for additional information. The grounds for referral are put to the panel for discussion about the best way to meet the interests of the child and to consider whether the child is in need of compulsory measures of supervision. The Panel can make supervision orders and placement decisions and refer cases to the Sheriff Court. The majority of children and young people who are diverted into the Children's Hearing system are placed on home supervision orders and the local authority takes responsibility for their supervision.

A relevant person for the purposes of a children's hearing is any person who has parental responsibilities. It does not include an unmarried father unless a court order has given him parental rights or he has registered an agreement with the mother that gives him parental responsibilities and rights. Other relevant people may include any other adult with parental responsibilities and rights, for example grandparents, who have a residence order or perhaps a friend, relative or foster carer who has care and control over the child. The children's hearing can exclude parents or relevant people when it is in the child's interests to do so, for example when a child is distressed and can only speak freely in a parent's absence. However when the adults return to the hearing, they must be told the substance of what has been said in their absence. The hearings are not open to members of the public.

The children's hearing can recommend the appointment of a safeguarder for the child. Equally, a Sheriff can appoint a safeguarder when there is a conflict between the interests of the child and their parent. The safeguarder does not take instructions from the child and is not the child's advocate but puts forward to the court what is in the best interests of the child. *The Children (Scotland) Act* requires the courts and the hearings to consider in each case how to give the child a voice in any hearing about them, to ensure the best interests principle of the UN Convention on the Rights of the Child is met. Legal representation is not permitted in children's hearings; lawyers can appear as advisers however they are not legally aided. This is done to preserve the informal, non-adversarial, direct and participatory character of the Children's

Hearing system and its emphasis on the social and environmental aspects of children's problems rather than on legal factors.

The Act provides for child protection orders, orders sought from the Sheriff Court when the local authority believes a child is suffering significant harm because of ill-treatment or neglect and needs to be removed to, or allowed to remain in, a place of safety. The Sheriff can authorise a place of safety for the child; parents can apply to have the order set aside or varied by the Sheriff and this has to be heard in three days. The Sheriff can also make exclusion orders that require a perpetrator of harm to a child leave the family home, an alternative to moving the child. A child assessment order gives the local authority the right to see and assess a child or have the child see other professionals, for example, a general practitioner or a psychiatrist, to resolve suspicions that a child is suffering harm. The parental responsibilities order gives parental responsibilities to the local authority when children cannot live with their parents. There is also provision for adoption where a child can no longer return home and there is no other alternative.

Children's Interests

The Children's Hearing System offers an entirely different approach to children in need. There is a great confidence in the competence of professionals to respond to problems of child abuse. In marked contrast to Australia, the legislation provides clear structures and procedures for responding to child abuse and makes it plain that responding to child abuse is a shared, and community, responsibility. Again, in marked contrast to Australia, there is legislative emphasis on working with families on a voluntary basis. If the police are involved then the case is automatically referred to the Reporter and social services refers all emergency matters to the Reporter. However, the local authority and other agencies invest great energy in working voluntarily with families. Child protection intervention may be confined to case conferences and to developing a plan of action for a child, perhaps putting the child's name on the child protection register. When parents are prepared to work cooperatively with social services then there may be no need to refer the child to a Children's Hearing. Approximately only one in ten children are referred to a hearing as a result of a case conference.

However, concern has been expressed about the lack of independent advice for the child at Children's Hearings, and the need for such processes to conform to the European Convention on Human Rights' requirements about representation for children in matters that affect them is a challenge currently confronting the Scottish system. Whilst the Children's Hearing is an informal process children, while they have the support of social services, or family, or friends, they do not have the benefit of legal advice. Parents receive reports prior to the hearing yet there is no provision for the child to receive these reports. The child's views are not confidential, although parents may be asked to step outside during a hearing so that a child can speak to the panel but when the parents return the chairman is required to say what views have been expressed in their absence.

The authority of the Children's Panel to admonish children who have offended is also an expressed concern of some professionals because young people attend the hearing without representation. The selection of Panel members is therefore particularly important. It is essential to be certain that their attitudes to young offenders or parents who maltreat their children will not stand in the way of their ability to conduct a fair hearing and make just decisions about the children and parents who appear before them.

The system differences between England, Scotland and Australia also reflect how child welfare activity is viewed. Hetherington, Cooper, Smith and Welford (1997:15) describe the Scottish Children's Panel as an example of child welfare activity that is based on a social mandate, that the community sees it as its role to take responsibility for the care and control of children: 'the line between citizenship, professional concern and responsibility and child welfare is drawn not in terms of a division but an inclusion'.

This is characteristic of European systems where child protection is conceptualised as 'family support' and is given social authority by the community and the state. The Scottish system is perceived as combining a welfare orientation with the judicial sphere (Hetherington, Cooper, Smith and Welford 1997). In England and Scotland, statutory intervention in child protection is intended only when certain limits are reached and there is particular emphasis on voluntary measures. However, the English child protection system has found there is increasingly less room for voluntary intervention and more and more the courts are being asked, as in Australia, to regulate child welfare activity (Hunt and McLeod 1997).

The philosophy underpinning child protection intervention in European systems is based on principles of community responsibility and membership, and social connectedness, rather than regulatory authority, say Hetherington, Cooper, Smith and Welford (1997). This is exemplified in the French system which is described next.

European Approaches

The child protection system in France provides for the juges des enfants, a specialist aproach to both child protection and juvenile justice cases. Hallett and Hazel (1998) explain that referrals to the *substitut des mineurs* (who is a lawyer) can be made by children, parents and guardians. The substitut refers on to the juges des enfants the cases that have sufficient child protection concerns, or refers the matter back to the child protection administrative system for further information about the case. Those cases that involve serious or criminal factors can also be referred to a tribunal for prosecution. Child protection referrals to the judicial system, by the social services department, must be agreed to by the *Inspectuer*, a senior official in social services. The Inspectuer will support the referral only after there have been sufficient attempts to achieve voluntary agreements with parents. Hetherington, Cooper, Smith and Welford (1997:66) describe this administrative process of needing the agreement of the Inspecteur as providing an important negotiating space before referral to the judicial system.

There are no specific grounds for referral to the child protection administrative or judicial system. Rather, child protection matters are referred if the 'child's upbringing is seriously endangered and there is no effective cooperation from the parents' (Hetherington, Cooper, Smith and Welford 1997:66). The juges des enfants does not need legally admissible evidence of harm to justify statutory involvement. The legal process in the French system is inquisitorial and legal representation is not usual. The juges des enfants meets the children and parents in chambers and the emphasis is on informality and on working with parents to maintain their child in their family. The juges des enfants has responsibility for particular cases and hears any matter that arises in these cases, and usually reviews cases at six to 12 monthly intervals. The juges des enfants has the power to impose orders, to ask the police to remove a child from their home and to refer the case for prosecution. The juges des enfants gives social workers authority to intervene in families and obliges parents to heed the instructions of the social workers, with regard to the care of their children.

The juges des enfants can impose assessment orders (a three month order), supervision, or placement orders (placing a child in residential care or foster care). As much as possible the juges des enfants attempts to get parents to agree to the orders. The juges des enfants can determine the amount of contact a parent can have with their child and can decide where a child will live, even if the parents are not in agreement with this. The juges des enfants can also authorise adoption. Emergency child protection referrals are dealt with by the public prosecutor who uses the police to intervene and act to protect a child.

Germany is not unlike Australia in that it is a federation of states and the individual states have regionally developed organisations that offer child welfare services. However it differs significantly from Australia in that child protection services in Germany are primarily offered by voluntary or non-government organisations. Each district or region provides the Youth Office, a service that coordinates family, recreational, pastoral, child support payments, foster care and adoption services (Hetherington, Cooper, Smith and Welford 1997). The Youth Office has a statutory duty to support families in their efforts to care for and educate their children and to investigate and report to the court on child welfare and safety matters. Child welfare and safety matters are dealt with by the family and guardianship jurisdiction. As with the French system, the German system is inquisitorial in approach and professionally trained judges invite parents into their chambers to hear child protection matters. The emphasis is on encouraging parents to agree to work with family welfare services so that their children can remain in their parents' care. Parents can be legally represented at these hearings, and witnesses' views sought by the judge, but the grounds for child protection concerns do not have to be proven before an order can be made. Social workers and youth workers can represent the child's interests, or the child can appoint an adult of their choosing, or request legal representation. A guardian ad litem is appointed by the court when there is a conflict of interest between the child, the parents and the welfare services. As in France, judges can make orders that regulate parental contact, or order the involvement of services such as intensive family support or specialist children's services. Judges can also make orders that remove all or part of parental responsibilities, or restore these responsibilities. They can also make adoption orders, or appoint a guardian for the child, who might be an adult other than their parent or a district or welfare organisation.

In the Netherlands the majority of services for children and families are also provided by non-government organisations. The child protection system relies more on a medical or welfare model of intervention than on a justice model, as is the case in Australia. The Netherlands system provides the Confidential Doctor Service to help resolve child welfare matters. Any individual can contact the Service if they have concerns about a child's welfare and the Office of the Confidential Doctor has the authority to investigate a referral, and is not required to inform parents in the initial stage of the investigation. The service is staffed by doctors and social workers who listen to child welfare concerns and seek out information that verifies or negates the child welfare concerns. The Confidential Doctor Service coordinates child welfare services and investigates child protection referrals; it does not provide actual child and family welfare services. The Confidential Doctor, like the Inspecteur, also acts as an important intermediary between the administrative and legal systems that regulate child protection.

If the Office of the Confidential Doctor believes that there are parental issues which stand in the way of a child receiving proper care, then the Confidential Doctor Service reports the matter to the Child Care and Protection Board. If the Child Care and Protection Board believes the only way a child will be cared for and kept safe is with a statutory order in place, then the Child Care and Protection Board seeks a child protection order. The Board will also seek an order if the Office of the Confidential Doctor has tried to get parents to use intensive family support services, or other treatment services, substantially provided by non-government agencies, but this has not worked. The legal process that decides child welfare matters is inquisitorial and welfare based, with informal hearings so that parents can speak directly to the judge, although they can be legally represented if they apply for this. Judges can order that there is family supervision, and oblige parents to work with child welfare services; they can also suspend or terminate parental rights, and make emergency child protection orders.

The role of non-government and local agencies in both the Netherlands and Germany underlines the concept of subsidiarity that has shaped the policy and provision of these services. Local organisations or groups are deemed to be responsible for the welfare of their constituents, and they are to be supported by the state in the provision of these services. Hetherington, Cooper, Smith and Welford (1997:84) describe subsidiarity as a 'buttress against the threat of a 'corporatist' state', and is a model, or philosophy, that is the very opposite of the central government control over welfare that characterises Australian and English child protection services.

Child Protection and Social Responsibility

The European approach establishes the family as an object of social concern, rather than as a private domain as it is in the Australian approach. Hetherington, Cooper, Smith and Welford (1997:86) note that in the European approach, the state has an obligation to, and collective responsibility for, child welfare and ensuring child safety. It prefers to exercise this concern through the use of voluntary measures rather than turning to the legal system to regulate child welfare services. It emphasises informal discussions between parents and welfare and judicial decision-makers to resolve child protection matters. There is less emphasis on legal representation although there might be provision for the appointment of a Guardian ad litem to ensure a child's views are heard.

Notions of collective responsibility are notably absent in the Australian approach which enshrines individual rights and places less emphasis on social rights and responsibilities. The Australian and English approaches place great emphasis on getting procedural and legal aspects of a case right. Child protection workers must provide clear evidence of significant harm or risk to a child to justify statutory intervention. When the need for this intervention is legally established, any orders made and welfare services required must be clearly linked to parental responsibilities and negating the child protection concerns. This is less so in the continental European systems, say Hetherington, Cooper, Smith and Welford (1997), which concentrate more on identifying children's needs and improving parental care rather than on proving child abuse has occurred. Child welfare legislation in Australia is predicated on state intervention in family life as an undesirable activity. A high value is placed on personal privacy and individual liberty, and it is preferable to avoid the welfare system. Parton (1991) and McGrath (1997:25) confirm the generally held view that it is better not to need help, as being involved in the child protection system, and with social workers, is stigmatising and also undesirable.

The welfare function of the court in the European systems mentioned above suggests a different relationship between the individual citizen and the state. It also suggests a different view about what is meant by child welfare and child protection. Hetherington, Cooper, Smith and Welford (1997) locate child protection within the broader construct of child welfare in the continental European system: a child's requirements for their human development, their needs – for example for education – are as central to child protection as is their freedom from harm. The child's need to be connected to the broader community, and the community's responsibility to ensure this, is central to the philosophy that animates child protection. This is exemplified in the way in which voluntary organisations are structured into the child and family welfare system. In the European systems outlined above, there is less emphasis on parental rights, and children can be interviewed without their parents' knowledge to establish whether they suffering. There is particular emphasis on social services working in partnership with parents to address child protection problems. Social workers are given the authority by the courts to work with parents and children. Parents accept this, and social workers can have confidence in their authority. Yet, in England, and this would also be so in Australia, Hetherington, Cooper, Smith and Welford (1997:160) argue that child welfare has been reframed as child protection and this has further been narrowed down to be understood as 'intra-familial protection'. The need for child protection to be understood in terms of having broader personal, educational and social needs met, is excluded from the narrower construction of what constitutes child welfare and safety.

Responding to Children: In Summary

There is a widespread acceptance of the need for a separate and specialised jurisdiction for children and young people to deal with child protection and juvenile justice matters. This is based on the understanding that the state intervenes differently in the lives of children from the way it intervenes in the lives of adults, most particularly when parents are not providing appropriate care or supervision for their children. In Australia, there is such a specialised approach for dealing with children and young people. However, they are separated into justice and welfare systems and welfare concerns are secondary when a young person, about whom there are also child protection concerns, enters the criminal justice system. This differs markedly from the Scottish Children's Hearings system which combines law enforcement, social work and community involvement when dealing with children and young people who are both troubled and troublesome.

However, in Australia, the state of Victoria introduced pre-hearing conferences to provide for alternate dispute resolution, to involve parents in decisions about their children and to reduce, as much as possible, the adversarial nature of child protection disputes. The English system has also encouraged parties in family welfare (private law) matters to achieve, as much possible, a settlement away from the court and reduce the acrimony associated with court proceedings. The French, German and Dutch approaches described earlier also provide for what McGrath (1997:182) describes as 'a space before the law is involved, or even when the law is involved, to allow deliberation and negotiation'.

Despite the emphasis in Victoria on alternative dispute resolution, the Australian system is legalistic; it has the same combative and competitive characteristics that McGrath (1997) finds in the Irish system. The Australian system emphasises the role of judicial determination in assessing both the fault of the parents and the seriousness of the child protection concerns presented to the court. What the Report of the National Inquiry into the Prevention of Child Abuse in the UK, *Childhood Matters* (1997:8), found was that such a legalistic emphasis in child abuse matters obscures a child-centred response and fragments what should be a 'whole child' response to child abuse. It also fails to acknowledge what Spencer and Flin (1993:358) describe as the 'unjustifiable degree of stress' that children experience when involved in the legal system, most particularly when their rights and needs are in direct conflict with those of their parents.

In the adversarial system, parents have to deny allegations of child abuse in order to win their case, and in doing this, the truth of what might be their difficulties is obscured. Issues involved in child protection cases are rarely simple and McGrath (1997) suggests that the inquisitorial approach is more helpful in trying to determine the validity of child protection concerns. It is certainly seen as giving more attention to a child's needs and parent competence. A system in which the judge has an active role in gathering information about a case, and managing how it is approached, appears to provide the possibility for more therapeutic outcomes than the confronting approach of the adversarial model. It is a system in which the judiciary and the legal profession have a better understanding of the role of social workers and the extent of their responsibilities within child protection.

McGrath (1997:70) believes that 'the greater involvement of lawyers in the child protection system has brought changes ... a trend towards more legalistic and bureaucratic procedures', procedures that ' turn welfare professionals into social police' (ibid.). The view that those who intervene in child protection are seen as oppressors and not as agents of social care (McGrath 1997:68), mirrors the general lack of agreement that there is in the Australian community about what constitutes child abuse and how responsible the community is for its fellow citizens.

The *Childhood Matters* Report (1997) recommended that child welfare legislation define what is meant by parental responsibilities so that there is an established standard of care that children can expect from their parents, and this can act as a guide for parents themselves. Such guidance is notably absent from much of Australian child welfare legislation, yet its presence would surely reduce conflict in child protection matters about parental care and children's needs. What the Report (*Childhood Matters* 1997:19) also recommended was that: 'Advocates should accept responsibility for preparing themselves, through appropriate training, for work in child protection cases. Judges also need to be sensitive to the style and advocacy they allow when such cases come to court'. The English public law child welfare jurisdiction requires child representatives to have specialist training in order to represent children in child protection matters. This is not the case in Australia, and whilst in Victoria children aged seven years of age and over are independently legally represented in any proceedings about them, legal representatives are not required to have any specialist training. The general unfamiliarity of many legal professionals with child abuse matters combined with the adversarial requirements for due process and attention to individual rights, means legal procedures are more adult-centred rather than child-centred and children's accounts may be given less credence than those of their parents.

Victoria has initiated some of the approaches suggested in the literature about how the legal system can better respond to children at risk. Child representation and pre-hearing conferences are examples of significant initiatives. However, it is clear that a child welfare system, and legal system, that is based on fault rather than need, fails to provide the possibilities for partnership with parents to address child protection concerns. The varying systems outlined in this chapter indicate that where the community emphasises citizenship and social responsibility, and as much as possible voluntary resolution of child protection problems, and gives welfare professionals the authority to work with families, then children's needs and wishes are better protected. What the varying systems also indicate is that where child protection matters are resolved as much as possible by informal means, by inquiry and listening to children's accounts, then the truth of a child's needs and parental difficulties are established more readily than by a contested hearing. Australians prefer that state intervention in family life is as minimum as possible (Alder and Wundersitz 1994). The child welfare legal system has to ensure that this preference does not fail to ensure a proper response to children at risk. The implications for framing child protection as a socio-legal enterprise, and the need for a broader child welfare focus are discussed in the next, and concluding, chapter.

Chapter Seven

Conclusion

> Children are not helped by the fragmented and conflicting policies, values, objectives and responsibilities at national and local level. They suffer as a result of the lack of a powerful and coordinating government voice. Where there is cooperation, this is often despite, rather than because of, existing systems. Law, regulations, structures and policies must be harmonised with a concept of the 'whole child' in mind (National Commission of Inquiry into the Prevention of Child Abuse, *Childhood Matters*, 1997:7–8).

The Australian Law Reform report on children and the legal process found that Australian child welfare legislation fails to address the practical concerns of child protection (ALRC 1997). Child protection in Australia is framed as a socio-legal enterprise and this has significant implications for the legal and welfare professionals responding to children who need care and protection. The lack of agreement about what is considered harm has meant that, in Australia, the legal system looks for clear incidents of child abuse to confirm that a child is at risk or has been harmed and needs statutory help. Yet child abuse is not an absolute concept (Farmer and Owen 1995). What *Messages from Research*, the Department of Health (HMSO 1995:26) study in England, Wales and Northern Ireland of child protection practice found was that for the most part child maltreatment is a continuum of longer term emotional and physical harm to a child, that sometimes includes sexual maltreatment. Child maltreatment is rarely a single event and most behaviours that place children at risk need to be looked at in context: at the child's needs according to their age and developmental needs, at parenting style, at family structure, for example. Despite current understandings that it is a combination of social, economic and environmental factors that contribute to child abuse and neglect, the child protection and legal systems are 'preoccupied with abusive events rather than the processes that underlie them' (*Messages from Research*, HMSO 1995:22).

Thorpe and Bilson (1998) found, in their study of referrals in custody and access disputes in matrimonial matters to a local authority social services department in England, that the child protection service focused on investigating cases to substantiate concerns rather than looking to see what help a child might need. Child welfare concerns were more likely to be dealt with by mediation rather than compulsory measures if the allegations made did not provide clear evidence of harm to a child. The lack of agreement about the point at which parent behaviours constitute harm, or the child's living situation causes maltreatment, means in Australia that there are no agreed thresholds that are tied to child protection intervention.

Magistrates in the study reported on in this book confirmed that families who find their way into the child protection system are generally 'families overwhelmed and depressed by social problems' (*Messages from Research*, HMSO 1995:22). Magistrates believed the child protection service needed to concentrate on providing families with support rather than finding fault with parents; yet the child protection service is required to establish fault to justify intervention. The view that it is struggling families who predominate in the child welfare jurisdiction means that there is a tendency to minimise parental responsibilities and to overlook the significance of a child's need to be looked after. It is a view that fails to recognise that not all family difficulties can be explained by social problems and that problems of family violence or serious psychiatric disorder cannot be managed solely by family support services.

The Australian Law Reform Commission (1997:8) noted, in its report on children and the legal process, that in 1992, 22 per cent of Australia's population was children, who mostly 'live with their parents but as increasingly families break down and are refashioned, many children now live in blended families that include step or half siblings'. What this means is that children's experiences of family life will differ from those of previous generations and professionals will need to develop measures of children's well-being that accommodate changes in family structure. *The Children (Scotland) Act 1995* gives legislative force to parental responsibilities, to establish the standard of care that children can expect from their parents or responsible adults. This concept of parental responsibilities is absent from Australian legislation.

The Law Commission also drew attention to the different requirements that children have of the legal process and the need for judicial and administrative fora to ensure children's interests are heard. Magistrates in the study reported on in this book recognised that their work in the Children's Court was unlike magistrate work in other courts and that they had no specialist training for deciding what are essentially social and psychological matters, as much as they are legal matters. Magistrates however believed they could not always rely on information provided by the child protection service to assist their decisions. They were frustrated by the welfare bureaucracy which appeared to work in ways that created difficulties for the courts and did not conform to the requirements of an adversarial system. Some of the problems raised by magistrates are common to child protection wherever it is. Others were problems because of the way legislation, child protection and the courts conduct child welfare matters in Australia.

Magistrates confirmed that the adversarial system does not provide easy legal resolutions for the problems of social and economic deprivation and poor parenting practices which are typical of the cases brought to the Children's Court. Whilst Children's Court work did not call on their legal training, magistrates looked to the legal framework to assess and respond to child protection concerns. Magistrates were clear that decisions about a child's welfare had to observe legislative requirements. They were also clear that their remit in the Children's Court, unlike other adult courts, was to decide what was in the best interests of the individual before them. Although the criteria magistrates used to decide the best interests of the child were individual and varied, they all agreed that they looked to see whether serious harm to a child had occurred, or could occur, and whether the child would be safe if they remained in their parents' care. However the vagueness about what is considered harm to a child and the lack of guidelines to assist magistrates with decisions about what is an unacceptable risk to a child or significant harm meant the needs of the child were reduced to what conformed to legal requirements.

Professional Cooperation in Child Protection

The study of the Children's Court, Victoria revealed, as has related studies, that effective child protection is a shared enterprise amongst the professions. However, the strict adherence to legal requirements meant particular categories of cases often failed to qualify for statutory intervention. It also meant that there was an increased tolerance of some categories of child abuse. The child protection service's strict adherence to service guidelines, has also contributed to the greater tolerance of some child abuse. The need to defend its investigations and recommendations has limited its ability to respond to suspicions of child abuse. Farmer and Owen (*Messages From Research* 1995:114) found, in their study of child protection conferences in Bristol, that the focus was on whether or not a child had been harmed and this meant less attention was paid to broader child development and welfare needs, for example for education, health, stable family relationships and adequate parental care. They found that children who are referred for help on the basis of neglect or emotional abuse do not receive the help that is given to children in physical and sexual abuse matters. There is less support given to child protection workers to respond to suspicions of emotional abuse and a consequent tendency of statutory services to 'neglect' the neglect of children (*Messages From Research* 1995:114).

Magistrates in the study reported on in this book said they had to be mindful of the legal process as well as welfare concerns in their decision-making. Without case law to assist them, and given the significant tensions between legal and welfare practitioners, magistrates took a case-specific approach to child abuse matters. They varied in how they weighed case factors, and information. Without guidelines to assist them in deciding what information was relevant, magistrates relied on their own assessments and personal frameworks to decide what would assist them. Moreover, what magistrates might perceive as the 'real issues' in a case were often not the same as those that concerned child protection. Magistrates mentioned particular cues and views they developed to assist them to process the considerable amount of information they were presented in each case. However, magistrates said it was difficult to articulate, outside a given case, the criteria they used in child protection decision-making. The individuality of magistrates' decision-making meant there could be little predictability about court outcomes. Yet, coherent and collaborative approaches to child protection needs shared criteria about intervention and the child protection service needs clear reasons for why the court decides a case in a certain way to plan and prepare court matters.

Magistrates in the study said they were frustrated by the quality of child protection workers' evidence and their often unfamiliarity with court requirements. They were also frustrated by their inability to obtain all the information that would be useful to deciding a case. Yet magistrates have legislative provision (*Children and Young Persons Act* s82) to obtain information and direct proceedings, but appeared reluctant to take advantage of these options. Given that children's and family courts are increasingly being asked to resolve problems of family dysfunction it is essential that the professional groups who work in child protection develop criteria to respond to these social problems. Given the considerable ambiguity that surrounds child abuse, this cooperation is essential. Hallett and Birchall (1995) found that professionals were prepared to share information about suspected abuse at the initial stages of child abuse investigation. They were less willing to do this at later stages because of the lack of clarity about professional roles and responsibilities and because of the impact of the justice system with its different standards for evidence etc. The lack of agreed criteria about child abuse to legitimise child protection action contributes to difficulties with professional roles and responsibilities.

Magistrates said that they did not regard themselves as having any role in statutory planning in child protection matters and that the court appearance should not be considered as part of welfare intervention. Yet the court outcome in a child abuse case will define the role of the child protection service in the case and specify what actions parents and welfare services are to take to ensure children are safe. Magistrates said it was their role to make sure the child protection service could justify its intervention and to ensure parents are heard by the court and their rights respected.

Child protection workers believed that the highly proceduralised way in which child protection is conducted and the emphasis on individual rights meant adult rights predominated over the child's rights. The Australian Law Reform Commission (1997:18) found that the law and the conduct of the legal process consistently fails to provide justice and redress for children who have suffered abuse. Whilst child welfare legislation in Australia is child-centred in its intent, it is not child-centred in its professional approach to the resolution of child abuse problems. The formalities of court process mean that 'the rhetoric and intentions in child abuse policy' (Mason and Fallon 1999:12) give way to adult issues as the main focus of negotiations. The legal focus on specific instances of at risk incidents or harm to a child means that what the child's experiences have been may go unacknowledged; the 'emotional hurt' described by children, in the study undertaken by Mason and Fallon (1999:10) of children's perspectives on abuse, is left out of legal considerations. Child protection issues are not viewed within the context of the child's wider needs. The individual rights framework hinders the development and acceptance of authoritative knowledge about what is known to be harmful and hurtful for children (*Messages From Research* 1995:22).

There is no concept of parental responsibilities in Australian legislation, nor such benchmarks as the threshold criteria of the *Children Act 1989* for assessing what is appropriate care for a child when measured against what care is given to another child of the same age. There is no provision for the exclusion of adults who have sexually offended and have been convicted as there is in Scotland where a child cannot reside in the same household as a Schedule 1 offender (see Chapter Six for discussion about this). The parent's right to maintain their household appears to be given precedence over the child's right to be safe, despite what a child's views, and the views of professionals, might be.

A Child-centred Approach to Child Protection

A child-centred approach to child protection requires a greater emphasis on the prevention of child abuse. This would require more flexibility than the current system permits. It would also require a re-examination of child welfare legislation and debate about the community expectations from child protection and the courts. It would necessitate a distinction between children in need and child protection, between issues of child concern and child protection, which would allow welfare professionals to approach cases on the basis of need rather than possible protection. The legal process would need to regard this as important child welfare practice and support preventative action. Magistrates in the study emphasised the family's right to privacy and family autonomy appeared to be understood as parental autonomy. The emphasis on family preservation is supported by all; however what must be also acknowledged is that there are families in which children are at significant risk and families who do not respond to family preservation efforts (Gelles 1996). Effective child protection and court support for at risk children requires a reconceptualisation of child welfare as concerned with children's well-being, and this is measured not just in terms of protection and care but also in terms of education, health, social connectedness, and emotional and behavioural development. However this means child protection needs to be reconstructed as a shared and interprofessional responsibility. The legal system is one part of this approach. For such an approach to work in the Australian context, legislation and the legal response to children at risk must be based on children's needs. Child protection professionals will need to be given the authority to do this and not to be seen as part of a malign system that is best avoided. Principles such as the child's right to be looked after and be safe, to not experience fear and loneliness must be given primacy over adult rights. This will necessarily require professionals and legislation to take a more pragmatic view about family autonomy.

The National Commission of Inquiry into the Prevention of Child Abuse, *Childhood Matters* (1997:8) reported that children and families, and many professionals, frequently find the legal system hostile, confusing and traumatic when child protection matters go to court. Magistrates in this study noted that it was difficult to translate welfare concerns into legal facts that they could decide on. The adversarial process that directs their decision-making does not accommodate the differences that characterise child welfare matters. Nor does the legislation accommodate the multifaceted nature of child protection concerns. The 'one-off' nature of court hearings, and the need to deal with the case as it is presented on the day in court, fails to provide magistrates with an adequate process for responding to the difficulties of child protection cases. Nor, does the adversarial approach; a system in which parties present opposing accounts in court in reality does little to establish proof of child abuse matters.

The legalistic character of child protection in Australia means legal approaches, and professionals, are more favoured than welfare contributions in deciding child abuse cases. Yet the nature of child protection concerns means that the professional opinions of welfare professionals should be given more weight than they are. Magistrates, in the study reported, were resistant to the use of checklists about, say, indicators of emotional abuse, to achieve more consistent decision-making. Yet the acknowledged specialist nature of the court indicates that such information is important to understanding the validity of child protection concerns.

Child Protection: Towards an Effective System

The child protection legal system differences referred to in the previous chapter describe systems in which there is a better match between legal and welfare principles than is in the Australian system. The contribution of the guardian ad litem in England (and Wales and Northern Ireland) is clearly an important mechanism for providing the court with an independent source of child welfare information. Magistrates in the study reported in this book spoke about difficulties with the availability and utility of information about cases. Magistrates were not comfortable about relying solely on child protection court reports because of their views about the quality of the information and its legal acceptability. Magistrates were critical in their views of child protection workers as witnesses. Magistrates were of a view that child protection workers sought to influence court outcomes, and their discretion, and magistrates criticised this unwanted interference.

The guardian ad litem role is well regarded in England as the family proceedings court considers its role is to be welfare-minded and to give priority to the needs of the child as well as acknowledging the rights of the parents. The professional collaboration that precedes court confirms this welfare focus. Child protection conferences include teachers, health professionals, child welfare workers and families who debate child protection concerns and look at the child's needs rather than solely at instances of maltreatment or abuse.

The continental European systems operate very differently from the Australian system. Yet the Australian system could look to the operating principles of these systems to provide a child-focused system, to work in a collaborative manner, working within the judicial system yet in a welfare-minded way that makes the child's needs the system's priority. There is court support for child protection, more agreement about what constitutes child abuse, more understanding of the complex task of the child protection worker and greater community acceptance about state intervention in family life. Judges are more able, and more prepared, to seek specialist knowledge of child development and child abuse to assist decision-making. Welfare professionals saw it as their responsibility to provide such information.

Much of child protection work is grounded in concerns about the very poor parenting of children. There appears to be little legislative concern about long term family dysfunction and its impact on children's emotional and behavioural development. Yet this lack of concern is costly to the community: in costs met by adult mental health services, for example, for adult victims of child abuse.

The study of magistrate decision-making identified the role and approach of the Children's Court in child protection and the tensions that emerge between legal and welfare responses to child maltreatment. The Children's Court has a central role in this response and the community expects the court to ensure children are safe and their parents protect them from harm. Until the community accepts that child protection is a social responsibility, and that it must support interventions that identify and support vulnerable children, the difficulties that surround child protection decision-making, identified in this study, will remain. The legal and welfare systems must acknowledge that work in child protection is a partnership and make the system changes that ensure this. Finally, these systems must ensure that the legal process meets the needs of children so that child abuse policy is not just rhetoric but is committed to making a difference in the lives of children affected by abuse.

Bibliography

Adler, R. (1979), 'Child Abuse', Proceedings of a seminar on *Crime and the Family – Some Aspects of the Report of the Royal Commission on Human Relationships*, Proceedings of the Institute of Criminology, no. 4, University of Sydney.

Alanen, L., Kiili, J. and Satka, M. (1999), 'Indicators for Children's Well-Being: A Pilot Project', University of Jyvaslya, Finland.

Allen, N. (1990), *Making Sense of the Children Act*, Longman, England.

Alternative Dispute Resolution: Information Sheet (1996), The Tavistock Centre and National Family Mediation, a pilot study funded by the Department of Health, UK.

Amato, P. (1987), *Children in Australian Families – The Growth of Competence*, Prentice-Hall, Sydney.

Angus, G. and Wilkinson, K. (1993), *Child Abuse and Neglect Australia 1990–91*, Australian Institute of Health & Welfare, AGPS, Canberra.

Angus, G. and Woodward, S. (1995), *Child Abuse and Neglect Australian 1993–1994*, Australian Institute of Health & Welfare, AGPS, Canberra.

Arkes, H.R. and Hammond, K.R. (eds) (1986), *Judgment and Decision Making: An Interdisciplinary Reader*, Cambridge University Press, Cambridge.

Ashworth, A. (1983), *Sentencing and Penal Policy*, Weidenfeld and Nicholson, London.

Ashworth, A., Genders, E., Mansfield, E., Peay, J. and Player, E. (1984), *Sentencing in the Crown Court: Report of an Exploratory Study*, Oxford Centre for Criminological Research, Occasional Papers 10, University of Oxford, Oxford University Press.

Asquith, S. (1983), *Children and Justice: Decision-Making in Children's Hearings and Juvenile Courts*, Edinburgh University Press, Edinburgh.

Australian Law Reform Commission and Human Rights and Equal Opportunity Commission, *A Matter of Priority: Children and the legal process*, Draft Recommendations Paper 3, May 1997, Australian Law Reform Commission, Sydney, NSW.

Australian Health Ethics Committee (1993), *Assessment of Qualitative Research: Information for Institutional Ethics Committees*, a draft discussion paper for the National Health and Medical Research Council, Canberra.

Ayres, P. (1998), 'Significant Harm: Making Professional Judgements', *Child Abuse Review*, Vol. 7, pp. 330–42.

Babbie, E.R. (1993), *Research Methods for Social Work* (2nd edn), Brooks/Cole, California.

Bagshaw, D. (1995), 'Mediating family disputes in statutory settings', *Australian Social Work*, 48, pp. 3–12.

Bainham, A. (1990), *Children, the New Law: The Children Act 1989*, Family Law, Bristol.
Baldwin, J. (1976), 'The Social Composition of the Magistracy', *British Journal of Criminology*, 16(2), April, pp. 171-4.
Ballenden, N.R., Laster, K. and Lawrence, J.A. (1993), *Pathologist as Gatekeeper: Discretionary Decision-Making in Cases of Sudden Infant Death*, paper prepared for the Victorian Institute of Forensic Pathology and the University of Melbourne.
Bartle, R. (1985), *Crime and the New Magistrate*, Barry Rose, Chichester.
Bates, F., Blackwood, J.B., Davidson, A.P. and Mackie, I.C. (1991), *The Australian Social Worker and the Law* (3rd edn), The Law Book Company, Sydney.
Batten, R., Weeks, W. and Wilson, J. (eds) (1991), *Issues Facing Australian Families: Human Services Respond*, Longman Cheshire, Melbourne.
Bean, P. (1985), 'Social enquiry reports: a recommendation for disposal', *Justice of the Peace*, 139, pp. 568-9, 585-7.
Bentovim, A., Elton, A. and Trantner, M. (1987), 'Prognosis for rehabilitation after abuse', *Adoption and Fostering*, 11(1), pp. 26-37.
Berger, P. and Luckman, T. (1967), *The Social Construction of Reality*, Penguin, London.
Besharov, D.J. (1981), 'Towards better research on child abuse and neglect: making definitional issues an explicit methodological concern', *Child Abuse and Neglect*, 5, pp. 383-91.
Besharov, D.J. (1986), 'Child Abuse: arrest and prosecution decision-making', *American Criminal Law Review*, 24, 2, pp. 315-77.
Birks, C. (1995), *Child Abuse in Europe*, Emwe-Verlag, Nurnberg.
Blackmore, R. (1986), 'The Judicial Perspective', Institute of Criminology Conference, Kuring-gai College of Advanced Education, Sydney.
Blackmore, R. (1989), *The Children's Court and Community Welfare in New South Wales*, Longman Professional, Melbourne.
Bogdan, R. (1975), *Introduction to Qualitative Research Method: a Phenomenological Approach*, Wiley, New York.
Bogdan, R. and Taylor, S. (1984), *Introduction to Qualitative Research Methods: the Search for Meanings*, Wiley, New York.
Bond, R.A. and Lemon, N.F. (1981), 'Training, Experience and Magistrates' Sentencing Philosophies', *Law and Human Behaviour*, 5(2&3), pp. 123-39.
Booth, Dame Margaret (1996), *Avoiding Delay in Children Act Cases*, July, Department of the Lord Chancellor, England.
Boss, P. (1980), *On the Side of the Child: An Australian Perspective on Child Abuse*, Fontana Collins, Melbourne.
Boss, P. (1987), 'History of Child Abuse in Australia', in R. Snashall (ed.), *National Conference on Child Abuse*, Australian Institute of Criminology, Canberra.
Boss, P. (1987), *Systems for Managing Child Maltreatment in Australia*, The Creswick Foundation, Melbourne.

Boss, P., Edwards, S. and Pitman, S. (eds) (1995), *Profile of Young Australians: Facts, Figures and Issues*, Churchill Livingstone, Melbourne.

Bostwick, G.J. and Kyte, N.S. (1985), 'Measurement' and 'Validity and Reliability', in Grinnell, R. (ed.), *Social Work Research and Evaluation* (3rd edn) F.E. Peacock Publishers, Itasca, Ill.

Bottomley, K. (1973), *Decisions in the Penal Process*, Martin Robertson, London.

Braithwaite, J. (1989), *Crime, Shame and Reintegration*, Cambridge University Press, Melbourne.

Brannen, J. (ed.) (1992), *Mixing Methods: Qualitative and Quantitative Research*, Avebury, Aldershot.

Braye, S. and Preston-Shoot, M. (1993), *Practising Social Work Law*, Macmillan, London.

Breckenridge, J. (1995), 'The Socio-legal Relationship in Child Sexual Assault', in Swain, P. (ed.), *In the Shadow of the Law: The Legal Context of Social Work Practice*, Federation Press, Sydney.

Brewer, H. and Hunter, A. (1989), *Multimethods: A Synthesis of Styles*, Sage, Newbury Park, California.

Brown, S. (1991), *Magistrates at Work*, Open University Press, Milton Keynes.

Browne, E. (1987), 'Social work – what went wrong? The Beckford Enquiry', *Australian Social Work*, 48(2), pp. 3–9.

Bryman, A. (1992), 'Qualitative and quantitative research: further reflections on their integration', in Brannen, J. (ed.) (1992), *Mixing Methods: Qualitative and Quantitative Research*, Avebury, Aldershot, UK.

Buckley, H., Skehil, C. and O'Sullivan, O. (1997), *Child Protection in Ireland: A Case Study*, Oaktree Press, Dublin.

Buckley, H. (2000), 'Working Together to Protect Children: Evaluation of an Interagency Training Programme', *Administration*, Winter, Irish Institute of Public Policy, Dublin.

Buist, A., 'Mentally Ill Families: When are Children Safe', *Australian Family Physician*, Vol. 27, No. 4, pp. 261–5.

Burns, R.B. (1994), *Introduction to Research Methods* (2nd edn), Longman, Melbourne.

Bullock, R., Little, M. and Millham, S. (1992), 'The relationships between quantitative and qualitative approaches in social policy research' in Brannen, J. (ed.), *Mixing Methods: Qualitative and Quantitative Research*, Avebury, Aldershot.

Burgess, R.G. (1982), 'Multiple strategies in field research', in Burgess, R.G. (ed.), *Field research: A Sourcebook and Field Manual*, George Allen and Unwin, London.

Burns, R.B. (1994), *Introduction to Research Methods* (2nd edn), Longman Cheshire, Melbourne.

Calvert, G., Ford, A. and Parkinson, P. (eds) (1992), *The Practice of Child Protection: Australian Approaches*, Hale and Iremonger, NSW.

Campbell, D.T. and Stanley, J.C. (1966), *Experimental and Quasi-experimental Designs for Research*, Rand McNally, Chicago.

Campbell, L. (1997), 'Decision making in child protection', *Child and Family Social Work*, 2, pp. 1–11.
Carney, T. (Chair), Child Welfare Practice and Legislation Review Committee (1983), *Child Welfare Practice and Legislation Review: Discussion Paper*, Report for the Victorian Government, Melbourne.
Carrick, M. (1985), 'Child Protection and the Court Process', in *Child abuse and the Criminal Justice System: Is there a need for change?*, Queensland Police Department, Brisbane.
Carlen, P. (1976), *Magistrates' Justice*, Martin Robertson, Oxford.
Carrington, K. (1993), 'The Welfare/Justice Nexus', in Mason, J. (ed.), *Child Welfare Policy – Critical Australian Perspectives*, Hale and Iremonger, NSW.
Carroll, J.S. (1978), 'Causal theories of crime and their effect on expert parole decisions', *Law and Human Behaviour*, 2 (4), pp. 377–88.
Carroll, J.S. (ed.) (1990), *Applied Social Psychology and Organisational Settings*, Erlbaum Associates, Hillsdale, New Jersey.
Carroll, J.S. and Johnson, E.J. (1990), *Decision Research: A Field Guide*, Sage Publications, London.
Carson, D. (1990), 'Reporting to Court', *Journal of Social Welfare Law*, 3, pp. 151–63.
Carter, J. (1983), *Protection to Prevention*, SWRC Reports and Proceedings, University of New South Wales, 29 January.
Carter, P., Jeffs, T. and Smith, M. (1992), *Changing Social Work and Welfare*, Open University Press, Buckingham.
Charlesworth, S., Turner, J.N. and Foreman, L. (1990), *Lawyers, Social Workers and Families*, The Federation Press, Sydney.
Chi, T.H., Glaser, R. and Rees, E. (1982), 'Expertise in problem-solving', in Steinberg, R. (ed.), *Advances in the Psychology of Human Intelligence*, Vol. 1, Erlbaum, Hillsdale, New Jersey.
Chi, T.H., Glaser R. and Farr, M.J. (eds) (1988), *The Nature of Experience*, L. Erlbaum Associates, Hillsdale, New Jersey.
Child Welfare Practice and Legislation Committee (1984), *Child Welfare Practice and Legislation Review*, v.2 *Equity and Social Justice for Children, Families and Communities*, Report for the Victorian Government, Melbourne.
Children and Young Persons Act 1989 (Victoria) (1993), Victorian Government Printer.
Children (Scotland) Act 1995, HMSO, Edinburgh.
Children Act Advisory Committee (1997), *Handbook of Best Practice in Children Act Cases*, HMSO.
Children Act Advisory Committee (1997), *Final Report*, June, Department of the Lord Chancellor, England.
Children Services News Supplement (1997), *Reporting to Court Under the Children Act*, 1997, Department of Health, England.
Cooper, A., Heatherington, R., Baistow, K. et al. (1995), *Positive Child Protection: A View From Abroad*, Russell House Publishing, London.

Cooper, S., (1996), 'Whether Child's Representation', *Child Rights*, The Children's Legal Advice Centre, University of Essex.
Chisholm, R. (1980), 'Children and the Law', in Brown, K.G. (ed.), *Children Australia*, George Allen & Unwin, Sydney.
Clark, R. (1989), *Reflecting on Decision Making in Child Protection Practice*, unpublished thesis, University of Melbourne.
Clark, R. (1986), 'Decision Making on Child Protection Work', conference paper, *International Congress on Child Abuse and Neglect*, Sydney, NSW.
Clark, R. (1995), 'Child Protection and Social Work', in Swain, P.A. (ed.), *In the Shadow of the Law: The Legal Context of Social Work Practice*, The Federation Press, Sydney.
Collingridge, M. (1991), 'Legal Risk, Legal Scrutiny, and Social Work', *Australian Social Work*, 44(1), pp. 11–17.
Community Services Victoria (1991), *Annual Report 1990/91*, Victorian Government Printer.
Community Services Victoria (1992), *Protecting Children: Standards & Procedures for Protective Workers*, Victorian Government Printer.
Community Services Victoria (1990), *Annual Report 1989/90*, Victorian Government Printer.
Conte, J. and Shore, D.A. (eds) (1982), 'Social Work and Child Sexual Abuse', *Journal of Social Work and Human Sexuality*, Vols 1 and 2, Haworth Press, New York.
Cooper, D. (1993), *Child Abuse Revisited: Children, Society and Social Work*, Open University Press, Buckingham.
Corbett, C. (1987), 'Magistrates and Court Clerks' sentencing behaviour: an experimental study', in Pennington, D.C. and Lloyd-Bostock, S. (eds), *The Psychology of Sentencing*, Centre for Socio-Legal Studies, Oxford University, Oxford.
Coull, V. (1992), *Evaluation of the Implementation of the Children and Young Persons Act: Trends in Protective Intervention*, Community Services Victoria, June.
Craft, J., Epley, S. and Clarkson, C. (1980), 'Factors influencing legal disposition in child abuse investigations', *Journal of Social Service Research*, Vol. 15, No. 1–2.
Craft, J.L. and Bettin, C.A. (1991), 'Case Factor Selection in Physical Child Abuse Investigations', *Journal of Social Service Research*, 14(3–4), pp. 107–23.
Craft, J.L. and Clarkson, C.D. (1985), 'Case Disposition; recommendations of Attorneys and Social Workers in child abuse investigations', *Child Abuse and Neglect*, 9(2), pp. 165–74.
Curnock, K. and Hardiker, P. (1979), *Towards Practice Theory Skills and Methods in Social Assessments*, Routledge and Kegan Paul, London.
Dale, P., Davies, M., Morrison, T. and Waters, J. (1986), *Dangerous families: Assessment and Treatment of Child Abuse*, Routledge, London.
Dawson, P. and Stevens, R. (1991), 'The Children's Act 1989: a new and exciting chapter in providing for the welfare of children', *Justice of the Peace*, Chichester, 155(11), 16 March, pp. 166–7.

de Vaus, D.A. (1990), *Surveys in Social Research* (2nd edn), Allen & Unwin, Sydney.

Denzin, N.K. (1970), *The Research Act*, Aldine, Chicago.

Denzin, N.K. (1991), *Images of Postmodern Society*, Sage Publications, London.

Department of Family and Community Services, South Australia (1990), *Guardianship, Long-term Legal Status and Related Issues: Policy Statement*, September, Adelaide.

Department of Health (1995), *Child Protection: Messages from Research*, HMSO, London.

Department of Health (1997), *Messages From Research*, HMSO, London.

Department of Human Services (1999), *Evaluation Of the Statewide Implementation of Family Group Conferencing*, DHS, Melbourne.

Department of Human Services (1996), *Family Group Conferences in Protection and Care: Program Document*, DHS, Melbourne.

Dhir, C. and Markman, H. (1986), 'Social judgment theory and mental conflict', in Arkes, H.R. and Hammond, K.R. (eds), *Judgment and Decision Making: An Interdisciplinary Reader*, Cambridge University Press.

Di Leonardi, J.W. (1980), 'Decision making in protection services', *Child Welfare*, Vol. 59, June.

Diamond, S.S. (1981), 'Exploring sources of sentence disparity', in Sales, BD (ed.), *Perspectives in Law & Psychology; Vol 2: The Jury, Judicial and Trial Process*, Plenum Press, New York, pp. 387–412.

Dingwall, R., Eckelaar, J.M. and Murray, T. (1983), *The Protection of Children: State Intervention and Family Life*, Basil Blackwell, Oxford.

Donzelot, J. (1980), *The Policing of Families*, Hutchinson, London.

Doob, A.N. and Beaulieu, L.A. (1992), 'Variation in the exercise of judicial discretion with young offenders', *Canadian Journal of Criminology*, January, pp. 35–50.

Douglas, R. (1980), 'Sentencing in the suburbs I: theft and violence', *The Australian & New Zealand Journal of Criminology*, 13(4), December, pp. 241–52.

Douglas, R. (1982), 'Case Structure, Participation and Verdict in the Melbourne Magistrate's Court', *The Australian & New Zealand Journal of Criminology*, 15(4), pp. 195–206.

Douglas, R. (1987), 'Do Lawyers make a difference', *Australian Journal of Social Issues*, 22, 1 February, pp. 377–89.

Douglas, R. (ed.) (1980), *Guilty your Worship: A Study of Victoria's Magistrate's Courts*, Occasional Monograph No. 1, La Trobe University Legal Studies Department, Bundoora, Victoria.

Douglas, R. and Laster, K. (1992), *Reforming the People's Court: Victorian Magistrates Reaction to Change*, Melbourne.

Douglas, R. (1989), 'A matter of small importance: SES and Magistrates' Court outcomes', *Australian and New Zealand Journal of Sociology*, 25(1), pp. 66–84.

Draper, H. and Ardley, M. (1989), 'The Children and Young Persons Act 1989: Stage 2', *Law Institute Journal (Victoria)*, October, pp. 937–9.

Drew, E.C. and Dalgleish, L.I. (1986), 'The relationship of child abuse indicators to risk assessment and to the Court's decision to separate', conference paper, *International Congress on Child Abuse and Neglect*, Sydney, NSW.

Dunnette, M.D. (ed.) (1976), *Handbook of Industrial and Organisational Psychology*, Rand McNally, Chicago.

Edgar, D. (1988), 'Child abuse: social forces and prevention', conference paper presented at *Prevention of Child Abuse Conference*, Adelaide, SA.

Edwards, Judge L.P. (1992), 'The Juvenile Court and the Role of the Juvenile Court Judge', *Juvenile & Family Court Journal*, 43(2).

Eekelaar, J. (1984), 'Legal systems and families: social change and family policies', *XXth International CFR Seminar*, Institute of Family Studies, Melbourne.

Ely, P. and Stanley, C. (1996), *The French Alternative: Delinquency Prevention and Child Protection in France*, an occasional paper published by Nacro, UK.

Epstein, I. (1985), 'Qualitative and quantitative research', in Grinnell, R., *Social Work Research and Evaluation* (2nd edn), F.E. Peacock Publishers, Itasca, Illinois.

Falkov, A. (1997), 'Adult psychiatry – a missing link in the child protection network: a response to Reder and Duncan', *Child Abuse Review*, Vol. 6, pp. 40–5.

Family Court of Australia (1982), *Child Abuse 1980–1981 Bibliography*, No. 7, March, Sydney, NSW.

Fanning, D., Draper, H. and Ardley, M. (1989), 'Have we finally got our act together? The Children and Young Persons Act 1989: Stages 3 and 4', *Law Institute Journal (Victoria)*, pp. 800–3.

Farmer, E. and Owen, M. (1995), *Child Protection Practice: Private Risks and Public Remedies-Decision Making, Intervention and Outcome in Child Protection Work*, HMSO, London.

Feely, M. (1979), *The Process is the Punishment*, Russell Sage, New York.

Finkelhor, D. and Korbin, J. (1988), 'Child abuse as an international issue', *Child Abuse and Neglect*, 12, pp. 3–23.

Fitzmaurice, C. and Pease, K. (1986), *The Psychology of Judicial Sentencing*, Manchester University Press, England.

Foddy, W. (1993), *Constructing Questions for Interviews and Questionnaires: Theory & Practice*, Cambridge University Press, Australia.

Fogarty, Justice J. and Sargeant, D. (1989), *Protective Services for Children in Victoria: an Interim Report*, Community Services Victoria, Melbourne.

Fogarty, Justice J. (1993), *Protective Services for Children in Victoria: A Report for the Victorian Government*, Melbourne.

Fogarty, Justice J. (1995), *Children First – The Rights of our Children and Young People*, Victorian Council for Civil Liberties Seminar Series, 9 August.

Folberg, J. and Taylor, A. (1984), *Mediation: A Comprehensive Guide to Resolving Conflict Without Litigation*, Jossey-Bass, San Francisco.

Foucault, M. (1977), *Discipline and Punish*, Penguin, Harmondworth.

Foucault, M. (1980), *Power/Knowledge: Selected Interviews and Other Writings*, Pantheon Books, New York.

Franklin, G. and Parton, N. (eds) (1991), *Social Work, the Media and Public Relations*, Routledge, London.

Freeman, M.D.A. (1992), *Children, their Families and the Law: Working with The Children Act*, Macmillan, Basingstoke.

Freestone, D (ed.) (1990), *Children and the Law*, Hull University Press.

Frost, N. (1990), 'Taking Child Abuse Seriously', in *Violence Against Children Study Group*, Unwin and Hyman, London.

Gale, F., Naffine, N. and Wundersitz, J. (1993), *Juvenile Justice: Debating the Issues*, Allen & Unwin, Sydney.

Gallagher, R. (1997), *Young People's Access to Legal Services*, Scottish Child Law Centre, Glasgow.

Garbarino, J. (1986), *The Psychologically Battered Child*, Jossey-Bass, San Francisco.

Garbarino, J. and Stocking, S.H. (1980), *Protecting Children from Abuse and Neglect*, Jossey-Bass, San Francisco.

Gelles, R.J. (1996), *The Book of David – How Preserving Families can Cost Children's Lives*, Basic Books, New York.

Giavonnoni, J.M. and Becerra, R.M. (1979), *Defining Child Abuse*, Collier Macmillan, London.

Gibson, D. (1998), 'Mediation of Family Disputes in the Family Court of Australia', Family Court of Australia, Melbourne.

Giller, H. (1986), 'Is there a role for a juvenile court?', *Harvard Journal of Criminal Justice*, 15, pp. 161–71.

Giller, H. and Morris, A. (1981), *Care and Discretion: Social Workers' Decisions with Delinquents*, Burnett Books (in association with Andre Deutsch), London.

Glaser, B.G. and Strauss, A.L. (1967), *The Discovery of Grounded Theory: Strategies in Qualitative Research*, Aldine de Gruyter, New York.

Glaser, D. and Frosh, S. (1988), *Child Sexual Abuse*, Macmillan Education, Hampshire.

Gochros, H.L. (1985), 'Research Interviewing', in Grinnell, R. (ed.), *Social Research Research and Evaluation* (2nd edn), F.E. Peacock Publishers, Itasca, Illinois.

Goldson, B. (1977), 'The Residualisation and Incarceration of Child and Young People: A New Surplus Populous?', paper presented at University of Stirling International Conference *On the Margins: Social Exclusion and Social Work*, 7–10 September.

Goldstein, J. and Solnit Freud, A. (1980), *Before the Best Interests of the Child*, Burnett Books, Andre Deutsch, London.

Gorrard, C. and Carew, R. (1993), *Responding to Children: Child Welfare Practice*, Longman Cheshire, Melbourne.

Gothard, S. (1989), 'Power in the Court: the social worker as an expert witness', *Social Work*, 34(1), pp. 65–7.

Grace, C. and Wilkinson, P. (1978), *Negotiating the Law: Social Work and Legal Services*, Routledge & Kegan Paul, London.

Graham, A. (1994), 'Parens patriae: past, present, and future', *Family and Conciliation Courts Review*, Vol. 32, No. 2, pp. 184–207.

Graycar, R. (ed.) (1992), *Dissenting Opinions – Feminist Explorations in Law and Society*, Allen & Unwin, Sydney.

Groenweld, C.P. and Giovannoni, J. (1977), 'Disposition of child abuse and neglect cases', *Social Work Research and Abstracts*, Summer, pp. 36–47.

Guba, E.G. (1978), *Toward a Methodology of Naturalistic Inquiry in Educational Evacuation*, University of California, Los Angeles.

Hall, G. (1989), *The Welfare of the Child: A Literature Review*, Family Court Custody and Access Research Report 1, New Zealand, Department of Justice.

Hallett, C. (1993), *Inter-agency Work on Child Protection and Parental and Child Involvement in Decision Making in NSW*, Child Protection Council Seminar Series No. 1, NSW Government Printer.

Hallett, C. and Stevenson, O. (1980), *Child Abuse: Aspects of Interprofessional Co-operation*, Allen and Unwin, London.

Hallett, C. and Birchall, E. (1992), *Co-ordination and Child Protection*, HMSO, Edinburgh.

Hallett, C. and Hazel, N. (1998), *The Evaluation of Children's Hearings in Scotland, Vol. 2: The International Context,* The Scottish Office, Edinburgh.

Hammersley, M. (1992), 'Deconstructing the qualitative-quantitative divide', in Brannen, J. (ed.), *Mixing Methods: Qualitative and Quantitative Research*, Avebury, Aldershot.

Hampson, R.E. (1986), *Sentencing in a Children's Court and Labelling Theory*, N.Z. Justice Department, Research Series, No. 5, Wellington.

Hann, R.G. (1973), *Decision Making in the Canadian Criminal Court System*, Centre of Criminology, University of Toronto, Canada.

Harder, M. and Pringle, K. (1997), *Protecting Children in Europe: Towards a New Millennium*, Aalborg University Press, Denmark.

Hardiker, P. (1977), 'Social work ideologies in the probation service', *British Journal of Social Work*, 7(2), pp. 131–54.

Hardiker, P. and Barker, M. (eds) (1981), *Theories of Practice in Social Work*, Academic Press, London.

Harris, L.J. (1983), 'Utah Child Protection System – Analysis and Proposals for Change', *Utah Law Review*, 1, pp. 1–97.

Harrison, M. (1988), 'The legal and social status of children' in Hatty, S. (1991) 'Of nightmares and sexual monsters: struggles around child abuse in Australia', *International Journal of Law & Psychiatry*, Vol. 14, pp. 255–67.

Hassall, I. (1996), 'Origin and development of family group conferences', in Hudson, J., Morris, A., Maxwell, G. and Galaway, B. (eds), *Family Group Conferences*, Federation Press, NSW.

Health and Community Services Victoria (1994), *Annual Report 1993–1994*, Melbourne.

Health and Community Services Victoria (1994), *Protective Services Statistical Report 1993/94*, Melbourne.

Henham, R. (1986), 'The influence of sentencing principles in magistrates sentencing practices', *The Howard Journal*, 25(3), pp. 190–8.

Henham, R. (1990), *Sentencing Principles and Magistrates Sentencing Behaviour*, Avebury, Aldershot.

Hetherington, R., Cooper, A., Smith, P. and Wilford, G. (1997), *Protecting Children: Messages from Europe*, Russell House Publishing, London.

Hine, J., McWilliams, W. and Pease, K. (1978), 'Recommendations, social information and sentencing', *Harvard Journal*, 17(2), pp. 91–100.

Hogan, M. (1993), 'Children's Courts: to be or what to be?', *Juvenile Justice: Debating the Issues*, Allen & Unwin, Sydney.

Hogarth, J. (1971), *Sentencing as a Human Process*, University of Toronto Press, Toronto.

Hogarth, R.M. (1987), *Judgement and Choice: The Psychology of Decision*, John Wiley & Sons, New York.

Holstein, J.A. (1985), 'Jurors' interpretations and jury decision making', *Law and Human Behaviour*, 9(1), pp. 83–99.

Holt, R., Grundon, J., Paxton, R. (1998), 'Specialist assessment in child protection proceedings: problems and possible solutions', *Child Abuse Review*, Vol. 7 pp. 266–79.

Homel, R.J. (1983), 'Sentencing in magistrates' courts', in Findlay, M., Egger, S. and Sutton, J. (eds), *Issues in Criminal Justice Administration*, Allen & Unwin, Sydney, pp. 109–25.

Hood, R. (1962), *Sentencing in the Magistrates' Courts*, Stevens & Sons, London.

Hood, R. (1972), *Sentencing the Motoring Offender: A study of magistrates' views and practices*, London, Heinemann

Hood, R. and Sparks, R. (1970), *Key Issues in Criminology*, World University Library, London.

Human Services Victoria (1998), 'Victoria's mental health and protective services working together: A Guide for Protective Services and Mental Health Staff', February.

Hunt, J. and MacLeod, (1997), *The Last Resort: Child Protection, the Courts and the 1989 Children Act*, Centre for Socio-Legal Studies, University of Bristol.

Jabes, J. (1982), 'Individual decision-making', in McGrew, A.G. and Wilson, M.J. (eds) (1991), *Decision Making: Approaches and Analyses*, Open University and Manchester University Press, Manchester.

James, A., Wilson, K., Parry, M. (1988), *Social Work in Family Proceedings: a Practical Guide*, Routledge & Kegan Paul, London.

James, M. (1994a), 'Child Abuse and Neglect: Incidence and Prevention', *Issues in Child Abuse Prevention*, No. 1, January, National Child Protection Clearing House, Canberra.

James, M. (1994b), 'Domestic Violence as a Form of Child Abuse: Identification and Prevention', *Issues in Child Abuse Prevention*, No. 2, National Child Protection Clearing House, Canberra, July.

James, M. (1994c), 'Child abuse prevention – a perspective on parent enhancement programs from the United States', *Issues in Child Abuse Prevention*, No. 3, December, National Child Protection Clearing House, Canberra.
Jamison, J.R., Thwaites, D. and Gamble, H. (1979), *Social Work and the Law*, Butterworths, Sydney.
Jamrozik, A., Drury, S. and Sweeney, T. (1986), *Innovation and Change in the Child Welfare System*, SWSC Reports and Proceedings No. 57, Social Welfare Research Centre, University of New South Wales, Sydney.
Janis, I.L. and Mann, L. (1977), *Decision Making: A psychological analysis of conflict choice and commitment*, The Free Press, New York.
Kadushin, A. and Martin, J. (1981), *Child Abuse: An Interactional Event*, Columbia University, New York.
Kahneman, D. and Tversky, A. (1975), 'On the psychology of prediction', *Psychology Review*, 80, pp. 239–51.
Kahneman, D., Slovic, P. and Tversky, A. (1982), *Judgement under Uncertainty: Heuristics and Biases*, Cambridge University Press, Cambridge.
Kahneman, D. and Tversky, A. (1986), 'Judgement under uncertainty', in Arkes, H.R. and Hammond, K.R. (eds), *Judgement Under Uncertainty*, Cambridge University Press.
Kapardis, A. (1981), 'Magistrates' opinions, characterisations and sentencing', *Justice of the Peace*, 145, pp. 289–91.
Kapardis, A. and Farrington, D.P. (1981), 'An experimental study of sentencing by magistrates', *Law and Human Behaviour*, 5(2–3), pp. 107–21.
Kaplan, F. and Schwartz, S. (1977), *Human Judgement and Decision Processes in Applied Settings*, Academic Press, New York.
Kellehear, A. (1993), *The Unobtrusive Researcher*, Allen & Unwin, Sydney.
Kelly, R.F. and Ramsey, S.H. (1984/85), 'Legal and other determinants of effective Court intervention in child protection proceedings: a policy analysis', *Journal of Social Service Research*, 8(2), pp. 25–48.
Kempe, C.H., Silverman, F.N. and Steele, B.F. et al. (1962), 'The battered child syndrome', *Journal of the American Medical Association*, 181, pp. 17–24.
Kiel, H. (1988), 'Child Sexual Abuse and the Family Court', *Australian Journal of Social Issues*, 23(1), pp. 3–13.
King, M. (1981), *Child Welfare and Justice*, Billing and Son, London.
King, M. (1991), 'Child Welfare Within the Law: The Emergence of a Hybrid Discourse', *Journal of Law and Society*, 8(3), pp. 303–22.
King, M. and Trowell, J. (1992), *Children's Welfare and the Law – the Limits of Legal Intervention*, Sage Publications, London.
Kirby, M. (1981), *Child Abuse: What can the Law do?*, 2nd Australasian Conference on Child Abuse, Mt Gravatt CAE, Toowing, Queensland.
Konechi, V.J. and Ebbeson, E.B. (1981), 'A critique of theory and method in social-psychology approaches to legal issues', in Sales, B.D. (ed.), *Perspectives in Law*

& *Psychology; Vol 2: The Jury, Judicial and Trial Process*, Plenum Press, New York.

Konecni, V.J. and Ebbeson, E.B. (eds) (1982), *The Criminal Justice System: A Social – Psychological Analysis*, NH Freeman and Company, San Francisco.

Konecni, V.J. and Ebbeson, E.B. (1984), 'The mythology of legal decision making', *International Journal of Law and Psychiatry*, 7, pp. 5–18.

Lagay, B. et al. (1994), '"... to seek the best possible outcomes": evaluation of pre-hearing conferences on the Family Division of the Children's Court of Victoria', School of Social Work, University of Melbourne, December.

Larcombe, H. (1981), 'Legal intervention: the role of the court', *Interdisciplinary Conference on Child Neglect and Abuse*, NSW Department of Youth and Community Services and Kuring-gai College of Advanced Education, Government Printer, pp. 395–406.

Laster, K. (1990), 'Judging the children', *Legal Service Bulletin*, 15(3) June, p. 137.

Laster, R. (1993), 'Juvenile Justice Reform and the Symbol of the child', *Juvenile Justice: Debating the Issues*, Allen & Unwin, Sydney.

Law Reform Commission, Ireland (1996), *Report on Family Courts*, The Law Reform Commission, St Stephen's Green, Dublin 2.

Lawrence, J.A. (1984), 'Magisterial decision-making: cognitive perspectives and processes used in courtroom information processing', in Muller, D.J., Blackman, D.E. and Chapman, A.M. (eds), *Law and Psychology*, John Wiley and Sons, New York, pp. 319–31.

Lawrence, J. (1987), 'Magistrates Thought at Work', paper presented at ANZAPPL 8th Annual Congress, Melbourne.

Lawrence, J.A. (1988a), 'Expertise in judicial decision-making', in Chi, T.H., Glaser R. and Farr, M.J. (eds), *The Nature of Expertise*, Lawrence, Erlbaum, and Associates, Hillside, New Jersey.

Lawrence, J.A. (1988b), 'Making just decisions in Magistrates' Courts', *Journal of Social Justice Research*, 2, 2, June, pp. 155–76.

Lawrence, J.A. and Browne, M.A. (1981), 'Magisterial decision-making: how fifteen stipendiary magistrates make court-room decisions', School of Education, Murdoch University, WA.

Lawrence, J.A. and Homel, R. (1987), 'Sentencing in magistrates' courts: the magistrate as professional decision-maker', in Potas, I. (ed.), *Sentencing in Australia*, Australian Institute of Criminology, Canberra, pp. 151–91.

Lawrence, J.A. and Homel, R.J. (1992), 'Sentencer and offence factors as sources of discrimination in magistrates' penalties for drinking issues', *Social Justice Research*, 5(4), pp. 385–413.

Le Sueur, E. (1990), 'Children's rights and the state in loco parentis', *Children Australia*, 15(2).

Leivesley, S. (1984), 'The police role in child protection in Queensland', Report for the Criminology Research Council and the Queensland Police Department.

Lovegrove, A. (1989), *Judicial Decision Making, Sentencing Policy, and Numerical Guidance*, Springer-Verlag, New York.
McBarnet, D. (1981), *Conviction: Law, the State, and the Construction of Justice*, MacMillan, London.
McBarnet, D. (1981), 'Magistrates' courts and the ideology of justice', *British Journal of Law and Society*, 8(2), pp. 181-97.
McClean, J.O. (1980), *The Legal Context of Social Work* (2nd edn), Butterworths, London.
McCracken, G. (1988), *The Long Interview*, Qualitative Research Series, 13, Sage, London.
MacCrimmon, K.R. and Taylor, R.N. (1976), 'Decision Making and Problem-Solving', in Dunette, M.D. (ed.), *Handbook of Industrial and Organisational Psychology*, Rand McNally, Chicago.
McGrath, K. (1997), *An examination of the Adversarial Legal System and its implications for Irish Child Protection*, unpublished thesis, University College Dublin, Belfield, Dublin 4.
McGrew, A.G. and Wilson, M.J. (eds) (1982), *Decision Making: Approcahes and Analyses*, Open University and Manchester University Press, Manchester.
McKnight, C. (1981), 'Subjectivity in sentencing', *Law and Human Behaviour*, 5(2&3).
McNiff, F. (1979), *Guide to the Children's Courts in Practice in Victoria*, CCH Australia, Sydney.
Markiewicz, A. (1996), 'The Pre-Hearing Convenor: A Skilled Practitioner Chairing Conferences in the Children's Court of Victoria', *Children Australia*, December, Melbourne, Victoria.
Marsh, P. (1990), 'Changing practice in child care – the Children Act', *Adoption and Fostering*, 14(4), pp. 27-9.
Marshall, C. and Rossmann, G. (1989), *Designing Qualitative Research*, Sage Publications.
Martinez, A.V. (1980), 'Social Workers, evidentiary testimony, and the Courts', *Journal of Education for Social Work*, 16(1), pp. 66-71.
Martyn, R. and Levine, G. (1998), 'If Your Worship pleases: an Australian perspective on the role of the magistrate in child protection', *Child Abuse Review*, Vol. 7, No. 4, pp. 254-65 (NB: Rosemary Sheehan was formerly known as Rosemary Martyn).
Mason, J. and Falloon, J. (1999), 'A children's perspective on child abuse', *Children Australia*, Vol. 24, No. 3, pp. 9-13.
Maxwell, G.M. and Morris, A. (1994), 'The New Zealand model of Family Group Conference', in Alder, C. and Wundersitz, J. (eds), *Family Conferencing and Juvenile Justice: The Way Forward or Misplaced Optimism?*, Australian Institute of Criminology, Canberra.
Meadows, H. (1995), 'Child welfare and the adversary system', *Law Institute Journal* Vol. 69, No. 4, pp. 307-9.

Medden, B.J. (1984), 'Criteria for placement decisions in protective services', *Child Welfare*, LXIII(4), pp.367-373.
Medden, B.J. (1984), 'The future of decision making in child welfare practice: the development of an explicit criteria model for decision making', *Australian Child and Family Welfare*, 9(3-6).
Melton, G.B. (ed.) (1982), *Legal Reforms Affecting Child and Youth Services*, Haworth Press, New York.
Miles, M.B. and Huberman, A.M. (1994), *Qualitative Data Analysis: a sourcebook of New Methods* (2nd edn), Sage Publications, California.
Mills, C. and Vine, P. (1990), 'Critical incident reporting – an approach to reviewing the investigation and management of child abuse', *The British Journal of Social Work*, 20(3), pp. 215–20.
Mindel, C.H. (1985), 'Instrument design', in Grinnell, R.M. (ed.), *Social Work Research and Evaluation* (2nd edn), F.E. Peacock, Itasca, Illinois.
Minichiello, V., Aroni, R. and Timavett, E. (1990), *In-depth Interviewing: Researching People*, Longman Cheshire, Melbourne.
Mohr, L.B. (1982), 'Organisations, decisions and courts', in McGrew, A.G. and Wilson, M.J. (eds), *Decision Making: Approaches and Analyses*, Manchester University Press, Manchester.
Morris, A. and Giller, H. (eds) (1980), *Justice for Children*, Macmillan, London.
Morris, A. and Giller, H. (1983), *Understanding Juvenile Justice*, Croom Helm, Beckenham.
Naffine, N. (1993), 'Philosophies of juvenile justice', in Gale, F., Naffine, N. and Wundersitz, J. (eds), *Juvenile Justice: Debating the Issues*, Allen and Unwin, NSW.
Naffine, N. and Wundersitz, J. (1991), 'Lawyers in the Children's Courts: an Australian perspective', *Crime and Delinquency*, 37(3), pp. 374–92.
Najman, J. (1992), 'Comparing alternative methodologies of social research: an overview', in Daly, J., McDonald, I. and Willis, E. (eds), *Researching Health Care: Designs, Dilemmas, Disciplines*, Routledge, London.
National Commission of Inquiry into the Prevention of Child Abuse (1997), *Childhood Matters*, NSPC, London.
National Council of Family Proceedings Newsletter, Summer 1997, University of Bristol.
Nicholson, Hon. Justice A. (Family Court of Australia) (1994), 'Mediation in the Family Court of Australia', paper presented at the *Families and Justice Conference*, Catholic University of Louvain, Brussels.
Nisbett, R. and Ross, L. (1980), *Human Inference Strategies and Shortcomings of Social Judgment*, Prentice Hall, New Jersey.
Norrie, K. McK. (1997), *Children's Hearings in Scotland*, W. Green, Sweet and Maxwell, Edinburgh.
Norris, L. (1993), 'The Family Court & State Department Approaches to Child Abuse', 4th Australian Family Research Conference, Family Court of Australia.

O'Connor, I. (1988), *Children in Justice*, Longman Cheshire, Melbourne.
O'Connor, I. (1987), 'Legal education for social welfare workers: has it made a difference?' *Legal Service Bulletin*, June, pp. 93-6.
O'Connor, I. (1988), 'Social work and the law revisited', in Chamberlain, E. (ed.), *Change and Continuity in Australian Social Work*, Longman Cheshire, Melbourne.
Oxfordshire Area Child Protection Committee Procedures 1996, Oxfordshire Area Child Protection Committee.
Oxfordshire Panel of Guardians Ad Litem and Reporting Officers Annual Report April 1995-1996, Nancy Druker, Panel Manager and Ursula Warnecke, Panel Administrator.
Page, Judge R.W. (1993), 'Family Courts: an effective judicial approach to the resolution of family disputes', *Juvenile and Family Court Journal*, 44(1).
Palmer, S.E. (1989), 'Mediation in child protection cases: an alternative to the adversary system', *Child Welfare* 68(1), January/February, pp. 21-31.
Parker, H. (ed.) (1979), *Social Work and the Courts*, Edward Arnold, London.
Parker, H., Sumner, M. and Jarvis, G. (1989), *Unmasking the Magistrate*, Open University Press, Milton Keynes.
Parsloe, P. (1981), 'The interface of law and social work', *Contemporary Social Work Education*, 4(3), pp.183-97.
Parton, N. (1986), *The Politics of Child Abuse*, Macmillan, London.
Parton, N. (1991), *Governing the Family – Child Care, Child Protection and the State*, Macmillan, London.
Parton, N. and Thomas, N. (1983), 'Child abuse & citizenship', in Jordan, B. and Parton, N. (eds), *The Political Dimensions of Social Work*, Basil Blackwell, Oxford.
Patton, M.Q. (1984), *Qualitative Evaluation and Research Methods*, Sage Publications, London.
Pennington, D.C. and Lloyd-Bostock, S. (eds) (1987), *The Psychology of Sentencing*, Centre for Socio-Legal Studies, University of Oxford, Oxford.
Platt, A.M. (1977), *The Child Savers: the Invention of Delinquency*, 2nd edn, University of Chicago Press, Chicago.
Plotnikoff, J. and Woolfson, R., *Reporting to Court Under the Children Act: A Handbook for Social Services*, Department of Health, HMSO, London.
Polk, K. and Tait, D. (1987), *The Use of Imprisonment by Victorian Magistrates*, a report prepared for the Victorian Sentencing Committee.
Potas, I. (ed.) (1986), 'Sentencing', in *Sentencing in Australia*, Summer, AIC, Canberra.
Pratt, J. (1993), 'Welfare and Justice: incompatible philosophies', in *Juvenile Justice: Debating the Issues*, Allen & Unwin, Sydney.
Rechtman, K. (1997), 'Synopsis of statistics for pre-hearing conferences January-July 1997', unpublished report, Pre-Hearing Conference Convenor, Children's Court, Victoria, September.
Reder, P. and Duncan, S. (1997), 'Adult Psychiatry – A Missing Link in the Child Protection Network', *Child Abuse Review*, Vol. 6, pp. 35-40.

Richardson, Right Hon J. (1984), 'Judicial decision-making: a New Zealand perspective', *Law Institute Journal*, 58(5), May, pp. 545–7.

Rizzo, C. (1989), *Questioning the Magistrate's Decision: Sentencing and Conviction Appeals from the Local Court*, NSW Bureau of Crime Statistics and Research, Attorney General's Department, NSW Govt. Publication.

Roberts, J. and Roberts, C. (1980), 'Social Enquiry Reports and Sentencing', *The Harvard Journal*, 21(2), pp. 76–93.

Ronnau, J. and Poertner, J. (1989), 'Building consensus among child protection professionals', *Social Casework*, 70(7), September, pp. 428–35.

Rosen, H. (1981), 'How social workers use cues to determine child abuse', *Social Work Research and Abstracts*, 17.

Ross and Hampson (1975), *Sentencing in a Children's Court and Labelling Theory*, Research Series No. 5, New Zealand Department of Justice.

Rowlands, Hon. Justice A. (Family Court of Australia) (1996), 'Reforms in Prospect' address to Canberra Lawyers, 12 December, Canberra, Australian Capital Territory.

Saks, M.J. and Kidd, R.F. (1980), *Human Information Processing and Adjudication: Trial by Heuristics*, Law and Society Review, 15, pp. 123–60.

Saks, M.J. and Hastie, R. (1978), 'Social psychology in court: the judge', *Law and Human Behaviour*, 2(4), pp. 255–67.

Sales, B.D. (ed.) (1981), *Perspectives in Law and Psychology; Vol 2: The Jury, Judicial and Trial Process*, Plenum Press, New York.

Sales, B.D. (ed.) (1981), *The Trial Process*, Plenum Press, New York.

Savoury, G., Beals, H. and Parks, J. (1995), 'Mediation in child protection: facilitating the resolution of disputes', *Child Welfare*, 74, pp. 743–63.

Schaffer, H.R. (1990), *Making Decisions about Children: Psychological Questions and Answers*, Basil Blackwell, Oxford.

Schlebaum, A. (1982), 'The Courts' contribution to child abuse', *Proceedings of the Institute of Criminology*, 54, pp. 79–97.

Schon, D. (1983), *The Reflective Practitioner: How Professionals Think in Action*, Basic Books, New York.

Schroeder, L.O. (1982), *The Legal Environment of Social Work*, Prentice Hall Inc., New Jersey.

Scott, D. (1989), 'Meaning construction and social work practice', *Social Service Review*, March, 1989, pp. 39–51.

Scotland's Children Speaking Out: Young Peoples Views on Child Care Law in Scotland (1996), The Scottish Office.

Scottish Child Law Centre (1995), 'Representing Children: Listening to the Voice of the Child', *Representing Children Conference*, Glasgow, November.

Seaberg, J.R. (1978), 'Disposition in physical child abuse', *California Sociologist*, 3(11), pp. 3–11.

Sellitz, C. (1976), *Research Methods in Social Relations* (3rd edn), Holt Reinhart Winston, New York.

Seymour, J. (1993), 'Australia's juvenile justice systems: a comment', in Gale, F., Naffine, N. and Wundersitz, J. (eds), *Juvenile Justice: Debating the Issues*, Allen and Unwin, NSW.

Sheehan, R. (1997), 'Mental health issues in child protection cases', *Children Australia*, Vol. 22, No. 4, pp. 13–21.

Sheehan, R. (1998), 'The administration of justice: the use of mediation to improve public access to dispute resolution and avoid court', *Administration*, Journal of the Institute of Public Administration of Ireland, October.

Sheehan, R., Rechtman, K. and Ban, P. (1998), 'The use of mediation in child protection: a report on the use of pre-hearing conferences in the Children's Court, Victoria, Australia', paper presented at the ISPCAN Congress, Auckland, 6–9 September.

Sheehan, R. and Trotter, C. (1999), 'Alternative Dispute Resolution in Child Protection Matters: The Victorian Experience', *7th Australasian Conference on Child Abuse and Neglect*, Perth, Western Australia, 17–20 October.

Smart, C. (1992), 'Law's Truth/Women's Experience', in Greycar, R. (ed.), *Dissenting Opinions – Feminist Explorations in Law and Society*, Allen & Unwin, Sydney.

Smith, C.R., Lane, M.T. and Walsh, T. (1988), *Child Care and the Courts*, MacMillan Education, Hampshire.

Smith, R. (1982), 'A consideration of some evidentiary and procedural problems in neglect complaints', *Child Welfare in the 80s*; Proceedings of the Institute of Criminology, No. 49, University of Sydney.

Social Work Services Group (1996), *The Children's Hearings System in Scotland: A Handbook for Children's Panel Members*, James Craig Walk, Edinburgh.

Sox, H.C., Blatt, M.A., Higgins, M.C. and Marton, R.I. (1988), *Medical Decision Making*, Butterworths, Boston.

Spakes, P. (1987), 'Social workers and the courts: education, practice and research needs', *Journal of Social Work Education*, 23(2), pp. 30–9.

Spencer, J. and Flinn, R. (1993), *The Evidence of Children* (2nd edn), Blackstone, London.

Stevenson, O. (1998), *Neglected Children: Issues and dilemnas*, Blackwell Science, Oxford.

Stevenson, O. (ed.) (1999), *Child welfare in the United Kingdom 1948–1998*, Blackwell Science, Oxford.

Stevenson, O. (1996), 'Emotional abuse and neglect', *Child and Family Social Work*, No. 1, pp. 13–18.

Stewart, A. (1986), 'Factors influencing decisions in child neglect investigations', conference paper, *International Congress on Child Abuse and Neglect*, Sydney, NSW.

Strauss, A.L. (1987), *Qualitative Analysis for Social Scientists*, Cambridge University Press, Cambridge.

Strauss, A. and Corbin, J. (1990), *Basics of Qualitative Research*, Sage, California.

Swain, P. (1989), 'Lawyer and social worker – can the marriage work?', *Journal of Social Welfare Law*, 4.

Swain, P. (1994), 'Natural justice and social work: what can social workers learn from administrative law?', *Advances in Social Welfare Education*, AASWWE.

Swain, P. (1995), 'Why do social workers need an understanding of law?', in Swain, P. (ed.), *In the Shadow of the Law: The Legal Context of Social Work Practice*, The Federation Press, Sydney.

Swain, P. (1997), 'Letting the family decide? Family Group Conferences and Pre-Hearing Conferences in Victoria's child protection system', *Alternative Dispute Resolution Journal* 7, pp. 231–7.

Tarling, R. (1979), *Sentencing Practice in Magistrates' Courts*, HMSO, London.

Taylor, R.N. (1976), 'Strategic Decision Making', in Dunnette, M.D. (ed.), *Handbook of Industrial and Organisational Psychology*, Rand McNally, Chicago.

ten Bessel, R.W. et al. (1985), *Child Abuse and Neglect*, National Council of Juvenile and Family Court Judges, Nevada.

Thomas, J. (1988), *Judicial Ethics on Australia*, Law Book Company, Sydney, NSW.

Thompson, J. (1990), *Social Workers and the Law*, Redfern Publishing Company, Sydney.

Thomas, J. (1992), 'The ethics of magistrates', *Judicial Review*, 1(1), September, pp. 59–79.

Thorpe, D. (1994), *Evaluating Child Protection*, Open University Press, Buckingham.

Thorpe, D. and Bilson, A. (1999), 'From protection to concern: child protection careers without apologies' *Children and Society*, Vol. 12, No. 5, pp. 373–86.

Tiffin, S. (1982), *In Whose Best Interest? Child Welfare Reform in the Progressive Era*, contribution to the Study of Childhood and Youth, No. 1, Greenwood Press, Connecticut.

Toseland, R. (1985), 'Research methods', in Grinnell, R. (ed.), *Social Work Research and Evaluation* (3rd edn), F.E. Peacock, Itasca Ill.

Trotter, C. (1999), *Working With Involuntary Clients*, Allen & Unwin, Sydney.

Trotter, C., Sheehan, R., Liddell, M. et al. (1999), *Evaluation of the Statewide Implementation of Family Group Conferencing*, Human Services Victoria.

Van Krieken, R. (1991), *Children and the State: Social Control and the Formation of Australian Child Welfare*, Allen & Unwin, Sydney.

Van Maanen, J., Dabbs, J.M. Jr and Faulkner, R. (1982), *Varieties of Qualitative Research*, Sage Publications, Beverley Hills.

Vickers, Sir G. (1965), *The Art of Judgement: A Study of Policy Making*, Chapman and Hall, London.

Wattam, C. (1992), *Making a Case in Child Protection*, Longman, Essex.

Webb, E.J., Campbell, D.T., Schwarz, R.D. and Sechrest, L., *Unobtrusive Measures: Non-reactive Research in the Social Sciences*, Rand McNally, Chicago.

Webb, K.R. (1978), 'Sentencing: a magistrate's viewpoint', *Sydney University Faculty of Law Institute of Criminology Proceedings*, 3, pp. 63–77.

Weber, R.P. (1990), *Basic Content Analysis* (2nd edn), Sage Publications, London.
Weil, M. (1982), 'Research on issues in collaboration between social workers and lawyers', *Social Service Review* 56(3), pp. 393–405.
Weinbach, R.W. and Grinnell, R.M. Jr (1987), *Statistics for Social Workers* (2nd edn), Longman, New York.
White, R., Carr, P. and Lowe, N. (1995), *The Children Act 1989 In Practice* (2nd edn), Butterworths, London.
Wilkinson, M. (1994), 'The social work and law debate: implications for social work education', *Advances in Social Welfare Education*, AASWWE.
Wilson, J.A. (1987), 'The Juvenile Court: a guide for effective social work practice', *Journal of Social Welfare Law*, May, pp. 180–2.
Working Together Under the Children Act 1989, 'A guide to arrangements for interagency co-operation for the protection of children from abuse' No. 8, Home Office, HMSO, London.
Yegidis, B.L. (1991), *Research Methods for Social Workers*, Longman Cheshire, USA.
Yin, R.K. (1984), *Case Study Research*, Sage Publications, London.
Zabar, P. and Angus, G. (1995), *Child Abuse and Neglect: Reporting and Investigation Procedures in Australia 1994*, Child Welfare Series No. 8, Australian Institute of Health and Welfare, Canberra.
Zifcak, S. (1995), 'Towards a Reconciliation of Legal and Social Work Practice', in Swain, P. (ed.), *In the Shadow of the Law: The Legal Context of Social Work Practice*, The Federation Press, Sydney.

APPENDICES

Appendix One

The Court Observation Sheet

The observation data was recorded on this sheet during the observation phase of the study.

Court Observation Sheet

1. Order being sought

2. i. Current placement of child

   ii. Danger child placed in

   iii. Nature of abuse alleged

3. Evidence of abuse alleged

4. Evidence produced by other side

5. Witnesses produced by other side

6. Legal representation of either side

7. Structure of family (include housing, money)

8. SE states

9. Ethnicity

10. Age of child

11. Magistrate

12. Family court matters

13. How disruptive is proposed change going to be

14. Magistrate decision and assessment is

15. Magistrate comments: please give .5 of a page

Appendix Two

The Interview Schedule

The structured interview schedule applied to the study participants.

Magistrates' Decision-making in Matters of Child Protection

1. What factors do d you look for when deciding child protection matters? (Given that the legislation gives specific grounds for dispositions but allows discretion).

2. How might it make a difference to the factors you look for if the case before you involves, for example,

    i) physical abuse or neglect
    ii) sexual abuse
    iii) if the allegations are concerning emotional abuse if the case arises out of parents' problems with
    iv) substance abuse
    v) psychiatric disorder
    vi) intellectual disability

3. When trying to decide 'the best interests of the child', what do you look for?

4. What do you look for to establish whether or not a child has experienced, or might experience 'significant harm'?

5. What constraints do you believe operate on you in deciding child protection matters?

6. How do these constraints limit the options you have, in deciding child protection matters?

7. In your experience, how aware are other professionals who work in this jurisdiction (eg legal representatives, welfare practitioners etc) aware of these constraints?

8. a. Which child protection decisions are the most difficult to decide?

   b. Which child protection decisions are most straightforward?

9. What changes have you noticed (or, did you notice) over time at the Childrens Court, in the kinds of child protection cases which come (or came) before you?

10. In your experience, are decisions in the child protection area more difficult to make than decisions in other jurisdictions?

11. What ideas, or beliefs, about families do you refer to when you make child protection decisions?

12. What sentencing objectives – for want of a better phase – or philosophical views do you refer to, when looking at the possible outcome for a case before you?

13. What common factors do you find in families who come before the Children's Court, in relation to child abuse issues.

14. Within which areas do you find yourself in disagreement, most often, with social workers, in child protection cases.

15. How often do you find yourself disagreeing with social work recommendation in consent matters?

    How often do you find yourself disagreeing with social work recommendations in contest matters?

16. a. Which professionals are of most assistance to you, in child protection matters?
    b. In what ways are they helpful?

17. What feedback do you get about cases you hear?

18. What research, or general information, would be helpful for you to receive about child abuse?

19. How do you weigh up ethnic attitudes or values when they are part of a case before you?

20. How long have you been (or, were you), at the Melbourne Children's Court?

    Were you a magistrate in the adult court before that?

    For how many years have you been a magistrate?

    What are the main differences you find between the adult and Children's Courts.

21. Age group   31–35   36–40   41–45   46–50   51–55   56–60

    Qualifications

Thankyou.

Appendix Three

The Survey of Children's Court Records

This appendix contains first, the data sheet on which information from the Court record was noted. The Court record comprised the Magistrate Decision Sheet and the Disposition Report. Second, the appendix contains the analysis sheet for the Survey of the Court Records.

Survey of Children's Court Records

MAGISTRATE DECISION SHEET

Case Name
Name of Magistrate
Gender   M /F

Length of time in jurisdiction

Order sought from Court   IAO

                                               PA

                                               IPO

                                               Custody

                                               Guardianship

                                               Other

Decision   IAO to family

                       IAO to family other than parents

                       IAO to Community Service

Guardianship : new
              : extension

Conditions attached

When did case first come to Court
Number of prior appearances

Action
_____
_____
_____
_____
_____

Legal Representation   Child   Y/N

                       Mother   Y/N

                       Father   Y/N

                       Mother and Father   Y/N

                       Dept. Human Services
                         : Court Unit   Y/N

                         : VicGov Solicitor Y/N

                         : Barrister   Y/N

                       Other _____

COURT REPORT

    Case features

1.   Date of birth

2.2.1   Grounds for p.a. _____

2.2   notification/apprehension?

3.   Reasons for seeking p.g.

4.   Family structure

    4.1   Genogram

    4.2   Family members

5.   Ages of children in family

6.   Children affected by allegations:
        number in family:
        position in family:

7.   Sources of information

8.   Reports provided by

9.   Reports supportive of child   Y/N

10.   Family status: intact/ married/ de facto/ blended

       single parent: female/ male

       grandparents

       Other

11.   Ethnicity

12.   Occupation: Mother

               Father

13. Income: Mother

               Father

14. Postcode

15. Relevant parent
    background

16. Prior department intervention/action

17. Current department action

18. Other agency involvement – current:
                    prior:
                    from order:

19. Problem location

20. Problem hierachy

21. 'Strength of case' assessment

22. Hearing   consent/contest/other

23. Department recommendation

24. Other comments